DATE DUE

DATE DUE

THE ADVANCE
AGAINST PAPERWORK
COMPUTERS, SYSTEMS, AND PERSONNEL

THE ADVANCE
AGAINST PAPERWORK
COMPUTERS, SYSTEMS, AND PERSONNEL

LEONARD RICO
ASSOCIATE PROFESSOR OF INDUSTRY
Wharton School of Finance and Commerce
University of Pennsylvania

BUREAU OF INDUSTRIAL RELATIONS
Graduate School of Business Administration
The University of Michigan
Ann Arbor

CONTENTS

INTRODUCTION

During the past fifteen years electronic computers have been introduced in increasing numbers to facilitate the processing of information in both private and public offices. Numerous changes and serious problems have challenged managements to integrate this new technology into their operations. The present impact and the future ramifications of computer technology are of immediate interest to all groups involved.

Many people from diverse backgrounds have said various things about automation and its implications. Unfortunately, diagnosis and prescription too often have been based upon conjecture. The lack of experience with automation accounts for but does not justify the generalizations which have been propounded by the extrapolation of tradition, the extravagant claims of machinery manufacturers and labor unions, and the soothing lullabies of managements.

Typically the impact of automation has been considered in its broad economic and social dimensions. This focus on the general contributes to the confusion that enshrouds the problem. It is because of this focus that much time and effort are expended debating whether automation is evolutionary or revolutionary in its impact. In many instances, the protagonists ask different questions and disagree over results. Some authors deal predominantly with the human factor, while others address themselves to the technical. The time perspectives of the reporters, too, are often different. And sometimes researchers have a vested interest in the conclusions they reach. This latter point is valid, for example, for the union representative whose constituency on any given automation problem may vary from one individual to the entire membership.

Significant changes have taken place in the research situation since the late 1950s. Many technical changes, previously in the planning stage, have been implemented. Further, many

7

pioneering companies now are able to furnish hard facts. As a result empirical research data are becoming available; these provide meaningful insights on the many managerial aspects of the automation problem.

The electronic computer produces a significant change in a firm's work methods, resulting in important qualitative changes in the process by which human resources are utilized. The task, therefore, is to evaluate the impact of computer technology on information processing, management, and personnel policies and practices. The objectives are to contrast and integrate library and field research data, and to outline the findings that apply to the computerization of office functions.

The firms surveyed were selected to obtain the maximum diversity possible (manufacturing, service, union, non-union, large, small, public corporations, and family-owned). Twelve Greater Boston area firms, all computer technology pioneers, were surveyed during 1959-1961. Initially the data were collected for a doctoral dissertation submitted to the Massachusetts Institute of Technology. During 1964-1965, data were collected from six Greater Philadelphia area firms, each with five or more years' experience with computers. In addition, during the summer of 1965, nine of the original twelve Boston area firms were visited again to evaluate their success in implementing computers. These latter interviews, many of which were held with the same managers interviewed initially, were particularly productive.

Evidence of change was sought by studying written material and making direct observations. Organizational documents provided an important source of data (e.g., charts, job descriptions, communications, policies, procedures, rules, and collective bargaining agreements). The other major source of information was tapped by intensive interviews with those employees of the firm most intimately involved and affected by the introduction of a computer.

Usually the initial contact was made with the manager in charge of personnel administration. The personnel administrator and his staff typically gave me the company background data that were requisite to understanding what was to follow. Next I usually met with the person in charge of the computerization program. Once I was oriented to the company and its computer and systems departments, I moved on to that operational area which would yield the most significant data on the effects of the computer. The final step completed the circle; I returned to the personnel administrator to discuss in more detail the impact of computerization on personnel policies and practices. Having become well acquainted with the impact on the organization and employees, I found this interview useful in evaluating the personnel function. Although this was the typical interviewing pattern, the amount of time spent at each firm varied considerably, as did the number of people interviewed.

The study is organized as follows. The first part encompasses marshalling forces for organizational change: the development and implementation of computers, the development of systems to utilize the new technology, the deployment of computers within a firm, and the operation of the computer center itself. In the second part managerial aspects of computerized operations are analyzed: the management of systems, the impact of computers on line and staff managers, and the management of organizational change. In the third part the impact of computerization upon the nature of office work, the staffing process, the compensation process and working conditions, and the new training and development needs are considered. In the fourth and final part of the book the present state of computerization is reviewed, and comments on future developments are offered.

I am indebted to numerous organizations and individuals for making the publication of this book possible. Professor Charles A. Myers, Chairman of the Industrial Relations Section at M. I. T., supervised the thesis from which this book derives and has encouraged my research on computerization. Professors Douglass V. Brown and Paul Pigors offered many constructive suggestions in the early stages of this study.

Professor Herbert R. Northrup, Chairman of the Industry

Department, Wharton School of Finance and Commerce, University of Pennsylvania, gave the encouragement and backing that was instrumental to the publication of this book. Professor George S. Odiorne, Director of the Bureau, also was helpful in this regard. It is unfortunate that the firms surveyed and the numerous employees interviewed cannot be identified. Without their cooperation and active participation, this book could not have been written.

I have received financial assistance from several sources. The Alfred P. Sloan Foundation supported the early stages of this study. Dean Willis J. Winn, through the Committee on Faculty Projects, Wharton School of Finance and Commerce, awarded me faculty research grants made available by the Ford Foundation. Finally, the Labor Relations Council of the University of Pennsylvania, under George W. Taylor, Chairman, also sustained my research efforts.

William H. Price, Director of Publications of the Bureau, had final editorial responsibility for the manuscript. He exhibited a degree of understanding and tolerance in that role for which I am most thankful. John J. Golda, a research assistant, conducted field interviews in the Philadelphia firms. Kathleen Ceriotti, of the Bureau staff, typed the final manuscript, and Pamela Gilson did the final proofreading chores.

Finally I acknowledge with thanks permission to use material published elsewhere. Chapters VIII and X are derived in part from articles which appeared in the *Industrial Management Review* and the *Management of Personal Quarterly*, respectively.

LEONARD RICO

Haddonfield, N.J.
November, 1966

PART I
MARSHALLING FORCES

Chapter I

ENTER THE COMPUTER

Every manager must today ask himself: What can you do that
a computer can't do?
— FREDERICK PAMP

An ancient abacus, a simple but efficient computer developed
in 3000 B.C., is displayed in a glass case mounted on the wall
of a technical institute's new $2,500,000 computation center.
A sign below the case reads: "Use in case of emergency." The
startling aspect of the story is the relative lack of improvement
in "abacus technology" until recently. The vast strides of the
past several decades, however, go far beyond just computation.

In 1959, the Massachusetts Institute of Technology established a Center for the Communication Sciences. Here gather
such diverse experts as physicists and linguists to collaborate
on such problems as the processing and transmission of information, the working of the nervous system, and the development of artificial intelligence. Within the short span of
twenty years the computer has been utilized to help man with
such varied problems as simple addition and mechanical
simulation of the human nervous system.

The serious application of the computer to paperwork dates
probably from the processing of the 1950 census data.[1] Commercial electronic data processing was begun about 1955. In
discussing the extent of computerization, it is useful to define
current installations by size and by cost as indicated in Table 1.

---

[1] Throughout this book "computer" refers to the general or digital computer
which is used in commercial data processing applications. Special purpose or
analog computers, used for scientific and engineering applications such as process
control, are not discussed although such computers may be part of a firm's
computer activities.

Table 1
On-Site Computer Systems

Computer Size	Total Quantity Installed	Installed in U.S.	Installed Outside U.S.
Large Scale Computers ($750,000 and up)	1,950	1,678	272
Medium Scale Computers ($100,000-749,999)	19,283	14,128	5,155
Small Scale Computers (Under $100,000)	9,109	7,288	1,821
Grand Totals	30,342	23,094	7,248

Source: Adapted from "On-Site Systems Top 30,000 Mark," *Business Automation*, 13:no. 2, 54-56 (February, 1966).

Over the past decade the manufacture of electronic data processing equipment has been extremely rapid and today comprises the largest segment of the office equipment industry. The nature of the growth to over 23,000 computer installations in the United States is illustrated in the following statistics. In 1957, 100 large-scale systems were reported in use.[2] By late 1958, 166 large-scale and 900 medium-to-small-scale computers were counted.[3] In early 1959 the Bureau of Labor Statistics estimated that there was a total of 2,000 computers of all sizes and for all purposes in both public and private use.[4] According to Diebold, as of mid-1960, there were 607 large-scale, 840 medium-scale, and 2,810 small-scale computers in use, or a total of 4,257 computers in use.[5]

The increasing computerization of paperwork is evidenced also by Federal Government statistics, which exclude certain military and classified uses. The number of computers of all

[2] Roger Nett and Stanley A. Hetzler, *An Introduction to Electronic Data Processing* (Glencoe, Illinois: The Free Press of Glencoe, 1959), Figure 2, p. 33.

[3] Felix Kaufman, "E.D.P. and the Disenchanted," *California Management Review*, 1:no. 4, 69 (Summer, 1959).

[4] "Adjustments to the Introduction of Office Automation," *Bureau of Labor Statistics Bulletin Number 1276* (Washington, D.C.: United States Government Printing Office, United States Department of Labor, May, 1960), 1.

[5] John Diebold, "Bringing Automation up to Date," *New Views on Automation* (Washington, D.C.: United States Government Printing Office, 1960), 116.

types increased from 414 in fiscal year 1959 to 1,565 in fiscal year 1964. The number of personnel directly involved increased during this same period from 14,445 to 50,997.[6] Diebold points out that the bulk of the non-government E.D.P. systems users are "...aircraft manufacturers, transportation, insurance companies, computer component manufacturers, financial firms, public utilities, other manufacturing, military and research, science and engineering."[7]

The insurance industry offers another excellent example of the increasing use of computers in data processing. Insurance firms pioneered in the commercial implementation of computers. Several companies began feasibility studies in the early 1950s, and at least two computers were placed in operation in 1954 (see Table 2). In the course of a decade the use of computers became widespread throughout the insurance industry; moreover, the degree of application was extensive.

Statistics on the growth of computer manufacturing is another way of determining the extent of computerization, the nature of its growth, and future prospects, as well as a guide to the controlling variables.

In 1950 Remington Rand made available the first commercial computer system. At present about twenty companies manufacture commercial computer systems, and eight companies build nearly all computer systems.[8] International Business Machines Corporation (IBM) is the dominant firm in the computer market. IBM offers by far the broadest product line. According to *Fortune*, as of January, 1961, IBM held 76 per-

---

[6] *Inventory and Cost Data Concerning the Utilization of Automatic Data Processing (A.D.P.) Equipment in the Federal Government for Fiscal Years 1959, 1960, 1961* (Washington, D.C.: United States Government Printing Office, the Executive Office of the President, United States Bureau of the Budget, May, 1960), Table 4. Also *Inventory of Automatic Data Processing (ADP) Equipment in the Federal Government* (Washington, D.C.: United States Government Printing Office, Subcommittee on Census and Government Statistics of the Committee on Post Office and Civil Service, House of Representatives, 88th Congress, October 25, 1963), Table 1, p. 13.

[7] Diebold, "Bringing Automation up to Date," *New Views on Automation, op. cit.,* p. 106.

[8] In late 1964, *Forbes* estimated that the top eight firms controlled 98 percent of the domestic E.D.P. equipment market. See "Little Big Honeywell," *Forbes,* 94:no. 10, 25 (November 15, 1964).

cent of the computer market. The Sperry Rand Corporation had 7 percent of the market. Radio Corporation of America was accorded third place, sharing the remaining 17 percent of the market with all other producers.[9] Standard and Poor estimates that as of May, 1966, IBM held about 70 percent of both the domestic and European markets for computers.[10]

The rapid growth of computerization is depicted aptly by the value of computers in operation and sold yearly. *Fortune* estimated that the value of general-purpose computers in oper-

Table 2

Number of Responding Companies with Computers and Total Number of Computers in Operation, by Year, 1954-63.

Year ending	Number of companies with computers	Number of computers in operation at some time during the year	Average number of computers per company
1954................	2	2	1.0
1955................	17	24	1.4
1956................	35	64	1.8
1957................	57	99	1.7
1958................	78	141	1.8
1959................	107	185	1.7
1960................	126	232	1.8
1961................	160	387	2.4
1962................	201	544	2.7
1963................	673*	226*	3.0

*Installed or scheduled for installation.

Source: "The Impact of Office Automation in the Insurance Industry," *Bureau of Labor Statistics Bulletin Number 1468* (Washington, D.C.: United States Government Printing Office, United States Department of Labor, 1966), 11.

[9] Gilbert Burck, "The 'Assault' on Fortress I.B.M.," *Fortune*, LXIX: no. 6, 115, 198 ff (June, 1964).

[10] "Office Equipment," *Standard and Poor's Industry Survey*, Section 2, P O 10, (May 12, 1966).

ation in January, 1961, was $1.8 billion; in August, 1962, $3.2 billion; and in January, 1964, $5.3 billion.[11] In Table 3, data on the value of both past and estimated future shipments of computers are shown.

Table 3

Total Shipments of Computers

In Millions of Dollars*

	1955	1956	1957	1958	1959	1960	1961	1962	1963	1964	1965	E1966	E1967	E1970
Business and Scientific	100	221	274	335	400	550	1,100	1,750	2,000	2,000	2,250	3,000	3,500	4,000
Special Military	300	360	440	550	700	900	1,200	1,540	1,750	1,900	2,025	2,500	2,700	2,600
Industrial Process	–	–	–	–	23	80	47	67	95	160	200	250	320	500
Externally Programmed	58	43	52	53	35	23	20	25	40	52	62	68	67	60
General Purpose Analog	–	14	18	21	25	28	32	35	39	42	46	48	48	35
Total Hardware	458	638	784	979	1,183	1,531	2,399	3,417	3,924	4,154	4,583	5,866	6,635	7,195
Computer Services	189	245	309	389	495	611	786	998	1,263	1,600	1,950	2,250	2,550	3,000
Total Industry	647	883	1,093	1,368	1,678	2,142	3,185	4,415	5,187	5,754	6,533	8,116	9,185	10,195

*Shipments are calculated on an All-sold basis. E—Estimated.

Source: "Office Equipment," *Standard and Poor's Industry Surveys*, May 12, 1966, Section 2.

11 Burck, *op. cit.*, p. 115.

Computer sales projections generally have underestimated the demand for E.D.P. equipment. Computer sales for 1965 totaled above $4.5 billion, while a 1960 forecast had speculated that sales would double to $2.2 billion in 1965.[12] The estimate of about $7.2 billion for 1970 may be too low, also. *This much is certain: computerization will continue increasingly to affect every facet of information processing.* Current trends indicate that probably every medium and large company will implement some kind of E.D.P. system in the not-too-distant future. Rapid and significant innovations in computer technology also provide a means for developing new applications and improving old ones.

Many powerful factors are inducing further office mechanization. The size of firms generally, and offices particularly, has been growing. The volume of information processed also has grown, and probably will continue to grow. Further, mechanization is encouraged by the rapid growth in both the number of white collar workers and in overhead costs. Finally, the changing participation rates of women in the work force, and such pertinent data as their age, skill, mobility, and attitudes tend to encourage computerization.

The rapid spread of information technology, according to Leavitt and Whisler, is due to top management's desire to centralize decision-making, to extend greater control over subordinates, to act on a wider range of problems, and to reduce the number of employees.[13] These desires, although modified, plus the pressures mentioned above — those connected with size, volume, growth, and change — can influence management's objectives in utilizing E.D.P.

A Bureau of Labor Statistics survey found cost saving to be the primary motivation of managements which have introduced E.D.P. systems. Clerical labor saving was listed by

---

[12] Alfred R. Zipser, "R.C.A. Sales of Data Systems Running 200% above '59 Level," *New York Times*, Section 3, p. 1 (September 25, 1960).

[13] Harold J. Leavitt and Thomas L. Whisler, "Management in the 1980's," *Harvard Business Review*, 36:no. 6, 43 (November-December, 1958).

eleven out of twenty companies as management's first objective.[14] In my own survey of twelve Massachusetts companies, direct cost saving was also cited by managers as a major objective in introducing E.D.P., but except in the formulation of feasibility studies, the less tangible benefits received greater stress in the interviews. One good reason for this is the fact that few firms ever have a net decrease in the number of clerical employees, not to mention the total number of employees. I will deal in greater detail with some ramifications of labor saving later. However, at this point, it is worthwhile to stress the economic objectives that are only indirectly measurable in order to emphasize how much room for E.D.P. advancement lies ahead. One E.D.P. manager put it this way: "The major objective of E.D.P. is not cost, but quality and service. Streamlining and improved efficiency is the major aim. There is, of course, an element of cost reduction there, but in large firms cost is not *the* factor."[15]

A lengthy but well thought out company document is useful in illustrating the objectives of a particular firm's E.D.P. program *beyond* direct cost reduction:

> These benefits fall into three broad categories—indirect cost reduction, improved customer service, and better management control. A discussion of each follows:
>
> a) *Indirect Cost Reduction*
>
>   1) Reduced Inventory Investment: Centralized control of_____ and warehouse stock should permit a reduction of finished stock inventory. The application of production control techniques should reduce work-in-process inventories.

[14] "Adjustments to the Introduction of Office Automation," *Bureau of Labor Statistics Bulletin Number 1276* (Washington, D.C.: United States Government Printing Office, United States Department of Labor, May, 1960), 10. This finding is corroborated in a recent report of eight case studies of firms which had installed computers: "Management Decisions to Automate," *Manpower/Automation Research Monograph Number 3* (Washington, D.C.: United States Government Printing Office, United States Department of Labor, Office of Manpower, Automation, and Training, 1965).

[15] Because of their confidential nature, company documents and/or statements by company personnel cannot be identified, except to the extent of identifying them as such throughout the book.

2) Production Economies: Reductions in production costs should be realized by the benefit of: centralized inventory control which will permit larger production orders for stock, better application of alteration and substitution rules for stock, and more economic choices of mold equipment and manufacturing methods.

3) Reduction in Errors: Clerical errors are inherent in any manually operated system. Errors reduce clerical efficiency and are embarrassing when undetected and called to our attention by a customer. These errors will be minimized in a properly conceived integrated data processing system. An example of a current error problem which will be corrected by the proposed system is the assignment of list price and multipliers.

4) Flexible to Volume: The speed and capacity of data processing equipment will reduce to a minimum the hiring and lay-off costs of clerical help caused by changes in business volume.

5) Audit Control: There will be an improved audit system for controlling the falsification of piecework coupons.

b) *Improved Customer Service*

1) Order Entry Within Eight Hours: It is the objective of this program to permit the complete processing of all_____ and warehouse orders within an eight-hour cycle, excluding the rating of piecework coupons.

2) Centralized Stock Inventory Control: Centralized inventory control aided by the Data Transmission System will permit service to any customer from any point where inventory is stocked.

3) Production Scheduling: The production control system will permit better scheduling and improve performance to promised delivery dates.

4) Shorter Invoicing Cycle: We should be able to reduce the current Traffic through Billing invoicing cycle from 5 days to 2 days, and eventually 1 day.

5) Improved Product Quality: Product quality should be improved by the issuance of accurate bond charts and mixing slips. The availability of

a computer will also permit improved statistical quality control applications.

c) *Better Management Control*

   1) Standardization of Policies and Procedures: One of the indirect benefits of an integrated data processing system is the complete review and standardization of all policies and procedures. These benefits are usually realized whether all phases of the program are successfully completed or not.

   2) Mathematical Aids: The availability of a computer facilitates the application of mathematical aids, such as—economic lot size 7 reorder point, alteration and substitution from stock rules, statistical quality control, sales forecasting, and other techniques associated with operational research activities.

   3) Management Reports: Data processing equipment will permit the issuance of more comprehensive and timely management reports. Many management reports will be modified to permit action by exception or variance to given standards.

In emphasizing the fact that the potential of E.D.P. has only begun to be realized, I do not mean to imply that direct cost saving in manpower, equipment, time, and space is insignificant. For instance, a comparison of fiscal 1956 (before E.D.P.) and fiscal 1959 (after E.D.P.) in the Treasury Department's check payment and reconciliation operation indicates that:

Although the workload increased 14 percent, employment declined 48 percent — with the result that output per employee more than doubled (up 120 percent). Unit labor costs declined 44 percent, while equipment rental per unit of output rose 85 percent; total unit costs declined 32 percent.[16]

The complexities and difficulties of conversion to E.D.P. should be at least alluded to for better balance at present.

---

[16] Richard W. Riche and William E. Alli, "Office Automation in the Federal Government," *Monthly Labor Review*, 83:no. 9, 934 (Washington, D.C.: United States Government Printing Office, September, 1960).

The psychological attitude of employees is crucial at all levels of the organization. The complexities of conversion include the risk of important organizational problems arising which necessitate top management planning, and dramatic shifts in lower managers' duties and responsibilities; this conversion often precipitates many forms of employee insecurity. Technically, also, each installation has unique features and demands which require the careful choice of machinery. Computer characteristics and abilities change rapidly, often making systems obsolete before bugs can be worked out. In some instances specific machine requirements present considerable barriers to further mechanization. Finally, the economics of E.D.P. can restrain mechanization. The uncertainty of savings and the considerable cost of the computer create an extra if not insurmountable problem for the small firm.

A survey of the literature and personal interviews indicate that management has no clear idea of the costs of computerization, or how to turn the computer into a profit-making investment quickly. McKinsey and Company, Incorporated, surveyed 27 companies in 13 different industries and found that only 9 firms were unmistakably successful in computerizing their operations. The evaluation in the McKinsey report was based on the rate of return on investment in computerization, intangible benefits accrued, and the range and scope of applications. Marginal results, at best, were attained in the other 18 firms. In 4 of the 9 high achievement firms, capital expenditures for computer systems were found to exceed 12 percent of yearly capital budgets.[17]

Some idea of computer costs can be gleaned by examining the purchase prices and the rentals of selected systems. The computers cited below are the most popular types currently in operation.[18]

average between $46,000 and $103,000 and rent for from $1,100 to $2,600 per month.

[17] John T. Garrity, "Top Management and Computer Profits," *Harvard Business Review*, 4:no. 4, 7-8 (July-August, 1963).

[18] "On-Site Systems Top 30,000 Mark," *Business Automation*, 13:no. 2, 54-56 (February, 1966).

Large Scale: I.B.M. 7070, 7072, and 7074 cost on the average between $1,150,000 and $1,400,000, and rent for from $24,000 to $29,300 per month.

Medium Scale: I.B.M. 1401 (all types) cost on the average between $90,000 and $420,000 and rent for from $1,600 to $8,200 per month.

Small Scale: Univac 1004, I, II and III cost on the

Precise data on the true total costs of computerization are scarce. It is especially difficult to determine the non-computer costs of computerization, both prior to and after conversion. Thus, to obtain a realistic picture of expenditures for computerization, the cost of such factors as the following should be considered: undertaking the feasibility study, installing the computer in proper quarters, conducting a systems analysis, programming the computer, manpower training, conversion, handling employee displacement, and debugging the new system.

Firms with unique information processing problems and small firms with capital problems have begun to have their particular needs met in several innovative ways. One approach was the creation of a cooperative bureau:

> One of the earliest groups of this type is SPAN, a group of fire and casualty insurance companies in Hartford, Connecticut. These companies installed a computer system in early 1958 for processing their paper work.[19]

The objective, of course, was to share the costs of a large-scale system in order to reap the economies of large-scale operations.

Another approach to the problem of small firm office mechanization was the establishment of computer service centers by computer manufacturers. R.C.A. announced in July, 1959 that it would open two such centers. One of the first applications planned was in broker back-office operations, where reportedly over 25 percent of the commission dollar is spent on

[19] Diebold, "Bringing Automation up to Date," *New Views on Automation, op. cit.,* p. 105.

paper work. IBM reacted quickly, and announced that in the first half of 1960 it would open about thirty "Data-centers" which would be open to all firms buying a minimum of fifteen hours per month of computer time.

Economical small-scale computers are becoming available to the small firm. For example, Univac has recently developed a faster, third generation computer with a low-cost memory device. The average rental charge is said to be about $1,200 per month.[20]

The demand for computer technology services by all kinds of organizations has grown rapidly since 1955, from $189 million yearly to an estimated $3 billion by 1970 (see Table 3). Computer services are defined to include payments for E.D.P. consulting, data forms, systems analysis, and programming and machine time rentals. It is predicted that this latter service, the creation of "information utilities," will develop into a new major industry. This development is being hastened by the delivery of a time-sharing computer, i.e., a computer which permits several separate programs to share its services simultaneously, rather than in sequence.[21]

Thus technical refinements and cost reductions have made E.D.P. equipment increasingly accessible to all firms. Such innovations as the cooperative bureau, the service bureau, and the information utility, as well as third generation small-scale computers, have all contributed to make this development possible.

Finally the unavailability of adequate supporting personnel is troublesome particularly to the small firm. The crucial roles that technical skill and training play in office mechanization are discussed later, but a new development is relevant to the small firm. Temporary employment of factory and office work-

---

[20] "Univac Thinks Small — But Fast," *Business Week*, 1921:173-174 (June 25, 1966).

[21] "Office Equipment," *op. cit.*, p. 10. For a more detailed discussion of this topic, see Lee L. Selwyn, "The Information Utility," *Industrial Management Review*, 7:no. 2, 17-26 (Spring, 1966). Also for a report on the establishment of the first business information utility see "Computer Time-Sharing Goes on the Market," *Business Week*, 1892:116 (December 4, 1965).

ers and management consultants through outside agencies is not new. But because of the rise of office mechanization, E.D.P. technicians are now available, even to the small firm. A typical advertisement reads:

> Hire us...then fire us...when the job is done. YOU don't incur the high costs of staffing-up for short term work....

The increased demand for high level technical skills in the office is, in a sense, only beginning — just as computer technology is, at present, in the toddler stage.

Some suggested uses of computer technology are startling: for instance, guidance of ocean shipping, translation of foreign languages, battlefield decisions, airfield instructions to five hundred planes simultaneously, medical diagnosis and patient care, expedition and clarification of the administration of justice, design and supervision of lesser computers, inter-machine communications over regular telephone lines, and long-range weather forecasts are all in various stages of development and implementation.[22]

Diebold maintains that automatic data processing "has arrived," but revolutionary organizational changes are unrealized as yet. Some developments in computer technology foreseen for management are the following:

> The American Telephone and Telegraph Company estimates that by 1970 its revenue from communication of data from one business machine to another, in different cities, will *exceed* its revenue from voice transmission over similar long-distance lines.

> By 1970 we shall see the commercial perfection of man-computer communications. Programming languages by then will be more like everyday language; and man will use voice communication and visual communication to direct computers.

> "Polymodular" systems will be a common mode of

---

[22] General Sarnoff states that "...computers will touch off an explosion in the social sciences comparable to that which we witnessed during the past half century in the physical sciences." See "The Social Impact of Computers," *Congressional Record*, 20:no. 149, A4051-A4053 (Washington, D.C.: United States Government Printing Office, August 3, 1964). See also, John Diebold, "The New World Coming," *Saturday Review*, XLIX:no. 30, 17-18 (July 23, 1966).

design. System modules (viz., functional "packages" of equipment) will perform in a number of ways: they will work separately or in tandem, communicate with a great variety of input and output devices, and process a great many programs simultaneously.

Programs will incorporate self-correcting features, permitting the machine to recognize its own malfunctions, correct them, or select a different path to solve a problem.

Heuristic, or self-organizing, systems will allow machines to develop their own problem-solving methods best suited to the management analysis or problem at hand. These systems will help achieve the goal of dispensing with formal programs altogether for certain decision-making processes handled by machine. The machines will tend more and more to "think" in the accepted meaning of that word.[23]

The computer developments forecast by Diebold underscore the fact that the *way* management manages and *what* management manages will continue to undergo significant modification in the near future.[24]

In the following section mechanization in the office prior to computerization is described.

OFFICE MECHANIZATION

The growing amount of paperwork in advanced industrial societies has been discussed widely. Sometimes the comments have been picturesque:

> As skyscrapers replace rows of small shops, so offices replace free markets. Each office within the skyscraper is a segment of the enormous file, a part of the symbol factory that produces the billion slips of paper that gear modern society into its daily shape. From the executive's suite to the factory yard, the paper webwork is spun; a thousand rules you never made and don't

---

[23] John Diebold, "ADP—The Still-Sleeping Giant," *Harvard Business Review,* 42:no. 5, 63 (September-October, 1964).

[24] For a survey to determine future developments in computerization in over 80 United States and European businesses, see John Diebold, "What's Ahead in Information Technology," *Harvard Business Review,* 43:no. 5, 76-82 (September-October, 1965).

know about are applied to you by a thousand people you have not met and never will.[25]
The omnipotent office, even for Mills, is a necessary evil because of the services it performs:

> But, however big or little and whatever the shape, the minimum function of an office is to direct and coordinate the activities of an enterprise. For every business enterprise, every factory, is tied to some office and, by virtue of what happens there, is linked to other businesses and to the rest of the people. Scattered throughout the political economy, each office is the peak of a pyramid of work and money and decision.[26]

The objective of paperwork — the treatment and transformation of information necessary for the efficient provision of goods and services — is achieved by four functions:

> The basic functions performed in an office may be roughly grouped under four main headings — classifying, computing, recording, and storing. Classifying includes the establishment of useful grouping of data, under appropriate headings or in some effective order for processing, and the sorting of incoming data in accordance with this system. Computing covers all calculating and accounting operations, including summarizing of the results. Recording may be interpreted broadly to include the operations of reading, transcribing and reproducing material processed. Storing is the function of keeping processed data readily accessible — in other words, file maintenance.[27]

The attainment of the paperwork objective through the economical performance of these functions has challenged managers increasingly over the last fifty years. Colorfully stated, managements must beware lest their ". . . production-marketing systems imposed by the office become a nightmare of paper shuffling — a dollar-draining necessary evil that tips a company into the red."[28]

---

[25] C. Wright Mills, *White Collar* (New York: Oxford University Press, 1951), 189.

[26] *Ibid.*, p. 190.

[27] "Effects of Mechanisation and Automation in Offices," *Report III* (Geneva: International Labour Office, 1959), 18.

[28] Lloyd E. Slater, "Instrumentation," *Office Executive*, 34:no. 10, 45 (October, 1959).

The office, like the factory, turned to mechanization as the only practical means by which it could hope to meet the expanding information needs of the activities which it served. Mechanization of office work is not new, computerization being only its newest form.

The earliest offices were rather simple by way of functions performed and manpower required. The office was generally small, reflecting the scale of production in most firms in the years before the last decades of the nineteenth century. Specialization of labor was slight because functions were few: the boss or partners made the decisions, the bookkeeper kept the financial records, the clerk handled correspondence and maintained the files, and the office boy was the system of communications. The office remained so until the "white collar girl" entered the labor force in significant numbers in the 1890s.

The focus of all activity was the ledger, and legal documents constituted essentially all the record-keeping. Employee relationships were intimate. Office employment was restricted to the middle class, while promotion often depended upon nepotism, influence, and privilege. A smattering of arithmetic, good penmanship, and cultural refinements were required.

The twentieth century ushered in the early stages of office mechanization.[29] The first office machines performed a single function. These machines are still important today, and many new forms of such mechanization continue to be used:

> The first mechanical appliances used in office work were designed to simplify and speed up operations in one particular area. Typewriters eliminated the tedious work of recording data by hand. Adding machines were invented capable of performing rapidly most of the simple calculations needed in clerical work. New methods of rapid reproduction of data by photographic or other means gave the office workers another handy tool which eliminated copy work. In addition, all sorts of visual filing systems and devices such as charge plates and key sort cards facilitated the sorting, inter-filing

---

[29] The prototype of punched card mechanical information processing equipment was developed in the Census Bureau in 1889, but did not have significant commercial application until the 1920s.

and looking up of data; while in more recent years microfilming has provided a new form of data storage which economizes greatly on space.... The handling of correspondence has been greatly facilitated by the introduction of addressograph and automatic stamping machines (postage meters), gadgets such as data stampers, and even, when large quantities of correspondence are handled, letter-opening machines and others which automatically fold out-going letters and insert them into the envelopes.

Machines of this nature involved no change in routines or operating procedures, and once their utility had been recognized they quickly achieved widespread acceptance.[30]

Increasing needs for business information, the rapid expansion of the clerical labor force, with consequent increases in cost, and growing specialization of work prompted introduction of office machinery. After the First World War the first multi-functional business machines were introduced, and since then these, too, have been improved upon:

A second stage in mechanisation began with the invention of machines which combine several functions, and can carry out without interruption two or sometimes a whole sequence of operations. Simple examples are the adding machine which computes and records, and the cash register which adds and stamps the bill. Others are a great deal more complex, such as the bookkeeping machines which print invoices at the same time as they perform the accounting calculations and post the data on a ledger card. Some of these machines are equipped with several registers, or built-in adding machines, which permit different classifications of data to be distributed, and they are capable of preparing 100 or more accounts per hour.[31]

The information processing system containing the types of office machines I have discussed so far is commonly referred to as part of a "manual processing system," although it may seem a misnomer. Yet, everything considered, clerical work until the end of the Second World War was highly labor in-

---

[30] "Effects of Mechanisation and Automation in Offices," *op. cit.*, p. 19.
[31] *Ibid.*

tensive. During the prosperity of the 1920s, and the surplus labor and curtailed operations condition of the 1930s, office mechanization lagged.

The information processing systems prior to 1945 had advantages as well as disadvantages. These systems involved less fixed capital and could be expanded or contracted flexibly as economic conditions demanded. Routines were relatively flexible, so that an "exception" could be accommodated more easily. Finally, records and documents were immediately accessible. The disadvantages were, however, still considerable. The probability of human error was high. The increasing size and the specialization of the clerical labor force made supervision more difficult and created many problems for managers as they became further and further divorced from the operating level. Replacement, training, motivation, resistance to change, and a myriad of other complicated problems also bore down increasingly on management.[32]

The powerful forces for further mechanization mentioned above increased with a vengeance after 1945. The third phase of mechanization involved the dramatic introduction of punched card equipment into the office:

> The invention of punched-card machines for offices introduced a new stage of mechanisation by providing compatability of equipment.... With this type of equipment, the punched cards serve as a common language medium between the different units — key punch, sorter, reproducer, accounting machine — each of which performs one or several of the basic functions.... While the intervention of the operator is still necessary in order to move blocks of cards from one machine to another, this system achieves a relatively high degree of intercommunication between functions. It is a near approach to a continuous process, and it requires severe discipline of procedures to be truly effective.[33]

This type of mechanization, commonly referred to as the

---

[32] R. C. Canning, *Production Control through Electronic Data Processing: A Case Study* (Washington, D.C.: United States Government Printing Office, United States Department of Commerce, Office of Technical Services, May 1, 1954), Table II, p. 14.

[33] "Effects of Mechanisation and Automation in Offices," *op. cit.*, p. 20.

"mechanized system" of information processing, was a major step forward. The machines were reliable, and the cards provided convenient, mobile, and legal records capable of being read by machine as well as by human beings. The cards, however, had to be taken from the files manually; to change a card it was necessary to re-punch it, and the amount of information that each card could contain was strictly limited.[34]

The current stage is, of course, that of computerization of clerical functions. The computer's abilities to operate at high speeds with precision, to store vast amounts of information, and to perform for long periods of time, have made a considerable contribution to office efficiency. The implications for management of office computerization are summarized by Bize:

> The intervention of electronics in a massive way into a field in which human work enjoyed until now a near-monopoly obviously brings about numerous modifications. It may be convenient to class them in four categories, which define, without exhausting the subject, the principal contributions of automation in this field. Automation puts at the disposal of the leaders of enterprise new possible uses for a multitude of information which he did not previously possess: it practically does away with time and space in office work — it makes it necessary to conceive of the enterprise as an integrated system and to reconsider the principles of scientific work organization — it necessitates the establishment of a system of homogeneous translation of all the activities of the enterprise — finally, it opens vast perspectives for the utilization of the scientific theory of decision, that is of operational research.[35]

These prospects for computerization will make possible an entirely new approach to information processing. The unsystematic approach at the turn of the century had been compatible with the small office, few employees, and highly personal and integrated social and work organizations. A change in approach became necessary as paperwork demands grew,

---

[34] Canning, op. cit., Table II, p. 14.
[35] Pierre Bize, "Automation and the Scientific Management of Enterprises," Views on Automation (Paris: Organisation for European Economic Cooperation, 1957), 4.

communication became more impersonal and complex, specialization was intensified, and multi-copy forms and reports from each functional area began to proliferate.

The era of fragmentation followed. Departmentalization, greater functionalization, and bureaucracy developed rapidly. Enlarged staffs and vested interests emerged as paperwork became more cumbersome.

The computerization of paperwork once again has encouraged and made possible an integrated approach in the office. The trend toward fragmentation has been reversed. Separate units and functions of a firm are being brought closer together by the integration of the increasing continuity of information flow and management functions.[36] Some aspects of labor market data and mechanization, as well as the intra-firm utilization of labor, will now be examined.

MANPOWER CONSEQUENCES

The decade beginning in 1960 offers many challenging opportunities for growth and change in the utilization of manpower in the United States.[37] Gross national product is expected to increase by 50 percent, resulting in a 25 percent increase in the standard of living, since the population will be 15 percent larger in 1970. During this same period, the number of available workers will increase by 20 percent, reflecting the postwar increase in births. There will also be a 30 percent increase in the number of part-time workers by 1970.

The predicted changes in labor force characteristics and the utilization of labor within the firm reflect most graphically the technological advances of the decade. These data offer keen insights for planning, and should be of particular interest to public and private officials concerned with manpower utilization.

---

[36] "Establishing an Integrated Data-Processing System," *Special Report Number 11* (New York: American Management Association, 1956), 16-18.

[37] The following labor force data, unless otherwise indicated, are from *Manpower Challenge of the 1960s* (Washington, D.C.: United States Government Printing Office, United States Department of Labor, 1960).

Significant changes in the age composition of the labor force are expected. There will be a dramatic increase in the number of workers under twenty-five years of age entering the labor force (nearly half), despite rising educational levels. The next largest increase will be in the number of workers over forty-five years of age, earlier retirements notwithstanding. Finally, there will be a relatively small increase in numbers in the twenty-five- to thirty-four-year age group. Because of the low birth rates in the 1930s, there will be actually fewer workers in the thirty-five- to forty-four-year age category. These figures do not reflect the sharp increase in numbers of female workers.

> By 1970, there will be about 30 million women workers, six million more than in 1960. This represents a 25% increase for women, as compared to a 15% increase for men. One out of every three workers will be a woman. Except for teen-age girls (most of them still in school) and women 65 and over (most of them either retired or past working age), at least two out of every five women in 1970 will be in the labor force. Among women whose children are in school or past school age the proportion who work will be much higher than now.[38]

This trend, to some extent, reflects the proportionately higher demand for workers in service industries rather than in manufacturing industries. Government, finance, insurance, real estate, plus "other services" (with the notable exception of construction) will issue the greatest demand by far for additional workers. The quality of the labor force, too, will change.

Reflecting the continuing trend of increasing high school and college enrollments, 70 percent of new entrants to the labor force in the 1960s will have *at least* a high school diploma. The increasing need for managerial, professional, technical, and clerical workers in the rapidly expanding industries will reinforce this trend toward higher levels of education for the work force.

The essential point is that, tomorrow, if not already

---

[38] *Ibid.*, p. 7.

today, more and more of the people in the normal traditional organization, in the day to day operations of a business, are going to be people who work with their minds rather than with their hands, people who are doing every day "line" work rather than special "longhair work" — and who yet are different in their background, different in their expectations and different in the way they work from the people who yesterday did these "line" jobs.[39]

In 1956 white collar workers outnumbered blue collar workers for the first time in industrial history. It is estimated that there will be an increase of 40 percent in the number of professional and technical workers from 1960 to 1970. Also, roughly a 25 percent increase in the number of proprietors and managers, clerical and sales, skilled and service workers is predicted. The number of unskilled workers will remain about the same, while the number of agricultural workers will decrease during the same period.

The composition of the firm's work force naturally reflects the labor force statistics mentioned above. A 44 percent increase of "upper executive manpower" from 1949 to 1959, for example, is reported. "The rise was ascribed to new concepts of management and organization, increased specialization of functions, corporate growth, the expanding complexity of business, and a trend toward decentralization.[40]

An investigation by Weber found that:

With the mechanization of data-processing, clerical and semi-technical employment in the two firms decreased numerically and relatively, while managerial employment increased numerically and relatively. The shift toward managerial employment was primarily

[39] Peter F. Drucker, *Managing the Educated* (Paper presented to the alumni of the Washington University Graduate School of Business Administration Management Development Conferences, January 14, 1959), 2. Also, for an examination of changes in educational levels of young male workers by occupation since 1940, see "The Rising Levels of Education Among Young Workers," *Monthly Labor Review*, 88:no. 6, 625-628 (June, 1965).

[40] From a study of 14,000 executive positions in 559 of the largest 1,000 corporations, reported by William M. Freeman, "High Executives Grow in Number," *New York Times*, Sec. 3, p. 5 (October 9, 1960).

attributed to the growth of administrative-professional personnel.[41]

Hill and Harbison, after investigating employment statistics of fifty firms, conclude that the ratio of highly skilled personnel to over-all company employment is increasing primarily because of innovation.

> In other words, the companies showing the greatest increases in non-production workers as a proportion of total employment were invariably those which had made the most spectacular or far-reaching changes in products, processes, and organization.[42]

These authors also conclude that "bureaucratic expansion" is not a primary factor in the increasing utilization of non-production employees of the firm, although the factor probably is present, especially during good times.[43]

Woodward found several interesting statistical relationships based on the type of production process. For instance, there were three times as many managers compared to all other personnel in process systems of production as in the unit form. Mass production had about twice as many managers for the same number of personnel as in the unit form of production. Thus, increasing mechanization seemed to lead to an increasing manager-worker ratio. In addition, the ratio of indirect to direct labor and the proportion of university graduates also increased with higher degrees of mechanization. Finally, the span of control widened and labor costs, as a percentage of total costs, decreased with technical progress.[44]

The importance of these changes in the composition and characteristics of the work force should be obvious to all concerned with the efficient utilization of manpower. A firm's manpower requirements are particularly affected by the application of computer technology to information processing.

---

41 C. Edward Weber, "Change in Managerial Manpower with Mechanization of Data-Processing," *The Journal of Business,* 32:no. 2, 163 (April, 1959).

42 Samuel E. Hill and Frederick Harbison, *Manpower and Innovation in American Industry* (Princeton: Princeton University, Industrial Relations Section, 1959), 54.

43 *Ibid.,* p. 55.

44 Joan Woodward, *Management and Technology* (London: Department of Scientific and Industrial Research, 1958), 16-17.

Manpower planning, under the above-described conditions, becomes increasingly necessary.

In summary, then, the rapid growth of the information processing function is transforming the small, personal office with its simple work functions into a highly mechanized, impersonal, and specialized work place. The development and use of computers for business is accelerated by the growth in company size, volume of information, and changing labor market conditions. The prospect is for greater availability of E.D.P. for every firm.

The changes predicted for the economy, the population, and the labor force indicate that manpower and organization planning will become a more important management responsibility. But more than hardware is involved. The computer moves hand in hand with method changes. The next chapter is concerned with the systems and procedures function and how of necessity it complements and accompanies computerization.

Chapter II

SYSTEMS TECHNOLOGY

A manager who believes that he can run his job without systems is mistaken. A systems specialist who assumes his system can run the organization is mistaken.
— ADRIAN M. McDONOUGH

Distinguishing between systems development and computer operations is important. Many writers consider systems plus computers to be equivalent to electronic data processing. In practice, systems analysis and computer operations obviously are closely related and very often are managed by the same individual. To appreciate their origins, current practices, future trends, and for clarity's sake, it is necessary to examine them separately.

Computerizing takes a long time. Generally, much planning and preparatory work is done by a business organization before the computer arrives. This planning and preparation usually involves systems analysis. Further, even after a particular procedure has been computerized, the functional distinction between systems and computer work remains. There is always systems work to be performed. You may add a computer, but this does not eliminate the need to devise new and revise old systems. Nor does an organization remain in a state of equilibrium for any length of time, either before or after a computer is introduced. This is noted by Mann and Williams in their study of an insurance company which had placed several procedures on the computer. They delineate the change process accordingly:

In studying a change of this magnitude and duration, it was found useful to identify seven different phases in the sequence of a change-over to E.D.P.: 1) relative stability and equilibrium before the change, 2) preliminary planning, 3) detailed preparation, 4) installation and testing, 5) conversion, 6) stabilization, and 7) new equilibrium after change.... The whole process appeared to start off slowly, gradually accelerate to a sustained level of high actvity in the installation and conversion periods, and then decelerate until the organization finally arrived at a new state of equilibrium.[1]

It is true, of course, that the conversion of even one procedure is a long, involved process requiring many new skills and much hard work. Nevertheless, there is some merit in viewing this single procedure conversion as part of the continuing process of change which accompanies, follows, or is quickened by the procedure conversion.

Finally, the division of systems design and computer operations sharpens another important distinction.

The master plan for developing mechanized data processing systems at our company is called "The Three-Phase Approach" — the study phase, the installation phase, and the operating phase.

In phase one — the study phase — the emphasis is on staff activity. Although contacts are set up with the departments concerned and department participation is sought in gathering facts, the effort is primarily a staff function....

At the end of phase one a proposal of the most advantageous system which can be installed is prepared. This system is advanced not only on the basis of the present-day economy but also on the basis of adequate longevity, both as to procedures established and equipment utilized.

In phase two — the installation phase — the emphasis is on team effort. The proposal outlined in phase one is developed in more detail. The staff project leader or

---

[1] Floyd C. Mann and Lawrence K. Williams, "Observations of the Dynamics of a Change to Electronic Data-Processing Equipment," *Administrative Science Quarterly*, 5:no. 2, 221 (September, 1960).

methods analyst manages the project and acts as the coordinating member of the team. . . .

In the third phase — the operating phase — the emphasis is largely on line activity. Members of the staff and team used during phase two play a continuous role in the actual setting up and in the initial operation of the new system, but this active role becomes less evident as the new system begins to operate in a normal fashion. In time, the team is discontinued and the role of staff reverts to a consulting service for the operating groups.[2]

This "master plan" is simple enough, but how is it translated into organizational practice? Is it realistic to discuss the many-faceted problems raised by computer mechanization in terms of a little more or a little less staff activity? The line and staff concept often loses its significance, but even if it does not, it is an insufficient means to describe or to evaluate the management of organizational change. The study, installation, and operating phases suggested as an ordered approach to mechanization are simple and neat, but of little help in studying organizational change. In the remainder of this chapter, the systems function in E.D.P. will be considered; the development of systems, its technical and human aspects, its modes of analysis, and its applications also are included.

DEVELOPMENT OF SYSTEMS AND PROCEDURES

Systems and procedures has only recently been accepted as a recognized and organized managerial function. Prior to 1945, the application of systems analysis to paperwork was minimal, except as industrial engineers, working on shop management problems, became involved indirectly. The Systems and Procedures Association, founded in 1947, had nine chapters by 1950. Ten years later there were sixty-three chapters. In mid-1966 the Association proudly announced that it had reached a "milestone of 100 chapters" and "growth prospects (were) undiminished."[3] The causes for this rapid growth in the num-

---

[2] Chester A. Swanson, "Functional Approach to Mechanized Data Processing," *Office Executive*, 34:no. 10, 42 (October, 1959).

[3] "Uncommon Denominator," *Systems and Procedures Journal*, 17:no. 3, 5 (May-June, 1966).

ber of chapters and the increased interest in systems work, according to Neuschel, are: 1) the growing size and complexity of business organizations, 2) the drastic increases in the number and cost of clerical workers, and 3) the growing interest in and application of computers by business.[4]

The increase in business computer applications has been paralleled by the development of systems departments. If the computer is thought of as crucial to advancing office automation, then systems can be thought of as a necessary prerequiste to the application of computers.

> A characteristic of all analyst positions was their relative newness. Many had been created within the past two or three years; none was reported to have existed as such prior to 1943. A few analysts reported that they had come from old job situations which were inherently "analysis" in nature although not so named and not, of course, concerned with systems studies from the current point of view. The reorganization and organization of so many systems departments within the past decade has been kicked off primarily by rumors of what electronic data processing (E.D.P.) can do. However, an organization must clean up its systems before it can think of E.D.P.[5]

The relationships among systems analysts, the approach of the methods men, and the procedures selected for computerization are crucial to the output of the newly mechanized operations. The approach of methods analysts to the problems of mechanization in large part derives from the degree to which prior planning and systems revision have taken place before E.D.P. begins. The problem arises, as stated earlier, to some extent because the expansion of systems work has been prompted by E.D.P.

In a 1957 survey of fifty-four companies, it was found that twenty-eight of the thirty-six systems and procedures depart-

---

[4] Richard F. Neuschel, *Management by System* (New York: McGraw-Hill Book Company, Incorporated, 1960), vii-viii.

[5] Irene Place, "Administrative Systems Analysis," *Michigan Business Report Number 28* (Ann Arbor: Bureau of Business Research, University of Michigan School of Business Administration, 1957), 8.

ments in existence had been established between 1950 and 1957.[6] The major reasons cited in the survey for the creation of these departments are similar to those offered for office computerization:

a) to develop electronic data processing applications and to increase general office mechanization, b) rising costs of clerical operations, c) shortage of clerical personnel, d) increase in types and quantity of information needed to operate business, e) a growing awareness of the need for work simplification, f) an increase in experience and knowledge of how to simplify and control clerical operations.[7]

Further, the activities of the systems and procedures departments were related closely to E.D.P.

The range of activities in which the analyst is most likely to engage comprises: a) office mechanization, b) systems, c) records management, d) forms control, e) office layout, f) communications, g) work measurement and standards, h) service units.

He may also become involved in training programs, the writing of procedures and manuals, management reviews, staffing surveys, and problems of organization and control.[8]

It should be noted that some of these activities were related more directly to E.D.P. than others. The more traditional concerns of systems departments, or their related antecedents, can be noted toward the end of the above-quoted list. It is only within the past fifteen years that the responsibilities of systems work have been recognized as important and distinct; and that the various people responsible for these activities have been drawn together and their activities organized more effectively. These comments modify but do not negate the fact that computers became the number one concern of the systems group, as indicated below:[9]

---

[6] *Ibid.*, p. 12.
[7] *Ibid.*, p. 70.
[8] *Ibid.*, p. 71.
[9] *Ibid.*, p. 14.

	Number of
Activity	Companies
Office Equipment Studies	
a. Electronic data processing applications	21
b. General mechanization and standardization	17
c. Punched card, tabulating, and statistical applications	6
d. Integrated data processing applications	5
	——
	49

The fact that office equipment studies, rather than computer applications, were the major activity reflected the state of the art in 1957 — the formative stage of development. Application rather than study is the major activity at present.

THE TECHNICAL SIDE OF SYSTEMS

The time required to implement computerization varies widely, depending upon the information needs, the size, and the organizational structure of a particular firm. According to Becker, a large firm may require from five to ten years to install a "total information system." The schedule he developed is based upon the key events occurring along the critical path of implementation. This schedule is depicted in Exhibit 1.

The systems analysis phase of computerization was lengthy in the surveyed firms. On the average about five years was required from the time the computer was planned for until specific procedures were ready to be separated from systems control. The general pattern of systems development with regard to computerization follows, and will be helpful in understanding the practices discussed later in this chapter.[10]

The initial overtures in the planning phase were made by various individuals and usually included a person engaged directly in systems and procedures work. As a firm was made more and more aware of computer technology, management either ignored the pressures for computerization, followed the

10 For an excellent general discussion of systems concepts, see S. L. Optner, *Systems Analysis for Business and Industrial Problem Solving* (Englewood Cliffs, New Jersey: Prentice-Hall, Incorporated, 1965).

EXHIBIT 1

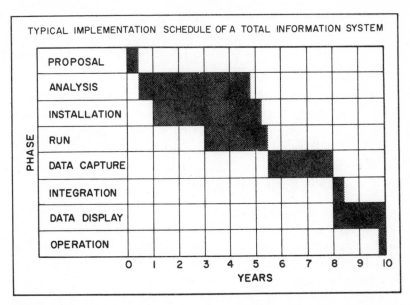

Source: James L. Becker, "Planning the Total Information System," Alan D. Meacham and Van B. Thompson, eds., *Total Systems* (Detroit: American Data Processing, Incorporated, 1962), 69.

example of other computerizing firms, or pioneered in applying the computer to its own business activities. Thus the rate of progress with regard to computerization varied, but at some point in time a firm formally organized its efforts to avail itself of this form of mechanization. Typically an E.D.P. committee was formed, perhaps consisting of division or department heads, which then entrusted to a small group of middle managers the responsibility of conducting a feasibility study. This small group was usually headed by a methods man who, even before the formal study stage, had been interested in computers and informally was keeping himself informed of their development and usefulness.

The feasibility study, which may have taken a year of intensive activity, was designed to answer two basic questions: 1) Is the computer useful and economically justifiable? 2) If so, what type of equipment best suits our particular needs? Some firms considered a third question: Should the equipment be purchased or rented? In any event, the decision to conduct a feasibility study constituted the formulation stage in which a new group of specialists were to be responsible for the application of computer technology to the firm's operations.

Another year passed, perhaps, and a formal recommendation was made to top management (without exception in my survey) to utilize computer technology. Top management approval led to the signing of an agreement with a computer manufacturer for delivery of equipment in from six months to two years, depending upon the type of equipment required.

The group initially in charge, as well as the chief sponsoring agency (usually the controller), really was in business then. A systems group was issued an "organizational hunting license" which outlined, with varying degrees of clarity and authority, the responsibility conferred by top management. The group began to develop an organization, to recruit and to train its staff, and to program its first procedure.

Computer program preparation by the systems group consisted broadly of four steps: analysis of the procedures, flow charting, instructions or coding, and testing. The first two steps — analysis and flow charting — usually had been completed during the feasibility study, at least for the simplest and most obvious first applications. These early procedures had been selected because they were easily adapted to computerization, and not necessarily because they would bring the greatest saving.

The third step — preparing instructions for the computer to mechanize the procedure — was a long, expensive process. Often this phase was extended because a thorough systems analysis had not been completed beforehand. This difficulty, as well as others, sometimes caused extreme frictions between systems work *per se* and programming, where these responsibilities were divided organizationally.[11] Programming the computer continues to be one of the most troublesome aspects of computerization, new programming aids such as simplified computer language packages (e.g., FORTRAN, COBOL, and ALGOL) notwithstanding. Firms also continue to experience delays in implementing computerized procedures when the time required to write programs for the computer has not been forecast correctly. [12]

The final step was testing the computerized procedure to insure that it produced the desired output. This de-bugging process sometimes took years, depending upon such factors as how good a systems job had been done, the degree to which the original procedure or input had to be changed over time, and how many modifications in the equipment were required. Throughout this period, the firm could elect to run two parallel systems (or some modification thereof) to insure uninterrupted output. All during this break-in period, the systems people not only supervised the running of these programs on the computer, but played an integral role as well in the line operations directly involved in supplying input to the program. Not until it was running routinely did the systems analyst in charge of the particular program relinquish control to the line operation (input) or computer operation (output) manager.

A fifth step is emerging which will constitute an important aspect of computer systems responsibility. Simon calls this step "systems design."

> Later on, when we understand the computer, we begin to think more about component adaptions. If we are going to do a task efficiently on a computer we find we need a different computer from the one with which we started. We may get to this stage of component adap-

[11] Some authors make a distinction between systems and programming responsibilities, just as I have elected to distinguish between systems and computer operations. For general discussion, unless otherwise stated, I will continue to consider programming as merely one responsibility of the systems group.

[12] For an excellent summary of the latest developments in computer "software," see "The Third Generation Computer," *American Management Association Bullletin 79* (New York: American Management Association, 1966).

tion very fast. . . . Then, when we have some experience on component adaption, we begin to fly free — we begin to understand systems design. I think we are just entering this phase now. We were shoved temporarily off the track in using computers because we had to select some things that we already knew and learn how to do them on the computer. We are just beginning a period that is suggesting to us new ways of constructing systems and new ways of making decisions in organizations. This is, in turn, suggesting new requirements in computer design, and perhaps new requirements in organization design.[13]

The advent of the "third generation" computer fulfills Simon's prediction with regard to computer technical developments. IBM's System/360 series, for example, is modular — that is, it can be modified to perform in a variety of ways to meet individual requirements. Using a System/360, a firm's computer complex may be changed by plugging in additional memory modules or by adding or subtracting peripheral units and input or output channels. A firm capitalizing upon these features may, with relative ease, adjust its computing capabilities to changed business conditions. Only a handful of System/360s currently are operating, but many have been ordered by firms wishing to implement on line real time systems. This general pattern of systems participation in computerization will be elaborated upon with survey data, but first a brief general discussion of the human and organizational factors involved in computer systems work is in order.

THE HUMAN SIDE OF SYSTEMS

Feigenbaum has commented that "The new industrial creed may well come to be termed: Improvement through integration of effort."[14] The essential parts of a system are comprised of both the physical and human assets of a firm — that is, its

---

[13] Herbert A. Simon, "Discussion and Summary," George P. Shultz and Thomas L. Whisler, eds., *Management Organization and the Computer* (Glencoe, Illinois: The Free Press of Glencoe, 1960), 94.

[14] A. V. Feigenbaum, "The Approach, Analysis and Design of a System," C. Gordon, ed., *Ideas for Management* (Forge Valley, Massachusetts: The Murray Printing Company, 1959), 55.

objectives, policies, organization, physical resources, manpower, financial resources, and procedures.[15] As McDonough and Garrett point out, systems analysis involves the integration of organization and information:

> One of the major opportunities is that of a blending approach which brings together the joint analysis of the organization and the information structure. [16]

Integration of effort does not apply to the physical or to the human spheres of the organization but rather to both. These are not two "irreducible" or autonomous areas, as one author believes:

> The head of enterprise finds himself therefore in the presence of two different organizations, irreducible to each other: that of machines, which have their demands — that of men, who have theirs; and the second are the most important precisely in the measure that machines are more perfected.[17]

To recognize the relatedness for systems analysis of the socio-technical arrangements does not mean necessarily that the human factor actually receives its due.

In the computerization of information processing, the systems practitioner is confronted with this problem. It becomes imperative to design, implement, and operate E.D.P., paying careful attention to organizational and manpower planning. This planning, generally neglected, is especially crucial during the systems development stage of office computerization or any other major technological change. Some firms, having learned from their past mistakes, are beginning to recognize this need.

> Since much of the data required to reach a decision is not readily available, a study is usually necessary.

---

[15] Ibid.

[16] A. M. McDonough and L. J. Garrett, *Management Systems* (Homewood, Illinois: Richard D. Irwin, Incorporated, 1965), 8. The authors amplify their approach on p. 18: "This book is neither an organization nor a systems book, but rather a book on the interplay between people in an organization and between the systems with which they work. Those who aspire to management positions in today's business world must be able to work with people and with systems relationships — and most importantly — with compound relationships between people and systems."

[17] Pierre Bize, "Automation and the Scientific Management of Enterprises," *Views on Automation* (Paris: Organisation for European Economic Cooperation, 1957), 29.

Early in its history, this study became known as the "feasibility" study, reflecting the major concern of the time as to whether it was "feasible" to use the equipment for the work. This term has undoubtedly been an un- fortunate one since it has tended to over-emphasize the machine aspects of the problem at the expense of many of the fundamental economic, organizational, strategic and other factors to be considered. It has likewise tended to underplay the value of preplanning for the preparation and introduction of the equipment, some- thing which has come increasingly to be a part of the initial study in order to provide greater assurance as to the practicality of the project.[18]

Laubach views the chief contribution of the computer as that of being a means to an end.[19] Through it a firm is enabled to re-think its objectives, organizational structure, and assign- ments of responsibility.

Members of upper levels of management find them- selves in the rare position of being able to review the organization. Long-standing routines can be questioned. Ancillary objectives, which have been added over time, can be reviewed and their contribution to the funda- mental purposes of the organization assessed.[20]

Typically, top management has not availed itself of this oppor- tunity. Systems men, being more concerned with technical matters and receiving little or no top management or staff assistance, have tended to work out "practical" solutions to the human side of systems. For example:

We have found that we sometimes must deliberately build human decision back into the system, even though it would be possible to run without it. We must do this in order to gain acceptance for the system. For example, we have occasionally tacked on a piece of hardware simply to gain acceptance. The device we have found useful is some sort of random access equipment such as

---

18 B. Conway, J. Gibbons, and D. E. Watts, *Business Experience with Electronic Computers* (New York: Controllers Institute Research Foundation, Incorporated, 1959), 20.

19 Peter B. Laubach, *Company Investigations of Automatic Data Processing* (Boston: Division of Research, Harvard University Graduate School of Business Administration, 1957), 258.

20 Mann and Williams, *op. cit.*, p. 223.

the RAMAC. When people can retrieve information from the system any time they want it, they feel they have it under control to a greater degree and therefore are more willing to accept it.[21]

Kaufman refers to the computer as a sort of organizational catalyst, and describes the "trojan horse technique" of dealing with organizational barriers to innovation:

However, as systems men will generally testify, we have all had experience with many situations where obvious improvements are long overdue, but cannot be achieved because of internal differences, organizational barriers, and other obstacles....

There are some situations — and I know of them — where electronic data processing has been undertaken by management knowing that it was the only effective way to eliminate archaic practices and modernize operations, even though careful analysis would reveal that other methods, perhaps less expensive, would do the job.[22]

A final example indicates how a systems analyst may be forced to operate on the principle of "hot pursuit" because of technical integration.

You may not go off limits to find a smuggler but, once on his tail, you may pursue him anywhere. In our organization we have adopted this principle. When we find a problem we pursue it wherever it may lead in the organization and, as a consequence, have in fact got into almost everything in the business, although we started in the production area.[23]

Obviously, as seen above, good technical work by systems analysts is not enough to insure that E.D.P. will be successful. The examples also indicate that systems analysts work out their own solutions to problems, and not necessarily to their firms' best advantage. The understanding, guidance, and active

21 John E. Hines, "A Department of the General Electric Company," George P. Shultz and Thomas L. Whisler, eds., *Management Organization and the Computer* (Glencoe, Illinois: The Free Press of Glencoe, 1960), 155.

22 Felix Kaufman, "E.D.P. and the Disenchanted," *California Management Review*, 1:no. 4, 70 (Summer, 1959).

23 Hines, "A Department of the General Electric Company," George P. Shultz and Thomas L. Whisler, eds., *Management Organization and the Computer, op. cit.*, p. 154.

cooperation of top management, as well as that of all persons directly affected by E.D.P., are essential if the objectives of the new systems are to be fully achieved.

The essential point...is that the decision which achieves organizational objectives must be both 1) technically and scientifically sound, and 2) carried out by people. If we lose sight of the second of these requirements, or if we assume naively that people can be made to carry out whatever decisions are technically sound, we run a genuine risk of decreasing rather than increasing the effectiveness of the organization.[24]

The growth in number of E.D.P. installations, coupled with greater systems sophistication, have made more and more systems specialists and managers increasingly concerned with the organizational implications of systems work. They recognize that E.D.P. systems have not achieved the economic goals predicted for them; computerization generally has not gone smoothly, and time schedules have been met only rarely. They recognize also that the success of computer operations can be affected materially by a firm's choice of systems approach. This aspect is discussed next.

SYSTEMS APPROACHES TO COMPUTER APPLICATIONS

A business system may be defined in various ways, depending upon the particular topic of discussion. Broadly speaking, a system can be defined as a series of procedures which are necessary to accomplish a given objective. These procedural relationships determine the organization of work in a firm, and when taken as a whole, or integrated, allow management to view the company as a whole, without regard to organizational impediments. Thus, a system may be seen as an interrelated network of subordinate procedures, developed with an eye toward the achievement of one, several, or all major organizational goals.

Systems analysis, too, can be defined in many ways, often depending upon the particular function given it in a particu-

---

[24] Douglas McGregor, *The Human Side of Enterprise* (New York: McGraw Hill Book Company, Incorporated, 1960), 170.

lar firm. Systems analysis, in short, is directed continually at improving business operations. Programming activities involve taking the systems plan and translating it into terms that make sense to a machine, i.e., into computer language instructions. The machine operations, with manual control of the computer, then process the information and complete the basic functions of computerization. In short, systems analysts define the problem and determine the desired solution, programmers adapt the solution for acceptance by the computer, and machine operators take the program and run it through the equipment.

The philosophy adopted by systems analysts has changed significantly over the past fifteen years. Systems approaches to computerization have gone through three stages of development, as delineated in the literature: electronic data processing (E.D.P.), integrated data processing (I.D.P.), and total systems, or management information systems (M.I.S.) phases.

E.D.P. Phase

Around 1955, when computers began to be applied to commercial data processing, firms employed the program-by-program or stepping-stone approach to computerization. The information network was rationalized and broken down into little pieces to be digested by the computer, one at a time. The previously existing procedure was literally transcribed (translated) in its conversion into a computer program.

Firms utilizing such rudimentary methods do not revolutionize management, organization, or work processes, although they usually do produce significant changes within these areas. One observer comments upon some of these possible changes:

> The computer may be used to reduplicate work in a business that is already being done by other means. This would suggest a simple transfer of work to a computer wherein the machine is programmed to do the present work of a business in part or in whole. Ordinarily those considering installing a computer will think first of this kind of application, for it is already being done....

But there is considerable deception in this point of view. Rarely are the functions of an organization such that they remain unchanged in a computerization program. Even what is potentially the same operation may change substantially in the overall results. It may prove uneconomical just to do present work when one considers that the computer system may yield much more. Unexpected by-products can result from computer runs. The information being processed may be found to have easily obtainable additional and parallel uses which reflection may find a need for. And from any of these, whole new frames of reference concerning use of the data may emerge to triumph over previous concepts.[25] This approach is open to criticism, nevertheless, because it may be employed by organizations which have the capability to engage in more ambitious systems revisions and would benefit from doing so. Rush makes just such a criticism:

> One of the ruts into which we have stepped is the tendency to develop highly specific programs or systems which lack the power of generalization. They fill needs by duplicating in machine systems the contents of existing manual systems, but they fail to capitalize on the opportunity to move to greater efficiency.[26]

In practice complete duplication of a particular procedure, even if intended, would be almost impossible to accomplish. Some degree of innovation, whether deliberately or inadvertently included, would most probably accompany computerization.

A similar approach would recognize the fact that some degree of innovation naturally becomes a part of any procedure placed on the computer. This type of systems approach as differentiated from the translation or E.D.P. approach is discussed by Conway, Gibbons, and Watts:

> Translation once again seems to be one of those catchy words with which E.D.P. is replete — a rather precise description, but not of what actually took (and takes)

25 Roger Nett and Stanley A. Hetzler, *An Introduction to Electronic Data Processing* (Glencoe, Illinois: The Free Press of Glencoe, 1959), 159.

26 Carl H. Rush, "Standard Oil Company (N.J.): Organizational Development," George P. Schultz and Thomas L. Whisler, eds., *Management Organization and the Computer* (Glencoe, Illinois: The Free Press of Glencoe, 1960), 207.

place. Most translations are 90% preservation and 10% innovation, or are 80% preservation and 20% innovation, or, perhaps, 70% and 30%. Very rarely is there 100% preservation of the status quo and even then it is normally a first step toward more imaginative and useful objectives.[27]

I.D.P. Phase

In the late 1950s, after several routine clerical procedures had been computerized, pressures began to build up to combine these programs to effect data processing efficiencies. Axsmith points out that:

> Many computers had been loaded with one task after another, each developed and processed very largely without reference to another.... In recent years, however, substantial efforts have been devoted to integrating the various data processing tasks into what ideally would be a single, unified system of data processing.[28]

In this approach the entire information processing system is conceived of as an interdependent whole rather than an amalgam of separate programs. Under I.D.P. there would be major revisions in the old procedures, so that the parts fit together to meet the expanded goals of the system efficiently. Ideally,

1) Original data are recorded *at their point of origin* in a mechanical form. In other words, all pertinent information is recorded once at the beginning of the clerical process.

2) From then on — whether on tape, cards, film, or whatever the medium may be — data are processed exclusively in a mechanical manner. The whole concept of I.D.P. is negated if at some station along the line data are again recorded manually.

3) All processing of data is integrated so that original

---

[27] Conway, Gibbons, and Watts, *op. cit.*, p. 101.

[28] Douglas J. Axsmith, "A Management Look at Data Processing: Promise, Problem, and Profit," Alan D. Meacham and Van B. Thompson, eds., *Total Systems* (Detroit: American Data Processing, Incorporated, 1962), 10.

data in mechanical form serve all subsequent applications.[29]

I.D.P., as a systems term in a field noted for rapid terminological changes, had a short life span, and was soon superseded by total sytems.

Total Systems Phase

Definitions of the term total systems are many, the following one by Kreithen being fairly representative:

The total information system can be defined as a system involving acquisition, processing, and communication of many types of information products and services required by both users and generators of information using the best combination of available concepts and equipment combined in an optimum fashion with attention to cost, efficiency, and growth factors.[30]

In the early 1960s, systems analysts began to chronicle the virtues of viewing a firm as one big system. By 1962 the idea of total systems already encompassed "traditional" and "current" interpretations. The old total systems approach had involved integrating on-going, routine computerized procedures, i.e., I.D.P.; the new one emphasized fulfilling managerial information needs for planning and control.[31] Analyses of the evolving concepts of total systems appear in the literature.

In 1962 Evans and Hague proposed a five-step, total systems "master plan" designed to insure that the economies promised

---

[29] "Establishing an Integrated Data-Processing System," *Special Report Number 11* (New York: American Management Association, 1956), 9.

[30] Alexander Kreithen, "Total Information Systems," *Data Processing Yearbook, 1965* (Detroit: American Data Processing, Incorporated, 1964), 121. Management information systems, for example, is one variant of the total systems approach currently being discussed. McDonough and Garrett define a M.I.S. as follows:

A management information system accumulates, processes, stores and transmits data to "relevant" people in the organization, informing them and thereby becoming information.

From McDonough and Garrett, *op. cit.,* p. 4.

[31] Richard DeLuca, "Understanding Total Systems," Alan D. Meacham and Van B. Thompson, eds., *Total Systems* (Detroit: American Data Processing, Incorporated, 1962), 31.

by the new computer technology would be reaped.[32] This master plan reached fruition with the creation of the Westinghouse Telecommunications Center, a time-sharing, central, corporate information system.[33]

The virtues of total systems have not gone unchallenged. Dale found, in his survey of thirty-two firms, that the "step-by-step" approach was being retrieved after firms had abandoned attempts at establishing a "total information system."[34]

The concept of a "total system" in which all major input data are available and can be used repeatedly for different purposes does not seem to have worked out anywhere. On the contrary, attempts to go the "total" route sometimes led to serious upsets and delays.[35]

John Dearden of Harvard University is probably the severest critic of the total systems concept of computer use. He maintains that the attempt by systems specialists to automate management information systems is at best nonsense and at worst may have deleterious consequences. In his opinion management should not attempt to systematize and automate a firm's strategic planning and control processes.[36] He holds, further, that a firm cannot and will not be able to develop a "...perfectly integrated, total system for management."[37] Regarding the utility of the third generation computer for management systems, Dearden has this to say:

It is my personal opinion that, of all the ridiculous things that have been foisted on the long-suffering executive in the name of science and progress, the real-

[32] Marshall K. Evans and Lou R. Hague, "Master Plan for Information System," *Harvard Business Review*, 40:no. 1, 92-103 (January-February, 1962).

[33] For a report on the Westinghouse system, see Jacob Ever, "A Corporate Time-Shared Computer System," *Industrial Management Review*, 6:no. 2, 71-79 (Spring, 1965).

[34] Ernest Dale, "The Decision-Making Process in the Commercial Use of High-Speed Computers," *Cornell Studies in Policy and Administration* (Ithaca: Cornell University Graduate School of Business and Public Administration. 1964), 6.

[35] *Ibid.*, p. 15.

[36] John Dearden, "Can Management Information Be Automated?," *Harvard Business Review*, 42:no. 2, 128-135 (March-April, 1964).

[37] John Dearden, "How to Organize Information Systems," *Harvard Business Review*, 43:no, 2, 65-73 (March-April, 1965).

time management information system is the silliest.[38]

McDonough and Garrett also warn the manager to beware of the total system: "The present quest for 'total systems' should be recognized as a hazardous quest for the ideal."[39] They raise some serious questions about the degree of integration as well:

> The question: Should certain systems be integrated? is just as important — if not more important — than: How can these systems be integrated? When nature puts certain odd systems together the result is often a freak, and managers must guard against integrated, but freakish, systems.[40]

These criticisms of total systems notwithstanding, the literature abounds with acclaim for the total systems concept. As Brooker points out, this wave of enthusiasm creates a feeling that "the totality of systems" approach is the one to follow:

> This assumption is translated into practice by writers who define the role of change agents such as systems analysts in terms of the total systems concept.[41]

Kaufman claims that with current computer technology a firm can build supersystems which cut across company boundaries. He feels that although companywide total systems "have been largely unsuccessful," and some firms may "reject the 'total system' outright, perceptive management needs to begin to consider the new possibilities for coordinating data processing *outside* its own organizational limits."[42]

In summary, systems approaches can be characterized as transcribed (literally or with some innovation), integrated, or total (internal or internal-external to the organization). The companies in my survey provide interesting contrasts when considered against the systems approaches outlined above.

---

[38] John Dearden, "Myth of Real-Time Management Information," *Harvard Business Review*, 44:no, 3, 123 (May-June, 1966).

[39] McDonough and Garrett, *op.. cit.*, p. 7.

[40] *Ibid.*, p. 8.

[41] W. M. A. Brooker, "The Total Systems Myth," *Systems and Procedures Journal*, 16:no. 4, 29 (July-August, 1965).

[42] Felix Kaufman, "Data Systems that Cross Company Boundaries," *Harvard Business Review*, 44:no. 1, 141 (January-February, 1966).

SYSTEMS APPROACHES IN THE SURVEY COMPANIES

The 1959-1961 survey of twelve representative firms indicated that by and large the only approach used by these firms was transcription with some degree of innovation.[43] The degree of change varied on the basis of the equipment selected, the nature of the procedure used, the training and experience of the systems department, and many other similar factors which were crucial to the type of approach adopted by a firm. In all cases the first procedures were placed upon the computer with little formal change. No firm then had in operation any program that could be classified as involving a revolutionary revision of the previously existing mechanized procedure. Nor did any company use a true I.D.P. approach. There was one exception, however, at the other end of the scale.

One firm came fairly close to literally transcribing its procedures onto the computer. But this, in its own peculiar way, was a special case in that no formal, written procedures existed in the firm before computerization! In this particular instance, an outside agency was given the task of formalizing procedures which until then had been informal.

Rationale

This cautious approach to applying computer technology may appear disappointing. The initial reasons for computerizing step-by-step are, upon examination, understandable. In any event, it should be emphasized that though less grandiose than popularly assumed, even these initial computer programs agitate an organization.

A practitioner explained directly and simply the major probable reasons for the program-by-program approach: 1) learn as you go, and 2) get productive work out of the computer as soon as possible. Another systems manager described more precisely the technical and human factors which neces-

---

[43] Obviously my comments on this topic are based upon incomplete data and non-exhaustive investigation. I have not studied all these various computer programs in detail, and I am not in a position to indicate quantitatively the degree of innovation which has accompanied computerization of individual programs. I shall relate some general observations.

sitated his firm's decision to employ a cautious systems approach. These impinging factors were carefully analyzed, and the decision was made to use fundamentally the existing procedure rather than attempt to innovate substantially. This program-by-program approach was taken because: 1) the firm had no employees experienced in E.D.P.; 2) it was difficult, if not impossible, to predict computer time required to do specific jobs; 3) parallel systems allowed for accuracy tests; 4) integration of systems would be much easier because all company records would be on magnetic tape, verified, and their precise location known; 5) the technical characteristics of the computers then in use would place severe limitations upon the firm's ability to integrate operations; and 6) even given the reasons already stated, the systems approach could have been more innovating, but this would have resulted in reassignment of top management responsibilities — why rock the boat since these managers would retire soon anyway? In regard to this last point the systems manager felt that any efficiencies that would have resulted from a more sophisticated systems approach would have been lost, in any event, because of personnel dislocations. These statements suggest the restraints both from within and from without a company which made necessary a conservative systems approach. What about developments since 1961?

New Developments

The systems approaches existing in 1965 obviously had grown out of the patterns established earlier. The particular approach chosen originally and modified to its 1965 state of development was determined, in large measure, by the changes which the systems function had undergone in the interim, e.g., its growing acceptance, centralization, and independence.

Several notable changes and trends were noted during the 1965 interviews. First, the geographical and organizational dimensions of systems coverage had been enlarged. The trend is toward a national or corporate business information system. (The Westinghouse Telecommunications Center was mentioned often as the prototype systems model.) This trend was referred to in different terms: total systems, central systems, a corporate concept of E.D.P., centralization of files, and a centralized systems concept. All of these represented, in some degree, an attempt to complete integration of computerized procedures, or I.D.P.

A systems manager reported that a tape integrated system had been established in his firm through the step-by-step approach. Currently he is working toward installing a M.I.S. using an I.B.M System/360. Another systems executive revealed that five years ago, under his predecessor, his firm was talking about a master plan. Both the master plan and its developer have long since been scrapped. Instead the firm embarked on a piece-by-piece approach and is now attempting integration.

In yet another case, a firm attempted to change from an essentially manual operation to a computerized I.D.P. system. Thus, from the start, the approach was to bite off a big chunk. This systems approach took longer to implement, and in fact was not completed until 1963. Two additional years were spent refining the integrated system, and the firm is now ready to reap the benefits. At present this firm is planning to install an I.B.M. System/360.

Another firm, however, was not as successful with its I.D.P. approach to a manufacturing planning and control system. The attempt failed because "it was developed without the understanding and cooperation of the line organization." As a result a short-run plan was developed to patch up the individual procedures. The long-run plan was to revise and to integrate the procedures. This was essentially accomplished by 1965, and the firm then turned to working on a total system.

A final example concerns a survey firm which, in 1961, had no systems function, written procedures, or approach to computerization. In the interim, a new systems staff has been recruited and a place found for it in the organization. Top management has been "sent to school" and "brainwashed" and now "understands" what E.D.P. is all about. The approach in this firm is simply to extend the intelligent use of the computer to new procedures.

These, in summary, are some of the major changes in the surveyed firms' utilization of computers. A major and noteworthy change occurred during the past five years: the approach is more sophisticated, that is, it involves a more creative use of computers. The true M.I.S. or total system, however, is still a pie-in-the-sky vision rather than a reality.

Within the companies, human restraints were pivotal. Systems and procedures work and technological changes required 1) major adjustments in attitude, and 2) the development of new skills in the organization. Training has been a necessary prerequisite to the exploitation of computers. Outside the companies the non-availability of suitable technical equipment to meet the needs of business has held back progress to some extent. In most cases, however, human factors determined to a great extent the systems approach taken.

Computerization is in a relatively early stage of development. Everything considered, the progress that has been made within so few years is astounding. It is only a matter of time until some of the more advanced systems approaches now being developed undoubtedly will supplant the somewhat limited systems approaches already described. The four principles quoted below, developed in 1952, indicate that systems approaches have lived up to much of their advance publicity:

> 1) An electronic computer should be applied to the whole job, not to some separately departmentalized piece of it. 2) Small jobs should be combined with others. 3) Source records should be combined with others. 4) Make all calculations at one time.[44]

In the next section the computer applications that have been implemented, as well as those now in the development stage, are discussed.

COMPUTER PROGRAMS

Firms are beginning to apply the computer to an ever-wider

---

[44] *Report of the Committee on New Recording Means and Computing Devices* (Chicago: Society of Actuaries, September, 1952), 22-23.

range of business problems. The pace of computerization, as measured by the number of programs placed on the computer, is gaining momentum. Moreover, not only is the total number of computer applications within firms rising steadily, but the structure of applications is becoming far more complex.

Early Applications

In an early survey of computer applications, Diebold listed programs then in use under these headings: 1) Business Data Processing Systems, 2) Analysis for Management, and 3) Scientific and Engineering Applications.[45] In order of frequency the survey results are listed below:

Survey Categories for Electronic Data Processing
Equipment Users

Business Data Processing	*Analysis for Management*
1. Payroll	1. Expense Distribution
2. Accounts Receivable and Billing	2. Budgeting and Estimation
3. Accounts Payable	3. Sales Analysis
4. Cost Accounting	4. Linear Programming
5. General Accounting	5. Simulation
6. Production Control	6. Market Research
7. Production Scheduling	7. Statistical Surveys
8. Inventory Control	8. Prediction and Forecasting

Ginder reported that regardless of size of E.D.P. systems, about 50 percent of all early applications were payroll programs, with accounts receivable the second most common program.[46] Diebold's and Ginder's findings are consistent with those in a survey made by the Bureau of Labor Statistics of twenty large computer installations:

The first applications of the computer were made on large scale, routine, repetitive operations which to a

---

[45] John Diebold, "Bringing Automation up to Date," *New Views on Automation* (Washington, D.C.: United States Government Printing Office, 1960), 101, and Chart C, 102.

[46] Charles E. Ginder, "Why Automation?," *Office Executive*, 34:no. 10, 12-13 (October, 1959).

great extent were already performed mechanically. Some examples are payroll preparation, premium billing, calculation of reserve liability, customer billing, revenue accounting, accounts payable and receivable, car accounting, mortgage accounting, inventory control, actuarial calculation, multiple correlation, and dividend calculation.[47]

In addition the Bureau of Labor Statistics listed several planned applications such as reports on sales, production costs, market research data, machine loading studies, commission accounting, statistical reports, stockholder records, production scheduling, general accounting, and sales forecasting.[48]

Examples of early computer programs in the Federal Government cited by Riche and Alli included payment and reconciliation of Treasury checks, auditing and accounting procedures in connection with United States Savings Bonds, and insurance records for 6,000,000 veterans.[49]

The results of a survey conducted in 1963 on office automation in the insurance industry are revealing. The data on computer applications indicate that the programs most frequently involved record-keeping tasks — i.e., high volume, labor intensive, data processing. For example, life insurance carriers had in operation only five programs, as reported by at least fifty percent of the eighty-six responding firms: premium billing, premium accounting, commission accounting (a by-product of the billing operation), valuation of reserves, and agency (producer) statistics. Property insurance carriers had seven programs in operation, as reported by at least fifty percent of the survey sample of ninety-three: unearned premium reserves, agency (producer) statistics, premium accounting, reports to statistical (experience rating) agent, premium billing, reserve

[47] Adjustments to the Introduction of Office Automation," *Bureau of Labor Statistics Bulletin Number 1276* (Washington, D.C.: United States Government Printing Office, United States Department of Labor, May, 1960), 9.
[48] *Ibid.*
[49] Richard W. Riche and William E. Alli, "Office Automation in the Federal Government," *Monthly Labor Review*, 83:no. 9, 933-934 (Washington, D.C.: United States Government Printing Office, September, 1960).

for unpaid claims, and commission accounting.[50] Some significant developments in computer applications during the last few years are highlighted in several surveys.

Recent Applications

Myers reports on a McGraw-Hill "Survey of Computers and Computer Usage" (dated April 9, 1965), based on data obtained from 650 prominent firms operating 5,000 computers. The survey included a breakdown of the most common computer applications:[51]

Program	Percentage of Companies
Accounting	99
Inventory Control	74
Production Planning and Control	58
Scientific and Engineering Applications	47
Business Forecasting	33
PERT	25

In an American Management Association survey of computerization in 288 companies of all descriptions, the following computer applications were listed in order of frequency:[52]

Program	Number of Companies
Payroll	247
Sales Analysis	235
Inventory Control	211
Billing Invoicing	195
General Accounting	197 (sic)
Cost Accounting	188

[50] "Impact of Office Automation in the Insurance Industry," *Bureau of Labor Statistics Bulletin Number 1468* (Washington, D.C.: United States Government Printing Office, United States Department of Labor, 1966), 16-17.

[51] Charles A. Myers, "The Impact of E.D.P. on Management Organization and Managerial Work," Working paper. Alfred P. Sloan School of Industrial Management, Massachusetts Institute of Technology, September, 1965, 1-2.

[52] M. Valliant Higginson, "Managing with E.D.P.: A Look at the State of the Art," *American Management Association Research Study 71* (New York: American Management Association, 1965), 38.

Accounts Receivable	183
Accounts Payable	152
Personnel	136
Production Control	133
Production Planning	128
Shipping Distribution	106
Sales Planning	95
Purchasing-Ordering	89

The respondents to the A.M.A. survey cited as the three most effective applications inventory or materials control, cost control, and production scheduling. It should be noted that no hard criteria were used to measure degree of program effectiveness. As was indicated in over 10 per cent of the replies, program effectiveness could not be estimated, since there was "no clear-cut method for measuring," and preliminary judgments were merely educated guesses.[53]

In a second A.M.A. survey of 110 manufacturing firms with a total of 799 computer programs, production and inventory control applications were found to predominate in the use of computers for manufacturing problems. The three most popular programs were inventory or materials control 74 percent, cost control 69 percent, and stock status reporting 68 percent. Production scheduling was next, with applications in 50 percent of the reporting firms. Some twenty-three other uses for the computer were reported by less than half of the survey sample.[54]

Frontier Examples

Computers continue to be of increasing aid to management in doing a better job. As reported in *Business Week*, several advanced computer applications have been made in the following areas:

---

[53] *Ibid.*, p. 16.
[54] J. N. Taussig, "E.D.P. Applications for the Manufacturing Function," *American Management Association Research Study 77* (New York: American Management Association, 1966), 10.

Computers, numerically controlled tools, and other advanced techniques are clipping months off lead times to make cars. Besides economies, they will be a marketing boom.[55]

The Bank of Delaware is pioneering a new era when cash, checks, and credit cards may become obsolete. But many obstacles remain before the concept can spread.[56]

Doubling the freight car's workday. That's what companies may be able to do, by rationalizing the movement of freight, and thus vastly increasingly railroad profits. They might even handle some operations.[57]

At Washington's Woodward and Lothrop, E.D.P. machines produce personalized information about customers — and free employees for carrying on the store's tradition of service.[58]

At Massachusetts General Hospital, information flows from hospital Teletypes into the computer. Data can be extracted via control typewriter at computer station — and eventually hospital will be able to tap file directly.[59]

I.B.M.'s new Recruitment Information System — IRIS — is most sophisticated electronic machine yet for matching men and jobs.[60]

A.M.A. survey respondents reported their plans for future computer applications to manufacturing procedures for the 1966-1968 period. The seven most popular types of applications proposed, in descending order, were forecasting, control, scheduling, cost analysis and cost control, planning, productivity, and management reporting programs.[61]

It is important to remember, pioneering efforts notwithstanding, that routine clerical applications predominate and represent

---

[55] "Finding New Ways to Make Autos," *Business Week*, 1880:190-198 (September 11, 1965).

[56] "Next in Banking: Pay Bills by Phone," *Business Week*, 1889:82-86 (November 13, 1965).

[57] "Doubling the Freight Car's Workday," *Business Week*, 1894:122-126 (December 18, 1965).

[58] "Where the Computers Care, Too," *Business Week*, 1906:140-146 (March 12, 1966).

[59] "Rx for Hospitals — Computers," *Business Week*, 1863:142-144 (May 15, 1965).

[60] "Computers Move Up in Personnel Ranks," *Business Week*, 1886:118 (October 23, 1965).

[61] Taussig, *op. cit.*, p. 38.

the bread-and-butter of computer applications. Nevertheless sales analysis and inventory control programs together now are more significant numerically than accounting applications. This development indicates a major change from the earlier structure of computer applications and the resultant managerial and organizational impact of computerization.[62]

A tendency always exists to exaggerate the value and rate of change. This is particularly true of computer applications. Dale reports the feelings of one chief executive on the matter:

These O.R. applications are based on drawing a straight line between unfounded assumptions and a foregone conclusion.[63]

Survey Data

Data on computer programs now operational, being readied for implementation, or being contemplated in the companies I surveyed are not inconsistent with the data presented above. There is a major difference, however, in that the firms I investigated were not quite as far advanced in these programs as their diversity might otherwise indicate.[64] Aside from this, the same general findings pertain to the surveyed firms.

Billing and accounts receivable constituted the most frequently implemented computer program in my 1959-1961 survey; the next most common program was payroll; the third was inventory control; and the fourth was comprised of a

---

[62] Gilbert Burck, *et. al.*, eds., *The Computer Age and Its Potential for Management* (New York: Harper and Row, 1965), 12; Jay W. Forrester, "A New Corporate Design," *Industrial Management Review*, 7:no. 5, 9 (Fall, 1965); and Higginson, *op. cit.*, p. 38.

[63] Dale, *op. cit.*, p. 6.

[64] The distinction goes beyond diversity to include individual company depth in its respective computer programs. Even including this point, however, Diebold talked of some programs as "becoming widely accepted" in 1960 which had just become operational in the firms I re-visited in 1965. Diebold summarized the early stage of computer program development thus:

Generally, payroll and accounting functions are most often cited as E.D.P. applications. Production and inventory control are becoming widely accepted for computer utilization as well as operations research techniques (used in simulation, distribution, and routing problems and production and inventory controls — to name just a few).

Diebold, "Bringing Automation up to Date," *New Views on Automation, op. cit.*, p. 103.

miscellaneous group of accounting functions. The latter included such programs as accounts payable, general accounting, special checking, reserve evaluation, dividend books, premium rate books, and statistical reports of various types. The following types of programs were being developed and debugged: corporate and personal trusts, all forms of bank loans, regular checking, production planning, and manufacturing control.

Later interviews with my original sample of firms during 1965 revealed a growing sophistication in applying the computer to business problems. While the computer was being used increasingly throughout the United States for inventory control, sales order processing, forecasting, and line balancing and production control, the major effort in the survey firms still was directed at extending the computer to additional routine clerical procedures, refining programs already on the computer, integrating two or more existing programs, and debugging and maintaining operational programs.

In general, accounting procedures were either on the computer or in the process of being programmed by 1965. The following are typical applications which are operational in the surveyed firms: demand deposit accounting, installment loans, loan interest, billing, payroll, freight payment, revenue accounting, inventory control, purchasing, maintenance and supplies, forecasting, market analysis and intelligence, premium accounting, status card changes, and personnel records.

Some applications begun during 1965 were: daily stock replenishment, portfolio analysis, over-all cash flow analysis, market analysis, and salesmen's quotas. Several programs were considered as likely future applications: factory profit and loss statements, exception reports, personal trust, commercial loans, and simulation of transit (i.e., check-clearing) operations.

A manager in a firm which is a major user of computer technology summarized his firm's program development in the following terms:

Pre-1955: punched card functional — the build-up of a master file

1955:   tape functional — period of consolidation and
           extension of computer programs
1965:   tape integrated — all facts pertaining to a
           given policy in one place and updated daily;
           next phase, all policies with one customer on
           a single master file
Future: System/360 — on line and real time manage-
           ment information system

Generally the initial programs in the survey firms were
simple, routine applications which had been the most highly
mechanized before computerization. These typically concerned
accounting procedures. The more sophisticated applications
which followed increasingly dealt with production problems.
Presently innovative applications augment and improve managerial information systems.

Chapter III

STRATEGIES FOR DEPLOYING COMPUTERS

The computer today is in a time of transition from initial acceptance to extensive exploitation by business.
— Douglas J. Axsmith

The use of computers in the ongoing "war on paperwork" has been accepted as a matter of routine. The altered man-machine relationship generated by computerization has resulted in the radical revision of the organization of work. The evolving organizational patterns designed to integrate computers and work is seen in the study of selected computerized procedures in the surveyed firms. Computer-deploying strategies and tactics are described by examining five variants of the "battle formation."

Computer strategies can be classified according to the relationship of the organizational units to the computer, the distinguishing characteristics being: generation of input, utilization of output, or both generation and use of input and output. There are five sections: input generation by the operating line departments, utilization of output by a staff department, electronic data processing and a warehousing operation, impact on line departments which generate input, machine process it, and utilize the output, and a corporate management-computer system.

LINE OPERATING DEPARTMENT

The major attributes and implications of four typical computerized procedures are considered separately below.

69

Billing Procedure

The major functions of the billing department are to collect premiums, to authorize commissions, and to process policy changes. The work is organized into three units: 1) accounting, 2) commission, and 3) policy changes.

Accounting Unit: The unit consists of teams of four accounting clerks under the direction of a senior clerk. There are two units and nine accounting clerk teams in the department. Each accounting clerk is responsible for handling one thousand items per day. Of these items, 94 percent involve checking the billing punched card against the receipt. The remaining six percent involve a change such as annual to quarterly payments.

A mode of payment change involves checking the journals, paid cards, and daily account listings files to insure that the change is not actually a mistake. The clerk then changes the billing card and refers the card to the policy change unit to update the record, which is maintained on magnetic tape. The accounting clerk does the keypunching on changes, also.

Four accounting clerks work as a team. Newcomers start with the easiest tasks. They are trained by the senior clerk and the other three members of the team. One supervisor thinks the jobs are suitable for people under thirty because of the necessity of frequently getting up and down and walking some distance to various files.

Commission Group: The commission group controls input and output to the computer. The group consists of a supervisor, two senior clerks, and thirteen commission clerks. This group provides a link to the computer. Matters of production control — time schedules, records, liaison with programmers — are coordinated in order to facilitate input and output from the computer. Error detection and correction are also handled.

Change Group: The change group handles all changes of policies that are in force at the time. There are a supervisor, two senior clerks, and eighteen change clerks in this group. It performs the same functions as the commission group, except that the change group has no liaison responsibilities.

After the introduction of the computer this department's operations were changed. The two master files (policy and address) are on magnetic tape. The organization structure of the department has been changed from a purely functional one to a group and team form. (Before computerization the department was divided into seven units, each with four invoice clerks, two file clerks, two account clerks, two account balancers, four change clerks, two commission clerks, three termination clerks, and four miscellaneous clerks.) The file clerk classification was eliminated, and the keypunch, account clerk, and balance clerk jobs have been consolidated into the present accounting clerk position.

Scheduling: The monthly invoice schedule coordinates the activities of the premium collection department with the activities of all other users of the computer. The schedule is developed by a supervisor from the collection department and representatives of the computer staff and other interested departments. The schedule contains information which directs and controls the activities of each employee in the department for the coming month's operations.

The Distribution and Use of the Schedule: Copies of the schedule are distributed to all supervisors in the department and to the three senior change clerks in the change group. The scheduling of activities includes the following:

1) Accounting unit — indicates billing cards due for processing by the computer.
2) Commission unit — no relevant information is provided.
3) Change unit — a) Dates are indicated when changes may be made in the invoice tape; dates and times are given when the master tape and the invoice tape may be altered (after cut-off date only the invoice tape is changed). b) Errors discovered by the computer come to the department on two lists. The lists indicate individual responsibility. Each clerk corrects her own mistake as indicated by codes on the error list. The computer list indicates the nature of the error. c) Corrections are sent back to the computer after cards are punched correctly. Invoices are

manually corrected, so that they may be mailed for the current month. Previously errors were detected only after the information had been forwarded to branch offices. The new master tape contains all pertinent information, so that mistakes are red-flagged and corrected before leaving the home office.

Manual of Operations: Each clerk in the department is given a manual which lists the code, a description of its meaning, and the location of the information. She soon memorizes the information that pertains to her function, so that merely by reading codes she can perform all the necessary operations or corrections. A sample instruction from the manual is quoted below to illustrate the language of management under computerization:

> Accumulated Dividend balances and Loan balances will appear on the billing notices. Therefore, codes 81 and 82 have been established which will permit the "C" Dividend accumulation balance or the loan balance to be changed. Blanks in either of the two fields on the #5 will not change the amount. Zero (0) punches will change the field to a zero and an amount in either field will change the amount.

According to a supervisor in this department, once the clerk has mastered the codes and terminology, she simply follows these directions, as indicated. Supervision under these circumstances becomes automatic.

Loan Procedure

The work of the loan department is primarily bookkeeping. The major functions in the work process are 1) coding, 2) conversion of information to paper tapes, 3) balancing of accounts, 4) corrections, 5) computer operations, and 6) final settlement.

Coding: The input to the system, an invoice or check, is coded. The jobs consist of unskilled duties related to bookkeeping. The work is menial. Two sets of numbers from two separate files are placed on the source document. In case the check does not bear the invoice number, it is obtainable from a ledger. Finally if a special deduction or allowance is in order, the information is noted.

Conversion: The information on the coded source document is converted onto a punched paper tape. Each operator, usually a former bookkeeper, does only a specific portion of the conversion. The job is a monotonous one, requiring little skill and no judgment.

Balancing of Accounts: In this operation the previous day's totals of invoices, checks, cash, applied and regular credits, adjustments, and miscellaneous transactions are checked against the punched paper tape totals. Then a corrected balance report is issued and remedial action taken for any mistakes indicated by the tapes. The balancer exercises some judgment in noting corrections and in checking the coding or punched mistakes by referring to the original source document.

Final Settlement: Typed tickets indicating the customer's payment status are dispersed to the customer, to the credit section, and to the payment storage section of the company. The adjustment portion of the report is analyzed and corrections are made by checking the journal to see how the Balancing Operation corrected the previously noted mistake. The reports are then dispersed as in the routine instance. Clerks use some judgment in the operations.

Differences: The major differences between the computerized procedure and the previous method are these: 1) Before, bookkeepers had performed the coding, recording, and balancing of the accounts individually. The bookkeepers also had prepared the tickets for dispersion. 2) Records had been maintained on punched cards. The data were transferred from the bookkeeper, placed on the cards, and then run off. The cards then were returned to the line department for record-keeping. The punched cards then were transported back and forth between the line department and the machine room, as needed. 3) The balancing function had been done by the machine room clerks.

Major Revision Necessitated: A breakdown in the procedure necessitated that some major changes be made in the work process described above. First, the coding operation was divided in two. One clerk now codes the source documents. Invoice numbers are now obtained by another clerk. This further specialization of functions was designed to provide greater control over errors. Second, the error report issued by the balancing operation was made to include information as to who committed the error as well as the nature of the error.

Payroll Procedure

The computerized payroll procedure of one firm is highly rationalized. Even though the payroll is becoming increasingly difficult to compute, e.g., there are forty possible deductions, the procedure has eliminated many problems. The payroll department had customarily worked overtime to get out the payroll on time. Vacations, holidays, and plant shutdowns also had resulted in much confusion. The only major problem is a new one: computer breakdown. In an emergency, however, the magnetic tapes can be transported to another machine operation to be processed.

Procedure:

1) Each employee has a clock card which is prepared by a machine center.

2) These cards, placed in time racks, are used as the punch-in cards for the week.

3) At the end of the week the foreman reviews all the cards for approval. Lost time and overtime must be initialed.

4) All cards are collected in a central location where they are separated by hand into hourly and salary groups. Any discrepancy or question is discussed directly with the foreman involved.

5) The cards then are sent to the payroll group. The section in charge of the hourly paid employees separates their cards into day and incentive groups. The salaried section checks the cards for absences and approved leaves and maintains the records on these matters.

6) After punched cards are created in the machine room

to take care of variable information, the straight, forty-hour payroll and the others are processed by the computer. First, there is a trial run. A discrepancy list of incorrect or missing information is generated. The payroll department then works to resolve the discrepancies. The final run by the computer prints the payroll checks.

Scheduling: These operations demand strict adherence to a schedule agreed upon by three organizational units: the payroll department and the two machine centers. Under a column entitled "Description," there are thirty-one separate steps that must be coordinated among these three units within a three-day period. The schedule lists the times for arrival and departure down to half-hour intervals.

Accounting Procedure

The implications of E.D.P. for jobs within a general accounting department are these. First, there had been greater reliance on policies, rules, and instructions for coordination of activities under the previous, manual system. Under computerization a highly rated clerk, appointed by management, coordinates all phases of accounting with the machine center. Second, the computerization process tends to eliminate some routine, paper-handling job tasks, which leads to combining of functions. The lines of differentiation between jobs are becoming less distinct. Third, clerks are more responsible for control and analysis of information. And fourth, more variety and responsibility are involved in the new clerk. jobs. While there is more variety, there is less individual security in the new routines.

STAFF SERVICE DEPARTMENT

The cost department, which does not feed input directly to the computer, is discussed here as an illustration of how its reorganization to provide better staff services to management was made feasible by E.D.P.

The major plant superintendent in the firm receives orders for work through a central ordering department. The superintendent then issues suborders to other superintendents in the plant for the various parts and subassemblies required for the finished product. Four major organizational units are involved in the manufacture of the product.

The cost department's responsibilities are: 1) to issue estimates for securing business (pricing), 2) to assist in controlling inventory by reviewing shipments and buildups, 3) to oversee labor costs, and 4) to analyze direct and indirect labor costs. The major functions, in summary, are inventory control, estimating, and analysis.

The Old Procedure

The old procedure of the cost department paralleled the major plant superintendent's subcontracting of work within the firm. There were four cost groups, each reporting functionally to the cost department and as staff specialists to the line managers. All four cost groups were situated in the production areas. Under the old procedure the cost manager attached to the major plant superintendent received the total cost estimate and subcontracted out the subestimates to the three other cost groups.

The Need for Change

The manager of the cost department felt that it was not as sensitive to the needs of the firm as it might be. There were numerous delays in meeting due-dates; a good deal of the time was spent in explaining why the department was doing badly and in ironing out difficulties.

The problems, according to the cost manager, were three. 1) An administrative problem — cost estimates frequently were required in a rush. This had a disruptive effect, since the pressures were aggravated by the procedure of subcontracting which caused pressures on the various cost managers to pyramid. 2) An authority factor—the subcontracting process made the cost manager, who always initiated the procedure, responsible for the end product (total cost), and yet he had no authority to get the task accomplished. 3) A pressure factor —

the department manager found himself too deeply involved in details which necessitated spending a good deal of the time coordinating the activities of his subordinates and telephoning line managers to exert pressure.

The Reorganization

The introduction of a new cost program and computerized operations provided the means by which the cost manager could reorganize his department. The cost department was consolidated to use employees in a more specialized fashion. All the separate cost groups were brought together and organized functionally according to the three major responsibilities of the department: 1) inventory control, 2) estimating, and 3) analysis. Subordinate managers for each of these areas were selected on the basis of merit, ability to maximize benefits from E.D.P., and capacity to work well with other staff departments. This last factor has become increasingly important as these managers no longer have to probe in the plant areas to get information for their work.

Gains from Reorganization

The stated gains from centralizing and functionalizing the cost department are these: 1) efficiencies because subordinate managers and employees now wear one hat, 2) the cost department manager has the ability to exert closer control over subordinates and to coordinate their activities (visual control), 3) the responsibilities of department members are defined more clearly, 4) a consistent routine exists for each of the three major responsibilities for all four plant areas, and 5) output has increased and is more satisfactory. Output will continue to rise as computerized procedures are refined and more advanced ones are incorporated.

WAREHOUSING OPERATION

The organizational unit in this case is a distribution center of a manufacturing firm. The products flow from the manufacturing plants to the warehouse operation, to franchised distributors, to dealers, and finally to the consumer.

The centralization of manufacturing some years back had led this firm to establish branch warehouses throughout the country. The warehousing function was decentralized to eliminate communication and transportation time delays. The advent of E.D.P. and economical delivery by airplane enabled the firm to recentralize its warehousing operations and to increase efficiency by a program eliminating branch warehouses.

The Systems

Three different procedures have been developed for use in centralized operations. These procedures are each designed to meet specific problems, but all are focused on shortening the order-delivery cycle.

System 1: This system handles 40 percent of the warehouse's volume. The procedure is as follows: 1) Salesman and distributor establish optimum inventory levels for all products to insure adequate stocks, to eliminate heavy investment in inventory, and to increase turnover. 2) Each package shipped to the distributor contains a prepunched information processing card. These cards are forwarded to the warehouse on a regular basis to replenish stocks automatically. This is a one-week, order-delivery cycle.

System 2: In an alternate procedure, the district sales offices receive orders and type an order form which simultaneously cuts a punched paper tape. This tape then is used to send information over a private wire to the centralized warehouse. The order form in tripicate plus a punched card are created automatically at the warehouse.

One copy of the order is sent to the order service department, another is shipped with the order, and the third goes to the billing department. The punched card is processed to determine the salesman's commission, taxes, market research information, and other statistics for management analysis. The goal of this system is to cut the order-delivery cycle to twenty-four hours.

System 3: This procedure is the most advanced. The distributor has two punched card files, one with his name and address, the other with the type of products he stocks. To order, the distributor dials the warehouse directly on a private wire, using a special but inexpensive devise. He then inserts both cards in the machine and depresses the proper buttons to indicate how many of a particular product he needs; the order then is punched automatically on cards at the warehouse for immediate handling. New product cards are inserted as needed. The goal of this system is to reduce the order-delivery cycle to twelve hours.

Advantages of Reducing Order-Delivery Cycle

Some advantages of reducing the order-delivery cycle are these. Distributor inventories are reduced, and warehouse sales are increased. Inventory savings allow the distributor to stock a wider range of products. Costly rush orders are decreased. Automatic reordering helps the warehouse to insure shipping its prior share of the distributor's volume. Sales statistics are improved. In summary, "...the entire order-receiving, shipping, and invoicing procedure will be greatly simplified with resulting substantial reduction in overhead costs. Inventory planning and control can be accomplished more accurately and more intelligently." Eventually the warehousing E.D.P. system will be integrated with production scheduling, so that efficiencies will accrue in production as well as in distribution.

LINE DEPARTMENT RESPONSIBILITY FOR INPUT, MACHINE PROCESSING, AND USE

Two computer installations illustrate how computerization of an inventory control procedure and a billing procedure may leave the work process relatively unchanged.

Inventory Control

The impact of using a computer in this firm was relatively slight. Files are maintained in the computer instead of on punched cards. The preparation of input still is handled by the machine center. Some additional information is being generated, but the operating departments have not been affected significantly by E.D.P.

There are probably three major reasons for this apparent lack of impact. First, the previous procedures were only slightly altered with the installation of the computer. Very little change has occurred in processing the information or in its final use. Second, the computer is utilized primarily to maintain inventory records. And third, the machine center had been highly centralized before the introduction of the computer. Payroll, inventory control, and financial accounting all were handled within the center. The line departments merely utilized the information generated and did not prepare it for machine processing.

Billing

This firm also changed little when its billing procedure was computerized. The installation involves the preparation of input, machine processing, and functional responsibility for billing under one manager. The computer is a small one. Input and output are punched cards.

The lack of a magnetic tape system precluded the storage of data. This prevents the consolidation of various large files and a cut-back in personnel. Consequently, three large groups of employees now maintain files, e.g., the ledger section, the cash posting section, and the accounts receivable ledger section (located in another division). There are forty clerks in the ledger posting section alone.

Consolidation of two machine rooms has increased efficiency of machine processing, but the work flow and jobs have remained relatively unchanged by computerization. Thus, there has been some centralization of operations, e.g., the preparation of the advanced billing card, and some consequent consolidation and decrease in size from the old functional, organizational setup. Also, accounts receivable clerical work and reports have been transferred to another division. In summary, only slight changes in the work process have resulted from the introduction of the computer.

ADMINISTRATIVE SERVICES DIVISION

The utilization of the computer in this insurance firm has facilitated major changes in its management organization. In an industry characterized by expanding product lines, it became imperative to centralize service to the customer and to consolidate management control to effect closer coordination of company operations. The computer-oriented total system is the means by which management hopes to achieve these objectives.

Organization

The three major functions in this insurance company were underwriting, sales, and claims. Since the introduction of the computer a fourth function, record-keeping and paperwork activities, has evolved. This is in keeping with the general trend in all industries recentralizing information processing.

About fifteen years ago, when the home office work load had become too heavy to handle efficiently, the processing function was decentralized and was handled by eight regional offices. There was also need to decentralize decision-making, because of the proliferation of insurance lines. In addition, decentralization was then very much in fashion. Thus, electric accounting machine tabulating centers were established in each of the eight processing centers to service forty-six sales offices and to feed data from them to the home office. In addition, each line of business, e.g., the underwriting, controller, and actuarial, had its own tabulating equipment.

In 1958, when its first computer was installed, this firm embarked on a vast plan to reorganize. Centralization of machine operations and systems and procedures work, and development of a step-by-step schedule to implement a total system were basic elements of this plan. The schedule was designed to include a system to 1) gather, 2) transmit, 3) compute, 4) store, and 5) retrieve relevant information. The implementation of an on line, real time information system was envisioned.

Thus by 1967 small computers will be located in each of the eight processing offices. These satellite computers will feed into the main home office computer center by transmission lines. By 1970 each of the forty-six sales service offices will be tied in with its respective processing office to further cut down the delay between obtaining new data, updating the files at the home office, and communicating with any field location. By 1967 the processing centers will have stopped producing their own management reports and will receive them instead from the home office.

These organizational changes are reflected in the changes in computer technology, past, present, and future:

1) 1958 — I.B.M. 705, Model 2 installed
2) 1960 — Second 705 installed
3) 1961 — I.B.M. 1401 replaces one 705
4) 1962 — Second 1401 installed and an I.B.M. 7080 installed
5) 1963 — Two I.B.M. 1460s replace the two 1401s
6) 1964 — Eight Model 30 System/360s ordered, one each for the eight processing centers, and two Model 50s and one Model 60 System/360 ordered for the home office computer center.

These management organization and information technology changes provide the framework within which computerized procedures are altering and will continue to modify the pattern of managerial work.

Information Systems Changes

To effectuate its long range computerization plan, this firm recently has computerized several key procedures, e.g., statistical information for management reports, investment analyses, and experimental simulation studies. The company's attempt to establish automated policy controls which are updated daily instead of monthly is a prime example of managerial reorganization. The goal is for an agent to be able to write up a policy, send it to the home office, and have nothing whatever to do with it thereafter. Billing and all other notices are to be handled directly from the home office to the customer for the life of the policy. Period changes and change notices are to be sent automatically to the agent. Policy control by the computer is already operational on automobile policies; it is being converted on home owners' policies; it is being planned for life policies.

With better and more timely data made available through computerization, the manager can plan and control more effectively. For example, data on actual performance for the past year now is available in January of the current year, rather than in July or August as before.

The goal of this insurance company is to broaden its outlook and increase its market effectiveness by thinking of its customers as entities and selling them package policies. The computer has been at the heart of this process and the chief means for its implementation. The pattern of computer deployment has affected significantly the evolution of the new information network and, thereby, management organization in this company.

Chapter IV

COMPUTER CENTER OPERATIONS

Management honeymoons with electronic data processing appear to be over; in some cases desertion has ensued; in most, though, management finds itself living with a bride it has not yet come to either fully understand or to fully appreciate.

— George J. Brabb
Earl B. Hutchins

The application of computer technology to business information processing has evoked a great deal of popular interest. The notoriety that attends the high priests of electronic data processing, their organizational maneuverings, and their cabals and protocols are recognizable in numerous places within the firm. The dedicated spirit and comradeship of the select few who are closely associated with the computer are immediately discernible to even the casual observer. Academicians, too, have contributed significantly to this seductive picture by their talk of "information technologists" and "tight little oligarchies."

Once systems activities are segregated from E.D.P. and the novelty and notoriety of the new machine operations have worn off, the machine processing of information is seen as a rather routine, mechanical function.[1] The preparation of data for computerized operations is quite tedious, since the changes brought about by increased mechanization generally have been in the direction of narrow specialization. In decentraliz-

---

[1] It should be kept in mind while reading the present chapter that no distinction is made between a machine center that does or does not prepare the input, e.g., code, keypunch, verify, collate, for the computer.

ing operations, the input and processing functions are separated organizationally.

The management organization of machine operations is discussed in this chapter. The concern here is with day-to-day computer operations. Input preparation is incidental to the discussion, and systems analysis is not considered at all. In this chapter four main topics are covered: 1) the growth of mechanized information processing, 2) the organization of computer operations, 3) the centralization of data processing in the firms surveyed, and 4) current developments in the management of computer operations.

DEVELOPMENT OF MECHANIZED INFORMATION PROCESSING

In the surveyed firms mechanized data processing is a phenomenon of the last twenty years. From 1945 to 1955 most of the firms were in the process of installing or refining their tabulating machine procedures. Only since 1955 have computers been in operation. Experience with mechanization in these firms varied widely, even within this short span of time.

In three firms the change from manual operations was a particularly big jump. In two of these firms the transition was from a manual to a computerized method of operations. The decision to convert to E.D.P. entailed major changes in organization and responsibilities. In the third instance a large firm converted from a manual to an advanced tabulating machine method of processing a large amount of data. This move to advanced tabulating equipment had been long overdue and preceded by only a few years the conversion to E.D.P. In this last case major changes occurred at the time of converting to tabulating equipment, when the procedures were designed with computerization in mind. These three instances, then, represent the firms in the sample surveyed in which major changes in the technological level of data processing occurred.

In six instances the introduction of the computer was made into the existing tabulating equipment machine rooms. In these firms existing machine facilities were expanded and modified in order to absorb the new technological level of office mechanization. Disruptive effects were minimal because the change involved a less radical innovation in technology. The firms' ability to cushion the impact was enhanced because the organizations' machine operations were not significantly altered. A seventh firm also expanded its existing machine room to absorb the computer, but differed from the six others in one respect. The machine processing of data was transferred from finance to the jurisdiction of the systems manager.

In two other firms the computers were installed within new and separate organizational units. In one case the computer machine operation was set up within a separate division of the company and processed data for the administratively independent unit which I studied. In the other instance the computer team was organizationally separate from the old tabulating group, although both units reported to the same manager. This last arrangement was in all other respects similar to a previous expansion of machine operations.

These, then, are the organizational adjustments which facilitated the introduction of computers. The pre-existing level of technology and location of machine operations played a major role in placing the computer within the firm. Computer technology is particularly dynamic, and the computers' integration within these firms is not stable.

ORGANIZATION OF COMPUTER OPERATIONS

Although the organizational status, scope of operations, and technological level of each installation vary greatly among firms, my 1959-61 survey indicated that the organizational control of E.D.P. was concentrated. In nine out of twelve companies the machine room was within the financial department's control. Two computer installations were in the administrative division, while the third firm utilized the computing facilities of another division for some of its programs. This indicates to some extent the nature and degree of computerization in these firms. The higher the organizational position and status, the more innovative is the systems approach and the broader are the applications; and the more advanced the equipment, the greater is the probability that organizational control will not be dominated by one functional area of a firm. Conway, Gibbons, and Watts have postulated that scope of work is the major determinant of the position in the organizational structure into which the machine center best fits.[2] They have found that the three typical ways in which a machine center can function are: 1) as an integral part of a major department, 2) as a separate service center, and 3) as a relatively independent department.

Part of a Major Department

Conway, Gibbons, and Watts summarize the major characteristics and implications of placing computer operations at a relatively low level in the organization, and under control of a specific program, such as billing:

> In the first instance, when the E.D.P. unit is placed organizationally within the major department it primarily services, there is a minimum of disruption of the existing corporate organization, at least on the departmental level. The E.D.P. unit is used as a form of departmental mechanization, much in the manner that a "captive" tabulating machine unit would be. The vast majority of the work is usually carried out for one department although some work may also be done for other departments at their request.
>
> No major organizational problems seem to arise in this type of arrangement, so long as one major department is, in fact the major user of the E.D.P. services. However, when several major departments require a great deal of E.D.P. work, a choice must be made as to whether to continue E.D.P. operations according to this concept and therefore to establish separate, individual E.D.P. units within the several major departments.[3]

---

[2] B. Conway, J. Gibbons, and D. E. Watts, *Business Experience with Electronic Computers* (New York: Controllers Institute Research Foundation, Incorporated, 1959), 144.

[3] *Ibid.*

In the Boston sample four of the twelve installations initially conformed to this type of organization. They, like their systems counterparts, were probably the least developed organizationally or technically of all firms studied. Recognition of this fact lends support to Rush's statement as to the then-current impact of machine centers:

> At the present time [1960] it would be difficult to point to instances of radical organizational changes which can be attributed to increased sophistication in information systems. But there are signs of pressures which are building in such a way as to challenge the efficacy of existing organization structures. Computers and their staffs have been assimilated into existing structures, usually the controllers' departments....[4]

This assimilation process, as one might surmise, tends to blur the threefold typology of machine center control. For instance, the difference between this and the service center arrangement, discussed next, is based upon the number of departmental users of the computer. Although the categories established on this basis may not be mutually exclusive, there are meaningful differences.

Service Center

Conway, Gibbons, and Watts summarize the relevant managerial considerations in establishing, under one functional area, a service center which also serves other departments:

> In most instances, where there are several major departmental users of the equipment, an attempt is made to establish a service center to serve all departments....
>
> As a rule, the service center approach does not interfere with the existing corporate organization structure on the departmental level, except perhaps in those instances where the E.D.P. unit reports directly to the man in charge of one of the major using departments. The service center in its pure form is not intended to move functions or responsibilities from one department to another. The E.D.P. unit is literally a service unit,

---

[4]Carl H. Rush, "Standard Oil Company (N.J.): Organizational Development," George P. Schultz and Thomas L. Whisler, eds., *Management Organization and the Computer* (Glencoe, Illinois: The Free Press of Glencoe, 1960), 198.

performing certain work for the responsible departments. However, there is often a feeling that a portion of the responsibility has been transferred to the E.D.P. center. When a center is responsible to another major department user, many department heads feel that they have lost some of their former authority and responsibility. This reaction can become fairly strong if the department supervising the operation of the service center is primarily concerned with some other essentially incompatible function. There is, for example, a natural reluctance for a production control department to turn over a major part of the production control function to a machine center supervised by the financial department, or vice versa. The broader the scope of the program, the greater the reluctance appears to be.[5]

Five firms in the survey sample essentially organized computer operations this way. Their programs were somewhat more sophisticated than the first group's. The size and technical proficiency of the machine centers were greater also. Employee fears and frictions accounted in large measure for the reluctance of the surveyed firms to establish the third form of organizational arrangement.

Independent Group

This arrangement was the most radical, at that time, organizationally speaking. Most E.D.P. managers felt it would be the inevitable organizational form of the future. Conway, Gibbons, and Watts have evaluated this arrangement.

The E.D.P. unit can also be established as a relatively independent major department whose function and responsibility become one of processing data from raw to final form, according to general corporate rules, policies, and practices. In this case the E.D.P. department would be responsible for taking approved input data from a department, such as the financial department, for example, and producing the required information for the financial, purchasing, production control, and other departments in the manner in which it felt best. This approach, which is in some ways subtly and

---

[5] Conway, Gibbons, and Watts, *op. cit.,* pp. 145-147.

in some ways strikingly different from the previously discussed approaches, is based in essence on the premise that the financial department is responsible for appraising and initialing the source data and for handling the final data, but that the intermediate processing is not its concern.

This concept is not widely accepted and it is quite probable that it will not be in the near future.... This concept can provide an opportunity to use E.D.P. very effectively, but it would entail more shifts in organizational lines of authority and in assignments of responsibility, etc. than most companies are ready to undertake when E.D.P. equipment is installed. It is likely, therefore, that this plan, where the relatively independent E.D.P. group reports to a neutral administrative officer and assumes important functions now assigned to major using departments, will meet with more general acceptance very slowly, it at all, in most companies.[6]

In four of the firms surveyed independent machine centers had been established. This did not happen by an evolutionary process in any one of the four companies.

In two cases a separate or higher corporate organizational unit provided machine time for processing its sub-unit's data. Both of these units, incidentally, operated smaller computers in the financial areas of their operations. A third firm, in making the jump from manual to computer operations, placed the machine operations center in a service division of the company. In the fourth case the tabulating department traditionally had been associated with a service division. After a jurisdictional dispute, the service division was expanded to accommodate the computer, and top management decided that the division's functional independence was to be maintained.

These then were the organizational arrangements for computer operations that prevailed in the surveyed firms in 1959-61. The arrangements, as I said before, have by no means remained static. Strong pressures forced many more companies to affirm the functional independence of the machine center.

---

[6] *Ibid.,* p. 147.

CENTRALIZATION OF INFORMATION PROCESSING

Economies of scale are particularly promising in information processing. Computer technology has facilitated the centralization of information processing in order to reduce costs, among other things. The fact to emphasize is that the decision whether or not to centralize information processing is dependent upon many factors other than technology. E.D.P. is not a sufficient reason to centralize machine operations, although it is a necessary precondition.

As of 1961, in three out of eleven firms surveyed, two or more machine rooms were consolidated upon the introduction of the computer. In each of these cases, small tabulating machine rooms attached to different departments were combined because of changed procedures and increased machine capacity. However, in four firms more than one machine room continued to function. The trend toward centralization of information processing is greater than these data suggest. As pointed out previously the computer has precipitated new machine installations, expansion of existing machine installations, and some transfer of machine installations, all of which have contributed to larger, more centralized information processing installations.

This is not necessarily an inevitable trend. Gallagher has discussed some of the factors to be considered by management when deciding how data processing machinery should be utilized within the firm.[7] The factors he mentions that govern the degree of centralization are: the size of the corporation and of each of its operating units, the extent of uniformity of accounting and reporting procedures, the information flow, the cost of each system, and the ability of each system to meet operating needs.

One of the systems managers interviewed listed the factors he felt were most important in determining the degree of centralization that would be desirable. His ideas, circulated in a

[7] James D. Gallagher, "Improving the Organization and Management of the Data-Processing Function," *The Changing Dimensions of Office Management, Report Number 41* (New York: American Management Association, 1960), 55.

company memorandum, are more computer-oriented than those of Mr. Gallagher:

> I believe that the decision as to whether computing facilities should be centralized or decentralized depends on many factors, among which are questions such as:
> 1) The size and speed of computer needed to do the work planned.
> 2) The volume of computer work to be done relative to the speed of the machine to be used.
> 3) The extent of the inter-facility data transmission that would be required with a decentralized computing facility.
> 4) The attitude of the managers involved concerning the need for vertical integration of facilities within each decision-making area.

These factors illustrate the complexity of the organizational arrangement of computer installations. Gallagher oversimplifies the situation when he discusses the question of centralized as opposed to decentralized E.D.P. centers:

> In designing a management information system,... the systems planner must consider the relative advantages and disadvantages of 1) a single, large data-processing facility established on a centralized basis to serve the data-processing needs of the various operating units of the company, and 2) a number of smaller, decentralized data-processing facilities each designed and located to serve the data-processing needs of one or more of the company's operating units.[8]

In practice these are not two incompatible, alternate organizational forms. The fact is they can be mutually supporting parts of a well planned information processing system. The key questions in regard to information processing centralization are not simply technical, e.g., big or small computer; rather they are also human, e.g., responsibilities and organizational structure.

Centralization of information processing is one of the first steps in breaking down a traditional departmental form of organization. The tremendous capacity of the computer de-

---

8 *Ibid.*

mands centralization of processing, which in turn draws to it many routine functions once performed by other departments. Jones comments on this chain reaction process set off by computerization:

> Electronic data processing equipment does not solve the problem of reprocessing information by each group (e.g., department) for its needs unless the organization for assembling and handling information is re-shaped to conform to the concept that all paperwork is inter-related. If each functional section retains its own peculiar forms and procedures along strictly compartmentalized lines, much of the value of centralized data processing equipment is lost. Multiple-purpose centralized handling means the surrender of some independence by each of the contributing areas, and usually means a migration of personnel and procedural authority from them to the data center. The easy movement of information is possible only when clerical procedures within department lines are superceded by common procedures and a pooling of data.[9]

One surveyed firm is well known for its philosophy of centralized information processing. In a public relations brochure this firm states:

> In the spring of 1956, a group of................ officials placed in formal operation a nationwide 18,000-mile private communication network and data processing system — linking all.............facilities — described as a "completely revolutionary concept of the application of automation in industry." The complete system analysis was performed by............. personnel. The system has as its heart a 25-ton electronic computing machine.
>
> Located at ...., the equipment receives and radiates vital data to every .... facility...to slash time-consuming computing...and rush projects to completion with incredible speed.
>
> Production management can obtain exact inventory of any product throughout the Company almost instantaneously. Complete accounting and statistical service

[9] Gardner M. Jones, "Organizational Consequences of E.D.P.," *Business Topics*, 7:no. 4, 25 (Autumn, 1959).

will be provided for all 11 operating divisions. Engineers can calculate complex technical problems in a few minutes instead of several days. The progress potential in research and development, engineering, finance, performance measurement, and personnel administration can scarcely be imagined now.

It is important to look beyond the public statements of this corporation to understand what it has actually done, and what the consequences have been. Naturally there are divergences from this somewhat idealized picture of E.D.P. in this particular firm, the most glaring one being the description of centralization as a "revolutionary" development. There are data which suggest quite the contrary.

This firm, like so many others after World War II, had decentralized responsibility and authority by establishing product divisions. However, because of increasing information needs and costs, the company concluded it could not afford decentralized information processing, even on a computerized basis. Therefore, top management centralized its machine operations with the help of a large private communications network. This information processing center is isolated physically and functionally from all other company operations. It has been specifically charged with processing data so as to provide useful information to all divisions and levels of the corporation.

This corporation has forty-five plants and twenty laboratories located throughout thirteen states. Although the firm is widely dispersed, certain procedures are centralized at the product division level. For instance, accounts receivable, accounts payable, allocation of costs, and inventory management have been centralized at division headquarters ever since that form of corporate organizational structure was adopted.

Prior to computerization, payroll had been centralized somewhat differently. Before 1955 each plant, warehouse, and laboratory processed its own payroll. In the next stage one division handled the payroll for all company locations within a radius of fifteen miles. Later the payroll for all plants of this division, another division, and corporate headquarters was handled centrally. Accounts receivable — handled by corporate headquarters in 1955 — was absorbed by the large-scale computer installation in 1956, as were all corporate payroll and accounts payable functions. Inventory management, billing, and production planning presently are processed at the division level.

Some managers in the divisions felt that the firm had centralized prematurely. The group established for processing corporate information did not engage in systems activities to expand or improve the systems feeding data to their installation. One division systems group set out to fill this void by improving the division's inventory management, production planning, and billing procedures.

This particular division has eleven plants and sixteen warehouses. Its inventory system had been inefficient and needed improvement. In theory the only function of the division machine room was to feed information to the corporate information center for processing. Division management felt that this was all right for accounting procedures, but better local control was required for inventory management. The objective of the local group was to reduce the eight-week paper handling cycle to seven weeks, thereby reducing idle investment. A formal proposal to achieve this objective was made to top management.

The proposal, fought by the corporate machine group, was passed over their objections in 1959. The local systems group viewed the decision as dividing machine room responsibilities between the corporate and division levels thus: the centralized, corporate installation would handle all accounting procedures while the division systems group would develop and supervise inventory control and production planning. These latter functions were considered locally unique and handled more efficiently on a decentralized basis.

Two facts undercut this reasoning. First, the local systems manager had been promoted subsequently and was to report to the corporate machine center. Although it had not been explicitly stated, he was to work on inventory control and production planning problems as a staff assistant for all divisions. The second fact is that at least top divisional financial management feels it is only a matter of time until these two "separate" procedures will be processed at the corporate level also.

This particular firm's approach to machine operations is well known and is often held as an example for other companies to emulate. Further, the computer is given the major credit for bringing centralization within the limits of economic feasibilty.

Computer technology does facilitate the centralization of information processing. As the foregoing data suggest, the trend is toward larger machine installations within firms. What should not be overlooked, however, are the *other* factors in addition to the computer that may be necessary prerequisites to successful centralization. As in the example discussed above, for instance, there were other important contributory reasons for centralization.

First, the firm has had a long history of centralized information processing. The individual company units traditionally have had very little control, especially over accounting procedures. Second, the nature of the firm's products, their labor content, product markets, and distribution systems have allowed the formation of a corporate structure which is conducive to centralization. Third, company forms, procedures, and reports are standardized; this has facilitated the easy flow and compatibility of data. And fourth, there is a practice of holding quarterly meetings of all systems analysts to discuss common problems.

The purchase or rental of information processing machines is another factor which facilitates centralization. Corporate management has delegated responsibility to the central machine center to authorize any equipment changes in any unit of the firm. Such authority can be a powerful weapon in conflict situations. In this firm the division was allowed to rent a computer to develop its inventory control program only after a hard fought struggle had taken place.

CURRENT MANAGEMENT TRENDS

As newer programs are implemented, traditional organizational arrangements undergo increasing strain. Any department involved may become dissatisfied if its information processing needs are not met impartially and efficiently. Such pressures may develop along with centralization of computer facilities as well.

At present, as indicated by my 1965 survey of the Greater Boston area firms and supported by data on selected Greater Philadelphia area firms in 1964-65, the management of the computer is still in flux. The two major issues continue to be who should be responsible for the computer, and where should it be located in the organization. The answers to these questions have changed since 1961, in conformance with the change in trends since that time.

Computers, first placed in the department of the major user (typically in finance, under the controller), are being moved in several directions: upward in the organization hierarchy, relocated and placed under some other functional organizational unit, or relocated as an independent service department reporting to top management.[10] The proliferation of computerized procedures and their integration, as well as the development of management information procedures, have precipitated these changes.

The initial placement of the computer under the controller was uneasy from the start. With the growing breadth and sophistication of computer applications, the corporate service nature of computerization is increasingly apparent. This trend is exemplified by a new emphasis in the firms that the computer center must "sell its services" to top management and executives in all the other departments and divisions for which it processes information. This type of thinking was manifested in several ways.

---

[10] M. Valliant Higginson, "Managing with E.D.P.: A Look at the State of the Art," *American Management Association Research Study 71* (New York: American Management Association, 1965), 9-13.

In all the Boston area firms revisited, machine operations had become more centralized. One company, for example, had had seven separate machine rooms in 1954. By 1965 it had only one. The executive in charge predicted that computer operations soon would be made a staff department reporting to the executive vice president, in order to service "captive customers" more efficiently.

In another firm, the computer operation gradually is being moved out of financial control because manufacturing applications have been increasing, and the firm itself is implementing a corporate/area System/360 organization similar to the Westinghouse model. The objective is to move systematically from plant- to division- to area-controlled satellite computers feeding into a corporate computer center. Another firm is on the same road — i.e., attempting to reorganize computer operations. Both these firms are multi-divisional and are 1) seeking the most economical means of utilizing computer hardware, and 2) developing a multi-divisional decision-making model to facilitate maximization of corporate goals.

Typically the computer group has moved up in prominence within the major user's department, usually finance. One firm has built a separate facility for its computer center, but it remains under the control of the major user. In another firm computerization led to a reorganization of the insurance policy maintenance function into a new division. The computer center was placed under the new organizational unit's control. In another firm computerization of new procedures resulted in the transfer of computer center control to the new major user.

Experience in the Philadelphia area firms supports these trends. It is evident in the six firms surveyed that while centralization of computer operations is taking place, in none has the transition been completed. In general these firms' experience conforms with the trend toward a centralized computer operation moving upward toward a service-oriented, nonfunctionally controlled position in the organization.[11]

In summary the organization of computer operations has gone through a series of evolutionary changes. First computers were located in a particular department. After expansion of application, computer groups became a departmental service unit, meeting the data processing needs of other departments as well as its own. At present there is still a trend toward the establishment of the computer center as an independent service department within a firm, i.e., *internal* information utility. Finally, third generation computers appear to offer the possibility for even higher economies of scale to be reaped in information processing. Time sharing techniques utilizing remote terminals will make it possible for computer operations to be performed by an independent, *external* information utility, established as a profit-making service.

---

[11] For a discussion of some of the prevailing reasons which account for the continuing centralization of data processing, see John Dearden, "How to Organize Information Systems," *Harvard Business Review*, 43:no. 2, 68-69 (March-April, 1965).

PART II
MANAGEMENT ENGAGED

Chapter V

SYSTEMS MANAGEMENT

Specialists have had too much responsibility for information systems, and operating managers too little.
— PHILIP H. THURSTON

The emergence, recognition, and acceptance of systems specification as a top level staff function is an accomplished fact today in commerce and industry. Systematic management techniques initially were applied to manufacturing problems. Since the advent of the computer, such techniques have been applied to information processing and managerial decision-making problems as well. The rationalization of managerial and clerical work is being accomplished by systems engineers acting as "human change agents" and computers acting as "technical change agents." The combined systems and computer technologies form a powerful team to effectuate organizational innovations.

Systems administration, as it relates to information technology, is focused upon in this chapter. Three areas are discussed: top management guidance to the systems group, the nature and type of organizational control of systems activities, and computerization and company policies.

TOP MANAGEMENT GUIDANCE

Theoretically the systems function affects every person and every aspect of company operations. In seeking a more efficient method of organizing work, it is of fundamental importance for systems people to know the guideposts top management has established for them. In practice, what philosophy, goals, and policies guide the systems group in the performance of its work? Specifically what objectives does top management prescribe for its systems group? In my investigations, the following prevalent conditions were recognized.

In the early stages of computerization — 1955-61 — formal, written policy statements conveying top management's thinking on systems development and implementation were nonexistent. The guideposts that did exist were all informal. Off-the-cuff management statements, the most important source of guidance, were an unsatisfactory basis for systems work.

Top management's role in computerization has been essentially one of control without planning. Computerization decisions have been made primarily on the basis of cost, with little consideration of personnel and organizational consequences. Once a feasibility study had been submitted and approved, top management rarely concerned itself with E.D.P., except under crisis situations. This was explained simply by one manager: "E.D.P. has had little effect on top management because they have no idea of the long run implications — they just have a cost control outlook." These cost controls have been loosely or tightly enforced, but in general a carefully developed schedule was used as a basis.

This form of planning consisted of fairly specific scheduling of delivery of the computer(s), the sequence of applications, and target dates for specific computerization jobs to be completed. An associate controller described top management as "...not conversant with operations in E.D.P.; they have to make their decisions on trust of what I tell them." In 1961 this was due, at least to some extent, to managerial inexperience with the complex technology that computerization entailed. The manager of a computer operation complained that "...before the computer, the controller could keep up with our machine operation. Now, we are operating beyond his ability to comprehend. The same is true for top management, only more so."

This lack of comprehension is reflected in a statement made

by the executive vice-president of a large organization after the purchase of a computer. He said it involved a big investment for the company, as well as a great deal of change, hoped for everyone's cooperation, and said no one could predict the eventual changes or total impact. He added that the systems manager would be around soon to request people to assist him in the conversion to E.D.P.

The nature of the above comments illustrates that it may be misleading to speak of top management in collective terms. Not *all* vice-presidents, division and department heads favor the introduction of E.D.P. or will cooperate with its proponents. On the contrary, various degrees of opposition can be expected from one or more sources. A method manager chronicled these pressures:

> There was much doubt by many top management people that the system could do what it proposed to do — even so, if true, so far away, nothing to worry about. This attitude has changed. Growing recognition of organizational changes necessitated by E.D.P. Line management beginning to have confidence and faith in the new system.
>
> V.P,s in the other divisions now behind E.D.P. — now for the first time *pushing* to get job finished. They are less prone to argue over incidental things. They are getting more of the "big picture." Petty bickering over forms, for example, now receding. Attitude at higher levels of acceptance of new principles.
>
> At present, problem of putting complicated dodads on systems at demand of top management.
>
> Some evidence of dragging feet at lower levels.

A systems manager faced all forms of resistance from two lower echelon managers who were or would be affected by his activities. In this case, his mandate from top management, that he was responsible for computer systems, had been of little help. However, the systems manager was assured by his boss that his superior, the executive vice-president, would intercede if the obstructionists ever actually threatened the survival of computerization. As the computer programs began to prove themselves despite the open resistance of the obstructionists, the executive vice-president bore down; the resistance then became passive.

Three examples illustrate the restraints under which systems analysts work and indicate the nature of top management guidance in areas other than cost control. The systems manager of a particularly paternalistic firm stated its governing philosophy: "No rough riding over employees, even if necessary to meet organizational goals." Another example is provided by a methods manager who reported the top manager's dictum with regard to systems development: "Conceived daringly, performed sparingly." Finally, a line manager informed me that although no formal, written policies had been issued by top management, an "informal" policy was communicated at top levels of the firm to the effect "...that functions may be taken over by the computer, but they will remain the responsibility of the old manager."

Admonitions and senseless guarantees of this type, along with fuzzy leadership, partially account for the initially slow rate of progress with E.D.P. Systems analysts are not cut loose from organizational restraints, nor given a free hand, nor a mandate to automate. The successful systems analysts still must possess and exercise the traditional organizational virtues, Hoos' comments notwithstanding:

A) E.D.P. personnel are not "organizational men." They do not attain status by good fellowship, manipulate others with subtlety, or move smoothly into executive positions by exercise of "personality." They are not so completely "other directed" that they always conform to the patterns of behavior laid down for up-and-coming men of the financial world....
B) For them, the basic ingredient of success is efficiency and not popularity. Unlike organization men who fit neatly into well-defined cogs of the machinery of a large enterprise, these "fair-haired boys" of the electronic age are in fact an anomaly. Theirs is an electro-centric universe from which emanate the waves of change.[1]

[1] Ida Russakoff Hoos, "When the Computer Takes Over the Office," *Harvard Business Review*, 38:no. 4, 109 (July-August, 1960).

Hoos' observations are contradicted in one firm's systems and procedures department. The top management believed that duplication of effort would produce the best results. Three groups, each under a different functional area of the firm, were assigned work on systems. In addition, the corporation headquarters maintained staff services for each of these functional areas. As one would expect, the situation was rife with "organization men."

The fact is clear that E.D.P. has progressed without top management involvement in planning. Top management has delegated, even abdicated, leadership in this area to younger middle managers who are willing and able to assume the risk and who possess the courage to move ahead with computerization.

A computer operations manager offered these reasons for the non-involvement of top management in E.D.P. 1) E.D.P. did not fit conveniently into the departmental organizational box, but rather cut across all departmental lines. 2) Older top management was not conversant with nor motivated to become familiar with systems technology or computers. As a result middle managers carried the brunt of policy and administrative responsibility for E.D.P. There is clear evidence that this situation is changing.

The degree to which middle managers still are in control of a firm's computer efforts is described in a recent American Management Association survey of E.D.P. Detailed questionnaires had been sent out "...to the executive having overall responsibility for E.D.P." Of the 288 letters returned, the greatest number, in a single job category, had been filled out by E.D.P. managers and other middle managers. However, the increasing control now exercised by top managers or their assistants is documented by the fact that they filled out the overwhelming majority of questionnaires.[2] It is important to

2 M. Valliant Higginson, "Managing with E.D.P.: A Look at the State of the Art," *American Management Association Research Study 71* (New York: American Management Association, 1965), 17.

remember that top management's efforts have been directed largely at control rather than planning.

Although lack of top management participation in E.D.P. activities is often cited as a problem, when the participants were asked who decided the major functions or projects for which computers are used in their firms, 224 of them gave the titles of top management executives. Another 31 named committees, most of which included top-level executives. In only 26 companies was middle management charged with the responsibility.[3]

Undoubtedly the increasing importance and rising status of the systems function within the organization hierarchy will insure greater top management guidance. In Exhibit 1 the relative position of computerization managers in the A.M.A. survey is depicted. The trend toward greater involvement of top management in planning systems specification is bound to be reflected in greater economic success with computerization.

EXHIBIT 1

Reporting Relationships of E.D.P. Executives
President

First Level:	5 E.D.P. Managers
Second Level:	117 E.D.P. Managers
Third Level:	110 E.D.P. Managers
Fourth Level:	49 E.D.P. Managers
Fifth Level:	6 E.D.P. Managers

Source: M. Valliant Higginson, "Managing with E.D.P.: A Look at the State of the Art," *American Management Association Research Study 71* (New York: American Management Association, 1965), 35.

---

[3] *Ibid.,* p. 35.

Computer Profits

The line management role in systems analysis appears to be the crucial variable determining the ultimate profitability of computerization. The unsuccessful firms "avoid top management involvement with E.D.P.," although that involvement is the key differentiating characteristic determining profitable exploitation of computerization.

> The size of a company, the number of computers it has, and the length of time it has used computers have little or no bearing on the company's success with E.D.P. The relevant factors are the support and interest of the company's management and its selection of activities to be computerized.[4]

McKinsey and Company conducted a study of the relation of top management's role in computerization to the economic success the firm achieves. Twenty-seven firms with from four to six years' experience were included in the survey. In all, thirteen different industries were represented. It was concluded that executive leadership, more than any other factor, determined the success or failure of computer systems.

> In many average companies, top management did actively participate in the original decision to build a computer systems capability and to pave the way for successful launching. But, viewing it as a one-shot investment rather than as a continuing dynamic force in the business, management then settled back and waited for results. Consequently, in spite of some early success, the effort tended to lose momentum and sense of direction to the point that the company has ended up bringing this high potential tool to bear "on whatever we can get whenever we can get it."

> In the lead companies, as their actions indicated and the results show, each one of the top managements has correctly assessed the computer's potential and has given it the continuing management direction and guidance it so badly needs and so much deserves. Having proved itself deserving of attention, computer systems now require that top management "take charge."

---

[4] *Ibid.*, p. 44.

The computer's challenge to top management is that it must direct, manage, and lead, if profits are to result.[5]

The surveyed firms in my own study generally conform to the McKinsey characterization of "average companies." Some notable developments indicate that top management is rectifying its neglect of systems. First, strong pressures have been operating to force greater top management involvement in systems: the rapidly increasing high investment in computer hardware and software; the failure to computerize significant procedures successfully; the rising level of managerial conflict (especially at the second and third levels in the management hierarchy); the prevailing strong, competitive inducements to reduce costs; the improved capabilities of computers; and the pioneering example of other firms.

Second, several strong forces are operative within the management hierarchy itself. Many younger line managers who have had direct experience with computerized procedures are reaching the executive level. They understand and appreciate computer operations and potential. Other young managers are being sent to schools run by computer manufacturers for orientation and indoctrination in computer technology. Management trainees, too, frequently have been exposed to computers in college. In addition the regular and early retirement of obsolescent or obstructionist managers has hastened changes in top management's attitude toward acceptance of its proper role in computerization.

ORGANIZATIONAL CONTROL AND SYSTEMS ACTIVITIES

To whom should the systems and procedures group report? This question involves three considerations: 1) the level of the organization to which the group should report, 2) the group's independence of functional control, and 3) the organizational relationship between the systems group and the computer operations group.

---

[5] John T. Garrity, "Top Management and Computer Profits," *Harvard Business Review*, 41:no. 4, 174 (July-August, 1963).

According to Neuschel, systems and procedures is a staff function. Its manager should report to the chief operating manager of a self-contained unit. Departmental systems and procedures analysts, on the other hand, who affect only internal operations, should report directly to their department head, while receiving functional direction and counsel from the general systems and procedures staff of the larger unit. Neuschel suggests that the problem of overlapping responsibilities can be met by drawing a line between *inter-* and *intra*departmental systems and procedures, and if further help be needed, by placing the general and departmental staffs physically side by side to insure maximum communication.[6]

As to the relation of systems work to computer operations, several views have been expressed.[7] The survey data suggest that organizational theory and the staff concept have not been strictly adhered to, and the organizational relationship between the systems and machine groups has varied.

The level to which the systems group reports appears to be a function of the following: 1) the traditions, accomplishments, and age of the systems group previous to the introduction of the computer, 2) the number and degree of sophistication of

[6] Richard F. Neuschel, *Management by Systems* (New York: McGraw-Hill Book Company, Incorporated, 1960) 62-63.

[7] Nett and Hetzler, failing to make a distinction between systems and procedures and computer operations, speak of this problem as one of over-all control of an E.D.P. systems program. Thus, they cite the following forms of control: 1. computer room-centered control, 2. third party control (separate staff activity), and 3. area of specialization control. In practice these forms have been modified to meet the demands of various relationships between systems and procedures and electronic machine operations in evolving and dynamic situations. From: Roger Nett and Stanley A. Hetzler, *An Introduction to Electronic Data Processing* (Glencoe, Illinois: The Free Press of Glencoe, 1959), 181-182; 185. Brabb and Hutchins report that computer job tasks are conventionally broken down into three components: systems analysis, computer programming, and computer operations. These three related tasks typically are located in an E.D.P. department. From: George J. Brabb and Earl B. Hutchins, "Electronic Computers and Management Organization," *California Management Review*, 6:no. 1, 35 (Fall, 1963). Throughout this book I have considered systems and programming work as being performed by the same work groups. Recently I have observed, however, that programming work is being performed by both the systems and computer operations functions, depending upon whether the programming activities are for new programs or for maintenance of old ones.

the computer programs, 3) the time lapse since the introduction of advanced mechanized and computer operations, 4)
the personal status and abilities of the manager who supervises the systems group, and 5) the importance which top
management ascribes to the systems function.

The resulting organizational forms fall into four categories:
1) the systems group independent of any functional and machine operations control, 2) the systems group under functional control but not responsible for machine operations, 3)
the systems group under functional control and responsible
for machine operation, and 4) the systems function nonexistent as such within an autonomous operating unit (a
temporary condition).

1) *Systems Group Independent of Functional and Machine
Operations Control:* The survey yielded but one example of a
systems group which reports directly to a chief executive (a
divisional general manager) of an independent profit center.
Further, this group does not have any responsibility for machine operations.

The systems group is built around its manager, who is known
as a maverick and blue-sky thinker within the organization. The
manager's curiosity and intellectual bent had led him to work
on various projects during his long tenure with the company.
Thus, when he exhibited an interest in computers and their
application to business problems, he was appointed systems
manager, that is, a special assistant reporting directly to the
chief executive. As the new systems manager, he selected a
study team which promptly embarked on a feasibility study.
After two years the team reported favorably on using a computer. The chief executive, in turn, directed: "Prove it will
work!" The team then grew rapidly as a test program was designed "to prove" the ability of the organization to utilize
computer technology efficiently.

Thus this systems group was conceived and developed as
a typical staff service. The reason for its creation and subsequent growth in size and influence was and is directly related
to computer technology. The systems group was charged with

studying the feasibility of computer technology and supervising the transition to computer programs whenever possible. The organizational picture, however, is not quite so neat. The systems group is not the only group within the organization which has responsibility for systems work, with or without regard to computers.

In this large corporation there are several corporate staff services which directly relate to the area of responsibility of the systems group in the division. Within the autonomous unit (profit center) itself, there are *four* other groups which have systems responsibilities related to the local staff group's activities. One of these four "other" systems groups is contracted for from within the company but is outside the organizational jurisdiction of the profit center; the other three are associated with functional areas, e.g., finance, within the jurisdiction of the chief executive of the profit center.

The local staff systems manager's conception of his responsibility is coincident with his personality and interests. The day-to-day needs of his unit are neglected, because he becomes bored once the exhilarating, intellectually challenging aspects of the program have been met, or if the problems are in areas in which he is not "interested." Hence the behavior of the local staff systems manager in addition to the chief executive's failure to assign systems responsibilities more specifically have diluted many of the benefits of an independent systems staff function.

The profusion of systems specialists has led to difficulties with regard to titles and organizational responsibilities. For instance, the local staff systems group, having assumed an organizational title similar to that of one of the corporate staff systems groups, was ordered unceremoniously to find another name.

In summary, although a staff systems group exists, it does not have exclusive jurisdiction for systems work within its organizational limits; it has not even been given exclusive rights to computer systems. In effect the systems group is assigned project work. As one would expect in such a situation, there are numerous organizational conflicts.

2) *Systems Group under Functional Control but Not Responsible for Machine Operations:* One company in this category has a systems department which is well established, with roots that date back to 1935. The systems group operates as a staff function and reports to the vice-president and controller of the organization. The systems manager indicated that his department was the "...right arm and right eye of top management for long-range planning to minimize costs."

The traditional tasks of the department prior to E.D.P. were research and planning, office machines, operating procedures, departmental layouts, and forms design and control. Its activities and utilization of manpower have been altered significantly by the introduction of the computer. Now the major responsibility of the department is to make recommendations on policies, programs, and conversion to E.D.P.

This major change in emphasis dates to 1954, when a department systems analyst was selected to study the feasibility of computers for the company's activities. The appointed analyst, deciding that the job was too big for one man, organized a group of interested parties *from various firms* to accumulate and share information. He hired an assistant and borrowed four additional men from the operating departments to get needed statistics. The first year of activity was taken up primarily with the gathering of facts relevant to the firm's operations.

The next year (1956) was devoted to analyzing the computers that were available to handle the specific data processing requirements of the firm. The systems analyst (who had been promoted during this period) concluded that the firm's operations were suited for computerization and recommended a specific computer to do the job.

After these findings were analyzed by an internal cost accounting group and two outside consulting agencies, an order for a computer was placed in 1956. Delivery was promised for

1958.[8] Once the purchase contract had been signed, the systems analyst (promoted once again) began building his team in anticipation of the increased work load involved in systems analysis, programming, and coding which was his responsibility as head of electronic systems work.

In this firm systems activities are entrenched within the controller's function. Tradition and individual interests preclude a spinning off of the systems responsibility in the near future. In no way does this detract from the internal organizational changes which have transpired within the department. The position, status, and influence of the systems analyst originally entrusted with the feasibility study have risen steadily as computerization has proceeded.

As one might suspect, the methods department prior to 1954 had been primarily concerned with cost control and equipment authorizations. A manager outside of the methods department described it in this way:

> Before the computer, systems were primarily developed within the individual line departments. The methods department was primarily interested in cost control and were primarily experts on office equipment. Now with the computer, the methods department is truly a staff department.

The split between systems work and machine operations responsibility which existed prior to the introduction of the computer has persisted, even though there has been some conflict in the organization in this regard.

The question of who should manage the computer was raised around the time of its delivery. The close relationship between systems analysis and computer operations motivated the methods department to seek control over computer schedules and operations. However, the tabulating machine group objected. Top management arbitrated the dispute in favor of

---

[8] It was estimated that the computerization of procedures would be more costly for the first two to three years than the old method. Thus, savings from applying electronics were not expected to reduce costs for possibly three years after the computer was delivered. Top managemnt did not want to pioneer, but felt that the longer computerization was delayed, the greater the change-over costs would be.

separation, dictating that operating responsibility for computer programs be given to the tabulating manager.

Of course this did not resolve the issue. As one manager put it, "In practice, we walk a narrow line." The methods department's responsibility for developing programs, supervising conversion, and de-bugging to the point that routine operation was possible necessitated close liaison with the computer group. On the other hand, the tabulating department felt, and quite rightly, "Giving in would give over our department to methods."

These operating difficulties with regard to computer control obviously were not resolved by the top management dictum separating methods responsibilities from tabulating and computer machine operations. A member of the methods department keeps a book scheduling the use of the computer, but since he is not made aware of changes in input to the computer his schedule bears little relation to operating reality. The tabulating department merely ignores the methods department's schedule.

In summary, the methods department, under the jurisdiction of the controller, has moved toward the status of an independent staff function with the advent of E.D.P. The reporting level for systems work has been moving upward, as has its manager. The traditional organizational distinction between systems activities and machine operations has persisted, although not without conflict.

3) *Systems Group under Functional Control and Responsible for Machine Operations:* This is by far the most prevalent arrangement. Eight of the ten formally established systems groups discussed in this section fall under this heading.[9] These eight systems groups represent the typical computer installation in that they are predominantly under the control of the financial function and report generally to a relatively low level of management. Although the department may

---

[9] The last arrangement discussed in this section deals with a computer installation which operated without any formal company systems activities.

be called the E.D.P. department, the leadership rests with a manager who by training and experience is systems rather than machine oriented. First I shall consider two groups at a relatively low level, and second, six groups which report to a middle level, noting the one exception where the controlling function is not finance.

The similarity of the first two systems groups is not the number of administrative layers which exists above their respective managers as much as the isolated and compartmentalized position of systems within the firms. This condition, in large measure, results from the pattern of growth and the objectives of the systems function in these firms. In both cases the organizational development of the systems function is paralleled by the advancement of the manager in charge.

The systems manager in the first firm had been an auditing clerk in 1945. He and one or two other men concerned themselves with general office procedures. In 1951, as a result of the group's activities, a work scheduling department was established, and the future systems manager assumed one of the minor supervisory positions created. In 1952 a procedures division was established in an accounting department. In 1956 a feasibility study was made, and a computer was ordered in 1957. As the requirements for systems and procedures work grew, the function was enhanced, and the systems manager was promoted twice more.

The first two programs placed on the computer were employee payroll and customer billing, in that order. Prior to computerization the general accounting department had had its own machine group and procedures division to handle its payroll and accounting functions. The procedures group was expanded to program the computer; machine operations were expanded with the acquisition of the computer. A year after the payroll had been computerized, the billing operation was computerized also. The billing machine room, formerly under the revenue accounting department, was absorbed by the computer machine center, and only the clerical functions relating to billing were retained in the revenue accounting department. In this situation systems considerations were subordinated to machine operations. The systems manager had responsibility primarily for programming selected procedures, for machine room operations, and for supervising two other general accounting sections employing eighty people.

Because the systems and procedures function in the second firm is almost identical in background, development, and current status with the first, the same summary applies to both. Although the systems function as such exists in these two companies, it has not developed as broadly nor as quickly as in other firms where it was not subverted by operating line responsibilities. As a result systems work *per se* has not received as much emphasis or energetic support as it has received under better circumstances. The young managers associated with systems work have had responsibility not only for data preparation and processing but also for the computerized programs themselves. Second, the pure systems function has received little organizational recognition. Further, the people entrusted with systems are engaged primarily in programming and coding procedures for the computer.

In five firms of the second group, the systems manager reports to the financial manager, e.g., the controller, at a middle level of the organization. In the sixth firm the systems group is part of an administrative division.

The five systems groups which share responsibility for computer operations represent the most typical E.D.P. organizational form. Each of the five managers is one or two levels removed from the top financial officer of the organizational unit to which he reports. Each supervises, basically, two groups of employees — the systems group (which includes programming and coding) and the computer machine operations group. All five managers are young and aggressive and have risen rapidly to their present positions.

In an interesting variant to the pattern, however, one of these five firms employed a corporate staff man to supervise the activities of the local systems manager. No one involved doubted that the consultant ran the show. His major objective, he said, was to design the system, implement it, and then train the local staff to run it.

In the sixth firm the responsibility for systems and procedures had been diffused widely prior to computerization. This resulted in part from the organizational philosophy of the firm. Briefly stated this company previously had been organized with a staff policy level for each functional activity, while the actual productive efforts of the firm were supervised by an administrative line organization. The head of the line organization was responsible for efficient operations, and staff services reported to him.

A systems man had been hired in the late 1930s to change data processing methods, but he refused to utilize the tabulating equipment being widely used for similar functions, even up to the 1950s. Hence paperwork was primarily a hand-labor process, with accounting machines used sparingly for only a very specialized function.

With a new president, a new systems manager, and a reorganization in the early 1950s, the stage was set for the study of the applicability of electronics to the firm's paperwork operations. The old form of organization was modified slightly. While the vice-presidential level continued to be the policy level and administrative managers continued to be responsible for everyday operations, one highly significant change was made. The sovereignty of the systems and procedures group was established by a document they had drawn up which was approved by top management and initialed by all affected division and department heads.

Although the organizational manual of this company continues to ascribe to the line managers the responsibility "...for the efficient operation of the assigned departments in accordance with policies, plans, and procedures approved by the vice president of the division," in reality, the activities of the systems group are centralized, and it delineates its own areas of responsibility. There is a charter to prove that this is so, witnessed if not approved by the affected areas!

The systems manager reports to the manager in the administrative division who is responsible for eight other functional activities also. The systems group itself has an interesting organization. It consists of a machine group and three methods groups, each designed to handle specific types of problems, any or all of which may be affected by a single computer program. The rationale for this form of organization is that it facilitates centralization and over-all control of systems activities.

4) *No Formal Systems Function:* In one surveyed company no one was involved directly in systems analysis for the computer installation initially. Its E.D.P. department was one of fifteen departments (functions) directly under the office manager who reported to the controller. The major function of the machine room was billing and inventory control. By the 1950s the tabulating equipment no longer could handle the increasing work load which had resulted from the rapid growth of the company. In 1958 I.B.M. was asked to make a feasibility study. After consulting with the machine room manager and the office manager, the controller accepted I.B.M.'s recommendation to install a computer. The machine room manager requested that a systems man be hired to work on systems and programming. An order also was placed for the installation of a more advanced computer the following year.

The I.B.M. representative assigned to the company to keep its computer operating, commented on the situation. As he saw it, the installation had grown rapidly with the business, but no one yet had attempted to formalize the basic operating procedures or to relate them into some coherent whole. Informal procedures were followed in accordance with the experience of individual employees; thus it was impossible to pin down the procedures or to translate them efficiently for the computer. Hence maintenance of the computer programs was extremely difficult and required the full-time assistance of the I.B.M. representative.

Interestingly enough, a so-called systems group did report to the controller. Its function was to "be directly responsible to the controller who will determine priorities and coordinate efforts between major departments." According to the machine room manager, this systems group in no way concerned itself with systems analysis.

In a follow-up interview it was revealed that many changes have taken place. A new information systems department has been created. Its manager reports directly to the financial vice-president. The systems manager is in charge of systems analysis, programming, and computer operations, as well as the the forms control and communications sections. This manager predicted that with an I.B.M. System/360, to be delivered in 1966, his department would become a separate service unit reporting to the president.

This firm provides a striking example of systems organization development. In the brief span of a few years the systems group has evolved to a top level function within this firm.

The power tactics that may emerge when a systems function, or any function for that matter, is badly guided and organized, are discussed next. The political aspects of such a situation are illustrated also.

COMPUTER PROGRAMS AND COMPANY POLITICS

General neglect of E.D.P. by top management is commonplace. Many executives prefer to turn over most E.D.P. planning and installation problems to "the specialists." The division of work and assignment of responsibilities for these specialists leave much to be desired. Such unsatisfactory management practices lead to much jockeying for position by the managers involved and, more importantly, usually are detrimental to the development of the computer programs.

Croome comments on this political dimension of business organization in a fluid, dynamic situation:

Inside the firm, there is little overt organization in the political party sense; but the formation of pressure groups and the quest for power are none the less familiar. "Political" considerations constantly influence, and more or less seriously distort, courses of action concerned with the firm's primary purpose as a working

organization. And they very obviously come into play
when that organization is in a state of flux owing to
new conditions.[10]

The introduction of computer technology creates precisely
this kind of fluid situation (power vacuum) which precipitates
"political action." The managerial and organizational ramifications of the introduction of E.D.P. are considerable,
although there is wide variation among observers as to the
exact degree and nature of the impact. Gustafson quotes an
insurance company executive's evaluation of the general
problem:

> "One of the most noticeable effects of this kind of
> shifting around is the mounting power of the man who
> directs the data processing operation" says Mr. Slater
> of John Hancock. "This may look like empire-building
> to some, and political problems may be intensified, but
> it means that top management will have to begin re-
> thinking key executive assignments and responsibilities,
> and do it early enough so that necessary adjustments
> and transitions can be made gradually and relatively
> painlessly."[11]

This top executive's awareness of this problem and willing-
ness to express his thoughts about it are refreshing. Many other
managers interviewed do not recognize the existence of any
divergent interests within the organization, and fail to bring
the undercurrent power struggles into the open. This is particularly true when the organization is undergoing extra pressures resulting from major shifts in responsibilities because of
technological changes.

Pretending these strains do not exist or trying to hide them
offers no solution. One permanent and effective solution to a
political power problem is to minimize it by good organizational planning and strong managerial leadership.[12] The reper-

---

[10] Honor Croome, *Human Problems of Innovation* (London: Her Majesty's
Stationery Office, Department of Scientific and Industrial Research, 1960), 19.

[11] Philip Gustafson, "What Management Is Learning from Computers," *Nation's
Business*, 46:no. 11, 39 (November, 1958).

[12] For a detailed discussion and a list of political strategies designed to further
executive careers, see Norman H. Martin and John Howard Sims, "Thinking
Ahead: Power Tactics," *Harvard Business Review*, 34:no. 6, 25f (November-December, 1956).

cussions of inadequate planning and unsatisfactory administration of systems were illustrated in the development of a
computer program in one of the companies studied.

Button, Button, Who's Got the Button?

In this firm the systems function was divided because top
management felt that duplication of responsibilities would
lead to the best results. A young manager, Mr. A, temporarily
assigned to an accounting function, concluded that the work
could be improved vastly by revising operating methods. He
felt that by revising the work process and utilizing a computer much duplication of work could be eliminated and sizeable efficiencies effected. On his own time, he worked out a
plan implementing his ideas.

Next Mr. A approached the machine room supervisor (also
in the financial department) for technical assistance in converting the general plan into a form suitable for machine
operations. These men collaborated and sent their recommendation to computerize to the chief financial officer who
approved it. All these activities had transpired without the
knowledge of 1) Mr. B, the systems manager in the finance
division, for whom, incidentally, the machine room supervisor
worked; or 2) Mr. C, head of an independent systems group
which was engaged, at that time, in applying computers to
the firm's operations.

The computer was rented, and Mr. B was placed in charge
of its implementation, even though he privately disapproved
of the entire project! Despite the fact that Mr. B had good
technical reasons to believe the project would fail, he let the
project proceed without protesting openly.

Mr. C was disgruntled too, but for different reasons. The
computer which the project was to utilize was technically
incompatible with the one used to process other company
programs already operational. Mr. C appealed to the top executive to overrule the financial officer on the project leadership assignment. The chief executive advised his second line
managers to work it out among themselves. The financial offi-

cer, who had already committed himself, refused to budge. The project was continued.

The systems manager, Mr. B, brought Mr. A into his organization and placed him in charge of the project. Throughout the time Mr. A worked for him, Mr. B gave glowing accounts of A's ability and rated him highly in performance appraisals. Mr. B did nothing to advance the success of the project.

Shortly before the delivery of the computer, Mr. A asked for and received a promotion to a different job in a different state. Then the systems manager was on the spot. With the delivery of the computer only a few months off, he had a potential failure on his hands and could not even blame Mr. A, after having rated him so highly.

Almost frantically Mr. B plunged into the project. He received some assistance in two ways: first, manpower was added from the affected accounting areas, and second, there was a two-month delay in delivery of the computer by the manufacturer.

Finally the computer arrived, and the program was put into operation. The work schedule entailed eighty-five hours of machine time, filled with chaos, problems, and mix-ups due to bad work. At this point the systems manager asked for and was given a position at corporate headquarters. Mr. D, a new systems manager, was quickly recruited to replace Mr. B. After three months of hectic, intensive work by every able-bodied man who could be spared and committed to battle, the program was de-bugged.

The savings originally predicted for the project were eaten up by the cost of revising the program to make it operational. Superficially developed and executed, it turned out to be a costly experiment with computer technology.

The end was not yet at hand however. It was decided that A's special program would be dovetailed into existing company programs and run on the same computer. A jurisdictional question was raised as to who would do the systems work to accomplish the transfer. Mr. D and Mr. C locked horns, and the outcome and the means thereto are interesting.

Mr. D insisted on doing the systems work connected with transferring the accounting computer program (the original project) to the older computer. He threatened to rent a *third* type of computer if he could not handle the desired systems analysis, and in fact actually got the equipment authorization and talked with various computer manufacturing representatives. His tactics bore fruit.

Mr. C gave in. He agreed to a compromise whereby systems analysis would be carried out by the financial systems people, while the programming and coding would be done by the staff systems group. Mr. D, who felt that systems analysis was 70 percent of the process and programming and coding were routine functions taking up only 30 percent of the time, was pleased. Mr. C was successful in maintaining most of his exclusive jurisdiction, although he had been out-maneuvered and did lose some ground.

The mediated truce lasted for a brief two years. A strong profit squeeze led management to create a task force to determine why computerization had failed so miserably and to overhaul it. This group recommended that 1) systems responsibilities be combined, 2) a new systems manager be hired, 3) Mr. C serve for one year as a consultant and then be retired, and 4) Mr. D be fired. During the past few years the newly centralized systems function has been directed by two successive managers. The nagging fact in this whole situation is of course that these battles need never have been fought. The skirmishes, although not entirely irradicable, could have been reduced in intensity and form by a better informed and more actively involved top management.

Strategies of Conflict

One of the devices employed in the power struggle just discussed was "computer blackmail," the use of a particular make of computer as a means of exerting pressure. This device is not subtle, and its use as a way of gaining one's ends is understood readily. Computer blackmail will be considered in connection with another device for business warfare.

An E.D.P. committee is typically created very soon after a firm begins to consider computerization seriously. The most common reason for forming such a committee is to coordinate E.D.P. activities from the initial feasibility study through conversion. Acting in their capacity as E.D.P. committee members, men often become involved in a struggle for power, because many management and organization questions have not been answered, nor are any relevant policy guides available as a basis for decision-making.

Members of an E.D.P. committee have various degrees of enthusiasm for E.D.P. The functional area representative, usually from finance, is often most enthusiastic and aggressive in furthering E.D.P within a firm. On the other hand, some of the other functional area representatives, fearing they may have much to lose, may become recalcitrant, pessimistic, and sometimes may even openly sabotage the efforts of the E.D.P. committee to carry out its assignments.

In one large firm surveyed, two functional area managers vied for over-all control of E.D.P. The issue was framed in terms of rival computer types. Once top management had decided on a particular computer, the functional area manager supporting that decision was put in charge of E.D.P. Essentially from that time on, the committee was transformed from a consultative body into a communicative device. The manager of systems and computer operations became the E.D.P. committee's dominant member, very often using the committee for his own personal ambitions, which may or may not have coincided with the objectives of the E.D.P. program.

A general accounting manager who had charge of a computer machine center and reported to the controller related another example of how the computer can become the focus of managerial conflict. The president had appointed a committee to study various new computers before replacing its old computer. The committee was made up of the controller, the administrative assistant to the controller for systems, the general accounting manager, and one or two lower management personnel. After a thorough evaluation of alternative computing systems, the committee was divided in its judgment: the controller favored the General Electric 625, the administrative assistant to the controller in charge of systems wanted the I.B.M. System/360, and the general accounting manager was caught between preferring the System/360 and supporting his superior.

As consensus was not reached by the committee, the president decided the issue. He endorsed and ordered the System/360. He also promoted the administrative assistant to assistant controller without prior consultation with the controller. The general accounting manager feels he faces an uncertain future, since in all likelihood the computer center will be transferred to the supervision of the new assistant controller.

In another company an E.D.P. committee was formed after the initial computerization program had been sabotaged by jurisdictional conflicts. The formal objective in forming the committee was to provide a means of coordinating the activities of all affected functional areas implementing E.D.P. The manager in charge of E.D.P. in the finance section thought of the committee as an orientation device for the managers of procedures he was readying for computerization. After top management had approved a broad E.D.P. program under the authority of the financial E.D.P. manager, the committee was dissolved. A bystander to this process commented: "I guess, in effect, the other managers on the E.D.P. committee have given up."

Another business conflict device is the exploitation of strategic location and information control. In one conflict situation, the systems manager strives to be at the "heart of the paperwork system." By controlling the design and stocking of all forms, by having the power to approve multilith printing activities, by determining the selection of office supplies, and by passing on requests for non-stocked items, this manager has immediate, intimate knowledge of his "adversaries'" activities. No communication need go in the other direction, giving this manager a tactical advantage. His position has been secured by the chief executive's company-wide directive authorizing the manager's activities. The systems manager admitted that the major objective of his maneuvers is to consolidate and expand his responsibilities and interests.

To give some flavor to the conflicts and strategies discussed above, interview notes describing this successful manager are included here.

Mr. X impresses me as a capable, driving, energetic, ambitious, and confident *operator*. He appears to enjoy the rough and tumble of business politics, and even thrives on battle. He has a good grasp of wielding power, and an excellent tactical sense of "taking the high ground."

He gives the impression of being somewhat ruthless, but the stakes are high, and it is all part of the game, anyway.

One indication that he felt he was in an invulnerable position was the fact that he was ready to talk frankly, straight from the shoulder, and not paint an erroneous picture of his situation. He took his present position at lower pay rather than another one he was offered, precisely because it entailed a difficult problem, and he considered it a challenge, and therefore an opportunity.

Chapter VI

THE COMPUTER AND THE STAFF ROLE

I consider that in the past decade a significant characteristic of information-systems work has been too great a degree of control in the hands of specialists. This situation has developed in part through the failure of top management to place controlling responsibility with operating managers.
— PHILIP H. THURSTON

The systems analyst is the chief staff specialist responsible for implementing computerization in a firm. The line and staff principle of organization is analyzed by examining the role of the systems analyst during and after a conversion to computerized operations. The focus of the discussion is upon the relationship of the systems analysts and the line managers whose departments' work procedures are being computerized.

The chapter is organized into three sections. In the first section data from the surveyed firms are drawn upon to describe and evaluate the line-staff relationship. Some of the issues involved therein are commented upon next. In the final section the future of staff jobs, especially under the imperatives of computerization, is discussed.

THE SYSTEMS STAFF SPECIALIST

The systems specialist participates in four stages in the computerization process: 1) determination of feasibility of the computer for a firm; 2) conversion, whereby information procedures are computerized; 3) testing, the stage at which a procedure is modified to eliminate unforeseen input problems or faulty design; and 4) achievement of smooth operation and

129

simple maintenance systems work required. A satisfactory relationship between the systems specialist and line management at all these stages is imperative for the success of computerization.

This relationship, ill-defined before the introduction of the computer, is strained by the pressures generated when computers are utilized for information processing. One line manager in a survey firm expressed it this way: "The computer helped to define our hodge-podge as far as organizational responsibility." Assignment of responsibility for the various phases of the conversion process, although seldom officially made, is crucial to its success.

The following activities were involved in one particular conversion process, according to a methods manager in one of the firms surveyed:

1) A detailed analysis of current operations, indicating the flow of information from its entrance into the system to its final disposition, regardless of department lines.

2) A sampling of all the forms of transmitting the information.

3) The development of an over-all flow chart, with a proposal including the forms and procedure and what is to be done in the program.

4) Detailing the job the computer will do — code and then de-bug the program, the *how* content of the job.

5) Providing the source of the data, where and how they can be obtained, and establishing *when* to convert.

6) Training of people in the affected department by pilot men, and conversion of historical records and new inputs for computerized operations to begin.

7) Establishing testing as a permanent program, and department and machine room operating normally.

Working Relationships

The assumption of these responsibilities once the conversion process is underway is the next consideration. Then the relationship of a systems specialist to the management of the computerized procedure can be discussed. Conway, Gibbons, and Watts state that a variety of relationships are possible between line and staff depending upon three important variables.

In practice, a variety of approaches has proven successful depending upon 1) the extent of the changes, 2) the manner in which changes in procedures and responsibilities are normally handled in the specific company, and 3) the presence or absence of systems groups, organization departments, etc. within the company to help decide upon the change which is to be made.[1]

Traditions, the nature of the change, and the type of groups involved in the change constitute the broad variables which structure the relationships.

Thurston provides another perspective to this same organizational subject. His focus is on the strengths and weaknesses that a line manager and a staff specialist bring to systems work.

The systems work of the specialist also has limitations. Foremost of these is the resistance of operating people. Operating people resist planning in which they have no part; they resist the efforts of the specialists to seek information or to install systems changes; and they delay accepting responsibility for new operating systems installed by specialists.

The flow of operating information to the specialist is blocked not only by the resistance of the operating people but also by the specialist's lack of familiarity with the areas he studies. He is slow to perceive unfamiliar work patterns and hence slow to gather the information he needs.

In addition, there is some suggestion that specialists may be limited by their own over-emphasis on systems change. That is, some specialists perceive the successful performance of their job in terms of change to the extent of disregarding the immediate needs of an operating situation and of underestimating the importance of cost and timing considerations.

In all, the systems work of specialists is influenced

[1] B. Conway, J. Gibbons, and D. E. Watts, *Business Experience with Electronic Computers* (New York: Controllers Institute Research Foundation, Incorporated, 1959), 131.

by their removal from operations, whereas the systems work of operating people is influenced by their close association with the work. The operating people possess detailed knowledge to be changed. This helps in assembling information necessary for systems decisions and in recognizing what changes will improve the immediate work situation. Further, once the supervisor in control of an operation is convinced of the desirability of making a systems change, his position enables him to effect the change with greater ease than could the specialist. Operating people make another contribution to systems changes through their strengths in manpower which enables them to give substantial support to systems projects in many areas at the same time. Operating people demonstrate weaknesses, too, in their systems work. They are limited in their knowledge of methods for handling information. They think in terms of existing areas of responsibility whereas the specialist has a broader outlook. And the operating people emphasize current operations, showing a reluctance to change existing work patterns.[2]

Many of Thurston's points are illustrated in the arrangements made by the surveyed firms to implement E.D.P.

Four basic patterns predominated in the conversion and operation of the new procedures: 1) no organized systems activity, the machine room manager and the computer manufacturer's representative shared total responsibility and the affected line management played no active role; 2) the systems specialists had full responsibility for conversion, the line for operations; 3) the systems, machine operation, and affected procedure all fell under systems control; and 4) the project approach with some specialist-manager cooperation for conversion established, and operations a line responsibility or not.

Case 1. No Organized Approach: Only one firm was in this

---

[2] Philip H. Thurston, *Systems and Procedures Responsibility* (Boston: Division of Research, Harvard University Graduate School of Business Administration, 1959), 98. These ideas are summarized by Thurston in a later article, "Who Should Control Information Systems?," *Harvard Business Review*, 40:no. 6, 135-140 (November-December, 1962).

category. Systems work was done by the equipment manufacturer. Conversion consisted merely of placing the existing unwritten procedures on the computer. The manager of the machine center participated, but the line managers were not consulted. Since little or no innovation had been made in the pre-existing information flow, and input preparation was not altered significantly, the affected line department's methods of operation were not changed.

Case 2. Specialists Responsible for Procedure Revision, the Line May or May Not Manage Operations: Two firms were in this category. The staff had full responsibility for the conversion of the procedure. The line operating management did not participate in any meaningful sense until the procedure had been perfected.

In the first firm a program was supposedly almost ready for testing. It was an extensive program which had been designed with extremely ambitious goals in mind. A composite view of the line-staff problem was represented by the opinions of the managers who had a vested interest in the success of the program.

A methods manager was in charge of developing the program. In his opinion most people (e.g., line managers) could not visualize the system; it took too much effort for line management to do so, and line management wanted the program delivered on a silver platter.

> They know my work. They know I will fulfill the requirements, even though I take two or three times as long. Because of line management's tight budgets and lack of time, they are willing to rely on me.

The methods manager said further that he did not particularly want to know what the line needed or wanted, and was developing the program independently. He explained, "It doesn't matter because the line doesn't know what they want."

For three years the methods group had been working independently on the conversion procedure. A subordinate manager reported that the line showed a lack of interest, was afraid of the program, exhibited hostility, but gave only passive resistance in face of top management's order to cooperate.

The top line manager of the department affected by the program felt that it was blue sky. He said that the line was helpless and was forced to leave everything to the methods group. A line subordinate who played a key role in the new program complained that he was not sure what needs he would be expected to meet. He said the program was complex and difficult to comprehend, and that he needed to be briefed on the input and output to the system. He needed this information from methods at least six months before the program could become operational. As he had had no contact with methods for three months, the projected date of the actual running of the program would have to be advanced.

Two other interested managers commented to me on the program. The first man was skeptical about its success, said that the program was being developed in a vacuum, and that communication between management and the methods specialists was minimal. He guessed that after three years the program would be sprung on line management. His colleague added: "Success or failure may determine the future responsibility for E.D.P."

Indeed, assigning responsibility for operation had not yet been faced. The top manager of the affected department thought that the systems group would manage the procedure "for a couple of years." The systems group considered the question of eventual operational responsibility to be unresolved but was prepared to run the program "for some time."

In the second firm an E.D.P. committee was formed to study the application of the computer to the firm's operations. This committee was chaired by the top methods manager. It included six line managers at the second and third levels of the organization and a three-member methods staff composed of a line manager from each of the two line areas to be most intimately involved with computerization and a methods specialist.

These three staff members, with the aid of a fourth man who had been lured away from an equipment manufacturer, conducted the first studies and did the initial systems work. No line management representatives were assigned to the staff in carrying out this work, although people had been requested numerous times. Most of the flow charting was done without reference to the line department. However, after the job had been completed, the charts were shown to the line management, and "they were permitted to make any corrections they wished. Not many corrections were made." The line was consulted only about the forms and reports required, and asked less of the new procedures than they were able to provide. After these procedures had been computerized, their operation became the responsibility of the line organization, although machine operations were to remain under the control of the methods group.

Case 3. Systems and Machine and Line Operations Responsibilities Coincide: In each of the two firms of this category one manager is responsible for systems activities, machine operations, and input-output generation. In both firms the payroll and billing responsibilities are completely handled by the manager in charge of systems and machine operations. Line and staff, under these circumstances, *has little relevance* to the process of conversion and operation. The pertinent responsibilities are completely integrated.

Obviously in these two firms there has been little or no change in the work methods employed, even though machine operations have been centralized. In one of the firms the affected functions, their managers, and employees were placed under the methods group. Otherwise the organization and responsibilities have not been drastically altered.

Case 4. The Project Systems Approach: Two firms in the survey sample utilized a project approach in implementing the computer. In each firm the purpose and form of the approach were different.

The first firm developed its project approach to computerization in order to meet the problems created 1) by the lack of a clear definition of E.D.P. responsibility, and 2) by line resistance to E.D.P. Prior to the introduction of the computer there was no formal systems group with jurisdiction over all departments. Therefore the introduction of the computer in the controller's department touched off a battle for control. A temporary compromise with another staff department led to a decision which later gave the controller full responsibility for information processing systems work and machine operations.

By the terms of the temporary compromise, an E.D.P. committee was established; it was to assign projects to be carried out by both staff specialists and line managers. When the success of E.D.P. was threatened by conflicts among these interested groups, a systems specialist was appointed chairman of each project.

The E.D.P. committee's major responsibilities were the phasing in of the computer, approving programs, and establishing target dates for the various pieces of the programs. To meet these objectives project teams were created. They were composed of both staff systems specialists and line representatives who had decision-making power to provide assistance and advice to the systems people. Part of the failure of past attempts at conversion had been the resistance of line management and its reluctance to assign line managers to assist the staff specialists.

The stated reason for and activities of these project teams are quoted below:

> The Data Processing Staff, with the cooperation of line and staff supervision, has been actively engaged in making a detailed study of the current clerical functions involved in the order processing cycle. This involves an intimate knowledge of the operations of such departments as Planning, Timekeeping, Factory Payroll, Cost, General Accounting, and various factory procedures, such as the piecework systems, manufacturing control functions, and production and inventory control procedures.
>
> To coordinate and direct these systems studies and establish lines of contact and communication with the various departments involved, 16 formal project assignments have been issued by the Data Processing Com-

mittee. These project assignments define the purpose
and objective of the particular study. Over 30 people
are directly assigned to these projects, representing 16
departments. The acceptance of the program and the
cooperation of the people have been excellent.

I questioned the methods manager as to his assessment of
cooperation. After much prodding he allowed that "cooperation
and acceptance have been as good as you could expect considering the impact on organization and responsibility."

The projects were formally presented with specific requirements listed. They were included in the E.D.P. feasibility
presentation to top management which led to the final resolution of jurisdictional problems. Top management assigned responsibilities for the computerization activities to the methods
department. In fact, after the presentation was approved by
top management, the E.D.P. committee was dissolved.

The contents of a sample project include, for example, the
project number, date assigned, completion date, the specific
line and staff managers responsible for results, project objectives, and expected benefits. Under the heading "Project Objectives" is a fairly specific list of the information, procedures,
rules, and records to be evaluated by the group.

The circumstances surrounding the birth and death of the
E.D.P. committee and the development of project groups suggest that they existed more to establish jurisdiction and control
than to form the basis for long lasting cooperation.

The second firm in this category also employs the project
approach, but the circumstances and form vary. Again the
line and staff problem and the attempt to resolve it are depicted first by summarizing the approach and then by para-
phrasing the attitudes of the managers directly involved.

This firm's methods group was divided into two major sections on the basis of the older and routine systems functions
and the newer electronic systems functions. The E.D.P.
methods group was also divided. One group was responsible
for the conversion of existing records onto magnetic tape. The
other group was responsible for feasibility studies, systems
work, and conversion of the department procedures to compu-

terized operations. Individual projects were worked on by several analysts in the initial stages, but during actual conversion one analyst was in charge. Most of the methods analysts had been selected from the operating departments. The men were expected to keep in touch with these departments, informing them of E.D.P. developments, and were to return to them to implement the new procedures.

After doing all the preparatory work, the methods analyst was transferred to the line department to begin the conversion. The initial conversion group in the department consisted of a supervisor and two or three key clerks who previously had had some training in preparation of input for information processing in the methods department. The methods analyst established a pilot operation to handle a small number of accounts under the new procedure. The pilot group was expanded as more and more accounts were converted to the E.D.P. system and as more people were trained in the department and absorbed into the operation. The rate of conversion depended upon the number of accounts to be converted, the nature of the information, and the rate at which suitable personnel could be trained.

In summary, the historical records for this particular department were converted in the methods department. Input for the computerized accounts was prepared in the line department under the direction of a methods analyst. Input clerks were recruited in that department and trained in the methods department. This nucleus established a pilot operation which was expanded as new people were selected and trained within the line department. The machine operations were handled by a separate department.

Several line-staff problems were precipitated by this system. The first major problem arose over supervision of the methods analyst. Selected initially by the line department manager in consultation with the personnel manager, the analyst was to be trained for systems work, and later for supervising the conversion. The methods manager objected to the selection, but the line choice prevailed.[3] When the analyst returned to the line department to lead the conversion, the department manager insisted that the analyst report to him, not to the methods manager. The line view was sustained again, but tempers were aroused.

A second problem, dimly recognized by the participants, arose because the methods analyst assumed sole leadership for the conversion process and supervision of the department employees engaged in preparing information under the new system. The analyst defined his own role, since no effort had been made by line management to do so. Neither was there any communication or conference among all concerned to outline the systems analyst's work objectives. Thus questions as to who would manage the procedure after conversion, what responsibility or authority the analyst had, and what was the most efficient means to accomplish the project were never even formally raised.

One result of this bad organization for conversion was the confusion of the supervisors directly involved. One supervisor said he reported to Manager A for procedure and to the systems analyst for conversion. Another supervisor said she reported to Supervisor A, but if she had a "real complaint," she saw either Manager A or the systems analyst. A third supervisor said that two supervisors were her bosses.

To eliminate the confusion a line manager finally was designated to take charge of the new procedure. This particular manager's behavior, prior to the formal announcement of his transfer, was especially interesting. This man had been tranferring his least capable employees to work on the new procedure. Unwittingly he was undermining his future area of responsibility. While his superiors knew of his impending transfer, they chose not to communicate it. This manager did

---

[3] This was typical of many firms. Line managers usually recommended the personnel whom they felt they would least miss, and, unfortunately, those least qualified for systems work. This practice forced a re-evaluation in many firms and led to more recruitment outside the firm to fill these extremely sensitive positions.

not play any part in the conversion and has inherited it as a going operation.

A final problem mentioned here concerns the future. Several departments in this firm used basically the same approach to conversion and operation of the new input-preparation operation. Each systems analyst pursued his job independently. This approach did not encourage the exchange of information or stimulate cooperation among the analysts to promote and facilitate a total systems concept. The emphasis of the job on line duties detracted from the pure systems duties of the analysts, and hindered their ability to function as staff specialists.

There were, then, four basic patterns in the conversion and operation of the E.D.P. procedures. The example below illustrates line-staff relations in dealing with a problem that arose during the conversion of a procedure in one of the surveyed firms.

A Conversion Breakdown

A problem over conversion arose in May. The group working on the new computerized procedure could not continue with conversion and still maintain the accounts already on the computer. A manager closely associated with the problem feared that the project deadline would not be met. The prospect of not meeting the deadline established by the methods manager and approved by the top executive worried the department line manager and the systems analyst in charge of the program. First they went to the top line manager of the department, then to the methods manager, and finally to the top executive. The result of all this activity was the dismayed executive's command to take another long, hard look at the problem.

A conference was called. For the first time the department line management, machine operations, methods, and personnel representatives[4] met to discuss the breakdown problem. Prior

---

[4] This marked the first time that the personnel department participated in discussing any operational problem associated with E.D.P. The personnel representative was there only because his approval was necessary to hire additional employees, i.e., via the control process.

to this time no effort had been made to coordinate the participation of these interested parties.

The threefold solution agreed upon included: 1) an extension of two and one-half months for completing the conversion, 2) the addition to the department of twenty newly hired employees, and 3) the assignment *for the first time* of a line manager to the systems analyst to help implement the procedure.

Some organizational problems then presented themselves. The first was whether methods specialists or department line managers should be responsible for the conversion and operation of the new procedure. In this case the methods manager set the date for conversion completion and was responsible to top management for meeting that date. However, the methods manager did not have direct supervisory authority over the managers involved in meeting the designated date.

A second problem arose because of a lack of planning. Top management was notified when a control mechanism signalled that the conversion might fall behind schedule. The chief executive did not investigate the situation to determine the underlying circumstances which had brought this kind of problem to his attention. No inquiry was made to determine the organizational arrangements which had precipitated the problem.[5]

Finally, higher levels of management were being forced to consider some organizational aspects of E.D.P. Also, both line and staff departments associated with the department undergoing conversion were being drawn into deliberations for problem-solving, if not for planning.

Reassertion of Line Authority

There is ample evidence to suggest that line managers are

---

[5] One manager explained the situation this way: "In order to bring things to a head, more time was requested than was needed, and the foul-up was allowed to build up to get some action from the higher-ups. The meetings which followed established commitments and understandings which will allow the conversion to proceed with increased speed and success." He also stated that the problem presented to the chief executive was framed in terms of "space requirements."

reasserting their authority over operations under their control. In 1960 both line and staff managers in the surveyed firms agreed that the brief, heady period during which systems analysts had usurped line management's leadership and called the shots is fading. Such staff specialist dominance is readily understandable, of course. The new machines had an aura about them which dazzled the uninitiated; their language mystified mortal managers. Under these conditions it was not surprising that computer technologists eagerly stepped into the void left by uninformed and fearful managers.

Things have changed, however! One young systems analyst who had risen rapidly within the firm on the back of the computer lamented:

> I don't get my way as much as I used to. Increasing management education in systems and computers has had and is having a tremendous impact on management's job, ability to utilize computers, and direct systems analysts.

A top executive reflected the general opinion of top management when he remarked: "We found that in the past the systems people made too many decisions." As a result,

> The president was forced to umpire decisions in the E.D.P. committee. We had to cut systems down to size and absorb them more naturally into operations. Through greater experience and understanding, the line manager is now doing two things: 1) comprehending and using computerized systems better, and 2) reasserting control over the E.D.P. specialists and the computer.

A third executive acknowledged that:

> Executives are participating more in the development of systems and exercising greater control over systems people. Systems specialists will follow the path of programmers soon and be a dime a dozen. The systems man is being absorbed into the organization without radical top management change. The systems specialist is a middle manager who must decide whether to stay in systems and level out his aspirations or go

into a line area of the firm for further advancement.[6]

These comments by surveyed firm managers characterize this highly significant management development: there is no doubt that the line manager is beginning to take charge of computerization in his area of responsibility. He is reasserting his authority and forcing the systems function to conform more closely to the staff role theory prescribes for it.

From the above discussion of the line-staff principle of organization under computerization, it appears that the principle is retaining its significance as an aid to the organization process. The line and staff principle provides a meaningful way to describe and to analyze relationships. The question as to how viable a principle it is cannot be ascertained easily. During conversion the traditional line-staff problems arose. Most of the initially computerized procedures also appeared to present few problems different from the sort raised in connection with line and staff before E.D.P. The reassertion of line management authority and the relegation of systems to a specialized staff role support the thesis that the line-staff principle is not dead.

In the next section the possibility of improving systems specialist-line manager relationships without changing the line-staff principle is discussed.

GENERAL COMMENTS ON RESOLVING LINE-STAFF PROBLEMS

The data from the surveyed firms suggest that at the present level of computer technology Thurston's conclusions are applicable and appropriate.

> There are four general findings. The first of these is that the systems work of specialists and operating people complement each other, leading to full use of supervisory and specialized abilities and to a balanced handling of systems projects.... The second general finding is the importance of the trial installation in

---

[6] John Diebold maintains, on the contrary, that the number of systems specialists will jump from the 1965 figure of 100,000 to 325,000 by 1970. "The Boss Will Always Be Human," *Business Week*, 1875:100 (August 7, 1965).

the development of the new system. The third finding
is the importance of continuing responsibility covering
both the planning and installation stages of a project.
And the fourth general finding indicates that, within
the capabilities of the people on the job and subject to
the special circumstances of some undertakings, leadership responsibility in systems projects should rest with
operating people.[7]

The fourth finding, that leadership should rest with line
management, is consistent with line-staff theory. It is interesting to note Thurston's criteria for the establishment of
systems responsibility.

> The important considerations, thus, in selecting lead-
> ership responsibility for systems work are: motivation;
> knowledge of goals, ability to interpret them and to
> judge prospective change within these goals; and ability
> to work with people to effect changes.[8]

As Thurston says, the first two criteria are most likely to characterize lower and middle operating management, while the
third is usually a function of top management. Thus the most
likely choice for systems leadership is line, not staff management.[9] Thurston's findings are based upon data gathered by
observation of various line-staff arrangements in systems work.
He observed four arrangements, from which he selects one as
the most productive.

> Two of the approaches may be disposed of easily —
> the two extreme approaches which centered all responsi-
> bility for systems installation and planning on either
> specialists or on operating men. These approaches lost
> the advantages of the contributions possible under a
> system encouraging joint effort by both groups. . . .
> Likewise, the third approach is not selected — the
> approach in which planning responsibility is assigned
> to specialists and installation responsibility to operating
> people. . . . This approach lost the advantages of the
> trial installation before the completion of the planning
> stage and the advantages of a continuing responsibility

---

[7] Thurston, *Systems and Procedures Responsibility, op. cit.,* p. 100.
[8] *Ibid.,* p. 106.
[9] *Ibid.*

covering both planning and installation. In fact, it proved to be the least satisfactory of the approaches examined.

There remains the fourth approach, the one in which responsibility for planning and installation is shared by operators and specialists.... The technical ability of the systems analyst plus his broader view of systems combined with the operating knowledge of the supervisor and the latter's control of the operations, permitted ready installation of a new system to fulfill promptly the systems project objective.[10]

The approach recommended by Thurston approximates one of two approaches implementing computerization discussed by McGregor. He distinguishes between the assumptions and the consequences of two alternative methods of utilizing staff specialists. Line and staff organization, as traditionally depicted, precipitates power struggles, resistance and sabotage, bureaucracy, and paternalism. The team approach, according to McGregor, is a more promising alternative.

In this approach line and staff managers belong to the same work groups. The E.D.P. specialist provides the data which allows more time for the line manager to manage. Although some operations are centralized, the opportunity for increased local autonomy increases. Finally, in this approach staff educates not dictates to the line on the basis that it knows what is best. McGregor expects neither approach to predominate. He simply outlines some consequences of the polar approaches.[11]

Conflict arises when a relationship of mutual cooperation and trust does not exist between line and staff. In this situation, as Fiock sees it, operating managers harbor strong fears about systems staff specialists and their activities.

Every aspect of an effective E.D.P. installation appears as an unwarranted—indeed ominous—intrusion to middle management.... The intense staff activity necessary to force policy definition exceeds any pre-

10 *Ibid.* pp. 103-104.
11 Douglas McGregor, "The Role of Staff in Modern Industry," George Shultz and Thomas Whisler, eds., *Management Organization and the Computer* (Glencoe, Illinois: The Free Press of Glencoe, 1960), 115-117.

vious attempts at such documentation.... The mere
presence of so much staff activity is disturbing to the
functional manager. He will not voluntarily seek the
specialized services of outside staff people. Their activity subjects the department manager to possible unsym-
pathetic outside criticism. Their analysis may scrutinize
his detailed procedures, which are sometimes defen-
sively designed because of "weaknesses" in other functional areas.... Thus, the entire company may be
shaken as a result of old wounds being opened and
some areas of uneasy compromise becoming outright
challenges. In some cases, this may appear intolerable
to various functional areas, and several may join forces
in a united front to resist the methods and procedures
staff.[12]

Hill and Wright depict their concept of the appropriate
management of systems as follows. They stipulate that systems
development can proceed from the top down. Top management
sets objectives, allocates resources, establishes priorities, develops standards, identifies information needs, and resolves
lower level conflicts.

Systems development can also proceed from the bottom
up, according to the authors. In this case the lower echelon
collects data and designs and implements systems gradually.
It is their thesis that there is a need for a "third force," a staff
function to coordinate the efforts of top management system
planning with lower management efforts at system designing.[13]
The systems staff function, or third force, "generates, monitors,
and modifies the A.D.P./M.I.S. program."[14] In effect, the systems group would be a central staff function entrusted by top
management to coordinate systems analysis and programming
functions for the achievement of corporate goals.

The survey data, in summary, emphasize the relative new-
ness of the systems specialist's function. As yet the staff spe-

---

[12] L. R. Fiock, Jr., "Seven Deadly Dangers in E.D.P.," *Harvard Business Review*, 40:no. 3, 91-92 (May-June, 1962).

[13] W. Henry Hill and Jack H. Wright, "Concept and Design of Integrated Management Information Systems," *Data Processing Yearbook* (Detroit: Ameri-can Data Processing, Incorporated, 1964), 117-118.

[14] *Ibid.*, p. 118.

cialist's position and duties are ill-defined. The line-staff friction generated under the pressures of computerization are recognized and are being met.

In considering the strengths and weaknesses of various organizational and working relationships between systems specialists and line managers, the project or team approach appears to offer the most promise in meeting the demands of systems development and management. The conversion breakdown example cited illustrated several problems that result from the failure to recognize line-staff conflicts and to plan and organize to minimize their effects.

Finally, some evidence from the literature and the surveyed firms suggests that systems leadership should rest with the line. This division of responsibility did not exist in any of the surveyed firms during the development phase, and in only some of the firms during the operational phase, yet the trend is definitely in that direction. All phases of systems activities should be shared by both staff and line representatives in order to maximize the strengths and to minimize the weaknesses that each brings to the job. What does all this imply for the future of staff jobs generally?

THE LINE-STAFF CONCEPT UNDER COMPUTERIZATION: ANALYSIS AND PREDICTIONS

The use of more advanced technology in information processing, the emphasis on systems rather than on functional management, and the increased specialization of management have enhanced the status of the staff role in the production process. The increase in the number and importance of staff specialists in a firm has prompted some new questions about their relationship to line management, i.e., executive, administrative, and supervisory personnel.

Generally researchers agree that the line-staff form of organization, as presently defined in most textbooks, does not adequately meet the demands of most firms with advanced technologies. These needs are summarized in Uris' statement:

The line-staff type of organization is seldom flexible enough for the new function and duties of the specialist. Where he's involved in line activity, functional relationships and flow of information often become fuzzy. Content of communications becomes more technical. Also, a split develops in the source of operating knowledge between supervisor and specialist.[15]

The inability of the line-staff organization to cope with these new demands has inspired various forebodings. Canter talks about the increasing influence of engineers and programmers in the day-to-day operations of the plant. In this case engineers are no longer staff, but rather represent the line of the production organization. Hence there is a drastic shift in the roles of various groups within the organization.[16]

The consequences of the developments Canter observed are elaborated in the concept of dual management developed by Miles and Vail.[17] They bisect the management group because they feel decision-making and supervision are being separated in practice. What emerges from this might be termed the "head and heart approach to organization," in which professionals (staff specialists) and managers (supervisors) have separate duties and characteristics. In this scheme "the professional would set the standards, make decisions, form policies, and assume control of projects — where the requirement is for specialized understanding."[18]

For his part, the manager should restrict himself to internal relations within the organization and to relations between his and other organizations. He would be enough of a materialist to realize how economic and material rewards can be used effectively, and conservative enough to accept the world of human beings as they are. He would have a personality big enough to absorb the tensions and stresses of those in his group

15 Auren Uris, "Fitting Today's New Specialist into Your Plant Organization," *Factory*, 117:no. 9, 226 (September, 1959).

16 Ralph R. Canter, "Automation's Impact on Future Personnel Policies," *Proceedings of First Conference, Research Developments in Personnel Management* (Los Angeles: University of California, 1957), 17.

17 Stephen B. Miles, Jr., and Thomas E. Vail, "Thinking Ahead: Dual Management," *Harvard Business Review*, 38:no. 1, 63 (January-February, 1960).

18 *Ibid.*, p. 154.

and to help them work better and so realize themselves more abundantly. A good manager would enjoy deflecting credit to his people, and be on the lookout for merit and brilliance among them, even when it puts him in the shade. Finally, he would be able to inspire, in order that he might integrate minds as well as bodies.[19]

Finally Miles and Vail conclude that "the chief executive should be a well-integrated combination of manager and professional."[20]

Whisler and Shultz describe the future role of staff specialists, i.e., information technologists, as that of a new managerial elite.

His relation to managers lower in the organization would seem to be prescriber of rules and planner. His relation to those responsible for innovation and commitment of resources is equally important and well-marked. He has at his command a combination of tools which help top management pretest new ideas before making a commitment to them. . . .

Whatever his line of entry, the information technologist's role in the organization seems likely to be an important one, with implications and contacts throughout the organization and with a base of operations near the top of the management structure.[21]

The staff role depicted above is similar to the one described by Atwood. The president of the Atwood Vacuum Machine Company tells how his company has "eliminated" staff.

We are presently organized into six divisions: Manufacturing, Finance, Sales, Personnel, Purchasing, and Planning. With this divisional arrangement, we have eliminated the concept of staff people. We have been able to avoid the kinds of problems that the existence of staff creates by simply not having staff around.

Planning, then, in our company, is a line function. It was not always such. We once had all kinds of staff people, but we could see no reason for continuing to

---

19 *Ibid.*
20 *Ibid.*
21 Thomas Whisler and George Shultz, "Information Technology and Management Organization," George Shultz and Thomas Whisler, eds., *Management Organization and the Computer* (Glencoe, Illinois: The Free Press of Glencoe, 1960), 12.

have the kinds of problems that staff people create. So we eliminated staff. We have simply taken the planning functions out of the other divisions and put them into this one. . . . The planning people do not "sell" any other division on anything. They go ahead and decide what the job is that has to be done and how to do it.[22]

Another suggested resolution of the line-staff problem is developed in McGregor's analysis of the changing nature and use of authority in organizations. He sees a new accommodation through the blurring of line-staff distinctions.

Perhaps the most important reason is that the nature of management is changing, and the line is beginning to look more like the staff. Formal authority, the traditional tool of line management, is becoming less effective as the dependence of subordinates upon superiors decreases. . . .

The significant point is that the managerial job — whether line or staff — is not limited to a single role. At other times the manager is a boss in the old fashioned sense, giving commands and telling others what to do. At other times he occupies other roles: teacher, helper, group member, expert, colleague, consultant, client. . . . Unity of purpose within the managerial organization is more important than unity of command.[23]

The substitution of unity of purpose for unity of command, according to McGregor, would allow an individual manager to assume a diversity of roles. His line and staff responsibilities would vary to meet situational needs.

All managers, whether line or staff, have responsibilities for collaborating in achieving organizational objectives. Each is concerned with 1) making his own resources of knowledge, skill, and experience available to others; 2) obtaining help from others in fulfilling his *own* responsibilities; and 3) controlling his own job. Each has *both* line and staff responsibilities.[24]

[22] Seth G. Atwood, "The Atwood Vacuum Machine Company," George Shultz and Thomas Whisler, eds., *Management Organization and the Computer* (Glencoe, Illinois: The Free Press of Glencoe, 1960), 237.

[23] Douglas McGregor, "The Role of Staff in Modern Industry," George Shultz and Thomas Whisler, eds., *Management Organization and the Computer, op. cit.,* p. 114.

[24] Douglas McGregor, *The Human Side of Enterprise* (New York: McGraw-Hill Book Company, Incorporated, 1960), 175.

McGregor's analysis of the line-staff problem in terms of superior-subordinate authority relations is applicable also when it is discussed in terms of functions and responsibilities. Then work groups or teams also require members to perform according to the needs of the group. In this case, however, each manager or specialist assumes the line or staff responsibilities needed for him to accomplish the purposes of the group. Specifically the project and systems manager or team approach employed particularly in some defense industries is an example of the group purpose approach. The participants of the team may, for example, functionally report to a staff service, but have temporary administrative responsibility in their specialties for a particular project.

Role flexibility may become a permanent adjunct if a team approach to organization is used, not only at the top of the organization, or for short-term projects, but at all levels and on regular, continuing operations. This form of organization would incur the two disadvantages of the "line and staff" principle cited below.

> The principle has, in fact, two possible disadvantages, the first of which concerns communication within the factory. Two types of rapid and effective communication are needed in automatic processes: first, between the machine-minder, maintenance personnel and technical specialists in the event of a machine breaking down; and the second, between the various technical specialists who set up the plant and correct faults in its operation. If the structure of management impedes communication of either kind it may have to be changed. . . .
>
> A second general disadvantage of the "line and staff" principle is that it encourages the growth of separate and rigid functional "empires," with ideas and objectives that are determined as much by specialist and professional interests as by the needs of the firm. Automation requires technical experts to be flexible and cooperative, rather than rigidly specialist and competing.[25]

---

[25] *Automation* (London: Department of Scientific and Industrial Research, 1956), 61.

Stahl poses a question which indicates his dissatisfaction with the current distinctions made between line and staff. His comments also support McGregor's thoughts.

> ...(W)ould it not make sense to divest ourselves of the abracadabra that divides "line" and "staff" into incongruous kinds of activity and to recognize that *all* such activities are simply specialized subdivisions of an organization's work? Because some of them, called staff functions, develop only by virtue of the existence of the organization and operate to sustain it does not detract from their necessity or their importance.[26]

The analyses of the line-staff principle of these observers are remarkably similar. They all agree that with the increasing use of highly complex production processes, the traditional distinction between command and counsel is disappearing. Authority, under these circumstances, may be exercised horizontally as well as vertically to a point where the distinction becomes nebulous. It should be noted that staff-like activities are becoming more important at lower levels of the organization, i.e., closer to the production line, because of the increasing complexity of the technical and human problems.

While the focus and terminology of the authors quoted above differ, their comments on the way in which the line-staff principle is changing and will change are quite similar. The traditional staff departments are more intimately involved with the functioning of the new production processes. As a result the tendency is toward a new division of managerial work, not on a strict line and staff basis, but by the management of things versus the management of people. McGregor suggests a significant alternative. In his concept of unity of purpose, he envisages an integration of roles, not a new division, to replace the line-staff principle of organization.

---

[26] Glenn O. Stahl, "The Network of Authority," *Public Administration Review,* 18:no. 1, 4 (Winter, 1958).

Chapter VII

THE COMPUTER AND THE LINE MANAGER

The computer and the new decision-making techniques associated with it are bringing changes in white-collar, executive, and professional work as momentous as those the introduction of machinery has brought to manual jobs.

— HERBERT A. SIMON

Line management is conveniently classified as top, middle, and lower management. Top management is defined to include the two or three highest strata of the organization, chairman, president, and vice-presidents, for example. These comprise the level which has final responsibility for company policies. Middle management includes managers of managers between top management and the first-line supervisor,[1] who usually supervises workers or professionals. Finally, lower management refers to first-line supervisors, the management representatives who directly organize and control the day-to-day work of employees in a face-to-face relationship.

One observer has described these levels this way:

top management — makes important decisions and knows it,

middle management — makes no important decisions but thinks it does,

---

[1] The term "first-line supervisor" is used here as a title encompassing heterogeneous status and managerial responsibilities. For an extensive discussion on the no-man's land of first-line supervision see Paul Pigors and Charles A. Myers, *Personnel Administration*, 5th ed. (New York: McGraw-Hill Book Company, Incorporated, 1965), 159-162.

lower management — makes no important decisions and knows it.

In this chapter line management and computerization are discussed in the context of these three levels.

TOP MANAGEMENT

Assessments of the impact of computerization at the policy level depend on the form of computerization at issue, in great measure on the imagination, bias, or viewpoint of the individual, and whether he is considering the present or the future. Predictions excluded and facts emphasized, there is no conflict between the literature and my findings.

On the level of prediction there is more room for controversy.

Policy Responsibilities

Forrester's view of the meaning of computerization for top management in the future is this:

> The executive of the future will be concerned not so much with actual operating decisions as with the *basis* for wise operating decisions. He will be concerned not so much with day-to-day crises as with the establishment of policies and plans that minimize emergencies.[2]

Not only will the need for policies be magnified, according to Forrester, but the policy process will be strengthened at the lower levels of the organization also:

> All of this will lead to a more decisive separation of policy making from operations, with the dividing line much lower in the organization than at present. New ways to predict the interaction between company functions will speed up the movement toward decentralized management. In the past power has been concentrated at the top in order to improve over-all integration and control. With increased understanding of the company operation, we can expect that improved definition of objectives and more pertinent standards for measurement of managerial success will permit managers at the lower levels to take on more operating responsibility. Senior executives will then be free to give more attention to product innovation, economic conditions, and the

---

[2] Jay W. Forrester, "Industrial Dynamics," *Harvard Business Review*, 36:no. 4, 66 (July-August, 1958).

organizational changes that will enhance man's creativity.[3]

Leavitt's and Whisler's analysis of the future impact of computerization on top management differs significantly from Forrester's. In their view the popularity of the participative management philosophy will decline. They discount the policy method of management and the need for facilitating change. They predict that the line dividing the policy and operations levels will be moved higher in the organization, and moreover, that this line will be sharply drawn, making upward mobility of middle managers more difficult.[4]

Consistent with Leavitt's and Whisler's prediction is Buckingham's revival of "management by exception."

> This new, timely information permits "management by exception."... Management need be concerned only with those instances where the standards are not being met. This is one way in which automation can take over the huge burden of routine administration and leave executives free to do what they are supposed to do — make decisions involving judgment, something a machine can never do.[5]

This method for insuring uniformity of decision-making is made feasible by E.D.P.:

> Much more of the work will be programmed, i.e., covered by sets of operating rules governing the day-to-day decisions that are made.[6]

---

[3] *Ibid.* Forrester amplifies these and related ideas in an excellent, thought-provoking article. See Jay W. Forrester, "A New Corporate Design," *Industrial Management Review*, 7:no. 1, 5-17 (Fall, 1965).

[4] Harold J. Leavitt and Thomas L. Whisler, "Management in the 1980's," *Harvard Business Review*, 36:no. 6, 41-42 (November-December, 1958). Whisler has revised his view somewhat in this regard. More recently he said that in the long run the authority structure would become more decentralized. Computerization, in the short run, centralizes control,

> But the functions of manager and machine will become increasingly different. In the long run, decentralization of creative management will be retained by men. Centralization of the operating functions will go to the machines.

From a speech delivered by Thomas L. Whisler and quoted in "Looking Ahead: Managing in 1980," *Iron Age*, 193:no. 13, 83 (March 26, 1964).

[5] Walter Buckingham, "The Human Side of Automation," *Business Horizons*, 3:no. 1, 21 (Spring, 1960).

[6] Leavitt and Whisler, *op. cit.*, p. 41.

Given this orientation, in unique or crisis situations minor matters necessarily will be handled at even higher levels of the organization.

Policy Management and the Computer[7]

In order to develop E.D.P. organizational policies a firm must first define its objectives and plan how those objectives are to be achieved. Policies make it possible to translate these goals and over-all plans into guides for day-to-day operational decision-making at all levels of the organization to minimize risks and maximize results.

Policies should be formulated at all management levels of the organization, although final responsibility for policy must rest with top management. The assumption is that the broader the base of participation (including the union, in organized firms) the greater are the advantages that will accrue.

Some advantages of policy management are that decisions will be made faster and better, especially during periods of rapid change or crisis; that greater efficiencies will result from an understanding of goals, a feeling of security and a sense of fairness, and a higher degree of participation, initiative, and motivation; and, that individual development and group education will be enhanced.

The policy method of management is based, in large measure on assumptions which closely approximate those in McGregor's Theory Y.[8] Essentially they are that people are not oblivious to organizational goals and needs; and that all people, to some extent, possess the capacity and motivation needed to further organizational goals.

---

[7] The following alternative approaches to management are characterized in the literature as "management by objective" versus "management by control" by Peter F. Drucker in *The Practice of Management* (New York: Harper and Brothers, 1954); as "Theory X" versus "Theory Y" by Douglas McGregor in *The Human Side of Enterprise* (New York: McGraw-Hill Book Company, Incorporated, 1960); and as "management by shared objectives and self control" versus "management by direction and external control" by Pigors and Myers, *op. cit.*

[8] McGregor, *op. cit.*, Chapter IV.

One final comment on policy management is relevant. Nowhere have I mentioned that the policy management approach involves people being made happy, employees having a sense of participation, the concept of democracy, or any goal other than greater efficiency for the firm. If, as a consequence of efficiency, employee satisfaction is greater, well and good, but the emphasis is correctly placed only on the attainment of organizational objectives.

Management by Rule and Regulation

The essence of this view is that management obtains the best results from employees by telling them what to do and how to do it, and by checking periodically to make sure that the assigned task is properly and promptly accomplished. All important decisions are discussed at the top levels of the organization and passed down the line for implementation. The goal of this management approach is to insure consistency through controlling decision-making and the activities of subordinates. There is little or no consultation with subordinates and very little upward communication, except through required or requested reports. Any matter not directly covered by rules and regulations, however, is immediately referred "upstairs" for consideration.

Some advantages of this approach are that managers have tight control over a firm's operations and are likely to be intimately involved at all times with "unusual circumstances" at the lower levels of the organization. Further, managers can be reasonably certain that the prescribed procedures are being adhered to because discretionary actions by individual employees are precluded or at least discouraged. Finally, the organizational structure, responsibilities, and authority are all defined clearly, so that there is absolutely no doubt as to one's position in the hierarchy, what activities one is responsible for, and the performance that is desired. Usually all these facets of the job are made explicit.

The assumptions about employees which underlie this approach of management by rule and regulation closely parallel the assumptions of McGregor's Theory X.[9] In summary, these assumptions are that employees dislike and avoid work, that only through coercive methods can organizational goals be met, and that most employees are interested in the *status quo*, and will avoid responsibility and seek security. It follows, then, that management must determine organizational goals, assign tasks, and establish reporting systems and controls.

Both views discussed above are in accord in predicting that top management will be able to spend more time on planning and innovation, but are at variance as to the underlying philosophy of and the approach to organizational problems raised by computerization. The survey data support the conclusion that E.D.P. allows top management more time for planning.

Survey Data on Top Management and Planning: The responses of top management to the question "How has the computer affected your job?" varied from "Not at all," to "It's beginning to." The danger in reporting data on this topic should be made explicit: the longer the question was discussed the more the manager felt that there *should* be some effect, and the more the answers tended to fit the predictions made in the literature.

One vice-president felt that his responsibilities have not been changed by E.D.P. He said his job primarily was "asking why in many voices, using my imagination to develop techniques, and enabling my subordinates to use their abilities to this end. Computerization has not altered my method of managing, but the tendency of E.D.P. to eliminate small elements of initiative and interest in the lower paid jobs has presented a challenge to my management philosophy." Middle management, according to this vice-president, knows more and learns it quicker; E.D.P. has stimulated their thinking and imagination.

The comments of another top manager are representative of the group who felt that the computer has had a more significant impact on their jobs. According to this manager E.D.P.

9 *Ibid.,* Chapter III.

has primarily changed the way in which data are generated. The lower in the organization one goes, therefore, the greater is the impact upon jobs.

The manager added that because of the speed and accuracy of the computer, he needs to spend less time on operations and has more time for other activities. This newly found time is devoted to such responsibilities as planning for personnel changes and counseling his boss. He attends to more creative activities, such as evaluation (budgets, cost activity, and financial analysis) and pricing. He now spends less time "looking over my subordinates' shoulders." Computers enable him to issue new reports to *lower* management, permitting them to assume more responsibility and allowing him to correct a bad trend before it causes much damage. In addition the new reports he issues enable his boss to make more timely decisions.

Another executive spoke for top management as a whole in stating succinctly the impact of computers on his job: "The computer does the dog-work, allowing me more time to use my judgment."

Many executives indicated that under computerization the quality of their planning has been vastly improved. The computer made this possible by providing a greater quantity of more reliable and timely information. The comments of two executives illustrates some job changes occasioned by computerization.

The general manager of a division of a manufacturing firm noted that the aspects of planning that had previously required intuitive judgment have become routine with computerization. Now he has time to concentrate on new planning areas, because he can handle medium and long range problems more quickly. The fact that his subordinate managers are better informed and are doing better jobs themselves also contributes to this executive's ability to plan better.

An insurance executive indicated that with the help of computers, jet aircraft, and improved communications, he is now able to make more planning decisions than ever before. Statistical data on his firm's performance for the previous year now are available in

January rather than in mid-summer as was the case in the past. Also, classification rates for automobile insurance can be determined more accurately, because the computer makes it possible to compile and arrange the necessary data economically.

While top level planning is facilitated by the computer, it imposes some new restrictions as well. The computerized system must be taken into account whenever a new idea affecting planning is evaluated by top management. A new idea must be judged on how its implementation will affect the optimum use of computer facilities and programs. Further, once a work element is put on the computer, there is a "locked in" feature to consider. No longer will a hurried call to a manager insure special customer service through exception handling. Finally, staff specialists are needed to help top management screen and evaluate information and to act as a liaison with the computer center. The role these specialists will play and the significance of these new positions for the planning process is not predictable.

From the foregoing discussion, it appears that top management has less to do with day-to-day operations, that more time remains for planning, and that the concept of policy management may not be inoperative under computerization. The degree to which computerization affects the locus of decision-making power is a crucial consideration bearing upon this question.

Top Management Decision Processes and the Computer

Lucking points out that decentralization means many things to many people.[10] He contributes to a better understanding of the question of centralization versus decentralization as related to computerization by depicting the forms decentralization may take.

Lucking lists four types of decentralization: 1) geographical dispersion, 2) responsibility transferal from functional com-

---

10 Walter T. Lucking, "The Function of Executive Management," from a forum, "Organization Planning — Decentralization Reconsidered," *Management Record*, 22:no. 4, 7 (April, 1960).

ponent to autonomous division, 3) organization by product or process, and 4) delegation of responsibility and authority.[11] In discussing the decision-making process in this chapter, the focus is upon the fourth type cited, delegation of responsibility and authority, which Lucking deliberately separates from the consideration of organization structure.

Machaver poses the most critical issue involving any discussion of computerization, decentralization, and decision-making:

> Are companies returning to older centralized forms of organization? Or is it possible that what is being called "recentralization" is really the setting up of those centralized plans and controls that are necessary for effective decentralization?[12]

The popular view is that decentralization of authority is a necessary evil which has been forced upon management by the rapid growth and increasing complexity of business. Top management, no longer able to keep in close touch with operating details, has been forced to delegate responsibility to the manager closest to the situation. E.D.P. reverses these needs to decentralize. Computer technology makes it both economically and technically feasible to establish computerized procedures which digest vast stores of complex information quickly and cheaply, so that management once again can recentralize decision-making at higher levels of the hierarchy.

The point stressed by advocates of this view is not that computers, themselves, are making these decisions, but that they are generating information for higher levels within the organizational pyramid in a form suitable for timely and effective decisions.

> A major change is that many decisions formerly based upon the judgment of the people at the middle level of management are being reduced, not to decisions within a computer, but to simple recognition of an existing condition. If we think of the flow of information within the typical organization as a triangular shaped

---

[11] *Ibid.*

[12] William Machaver, "Introduction," from a forum, "Organization Planning — Decentralization Reconsidered," *Management Record*, 22:no. 4, 6 (April, 1960).

affair with a broad base of facts moving upward to some point at which management reduces these facts by interpolation into decisions, then the effect of information technology is to move the level of facts higher in this triangle.[13]

An observer who feels that computers inevitably will lead to centralization of decision-making maintains that this fact is obscured in some measure because companies are reluctant to say that they are recentralizing:

For the past dozen years decentralization—along with management development, effective communication, and democratic supervision — has been very much in fashion. Among those who, until recently, were loudest in proclaiming its virtues, few now care to admit having gone too far in their enthusiasm.

"Recentralization is a dangerous word. We'd rather think of it as redefining regions of authority," says one company executive. Other companies speak of "centralizing policy while decentralizing administration." But what it adds up to is that decisions previously handled in the field, or not handled at all, are now being made at headquarters.[14]

Is a disbelief in the inevitability of top management making the most significant decisions based only on management's adherence to ideological fashions? I think the issue is not yet clearly defined, nor has any answer been sufficiently documented. An alternative view that E.D.P. may strengthen the

---

[13] Leonard F. Vogt, "The International Shoe Company," George Shultz and Thomas Whisler, eds., *Management Organization and the Computer* (Glencoe, Illinois: The Free Press of Glencoe, 1960), 148. In connection with this question of whether second generation computers have the capacity to make decisions, a quote from a memorandum written by a manager in one of the surveyed firms is informative:

I agree that present day computers cannot make decisions. The question as to whether computers can replace Middle Management then boils down to the question as to whether middle managers make decisions. I feel quite sure that we will find that middle managers make few decisions; what middle managers do is to exercise choices to implement decisions made higher up to the organization. To the extent that the work now done by Middle Management consists of choices between alternatives, it is programmable and can be done by computers.

[14] Edward McCreary, "Countertrend to Decentralization: Top Management Tightens Controls," *Dun's Review and Modern Industry*, 74:no. 1, 32 (July, 1959).

policy method of management, permitting even greater delegation of decision-making responsibility at lower levels of the organization, is a reasonable and viable possibility. This alternative is possible because:

Centralization of the physical process of data handling does not necessarily mean surrender of decentralized operating management. Branches, plants, or operating units supply basic data to the central processing group and use the information that comes back to them, just as if the information was processed locally.[15]

Burlingame takes issue with observers who cite the computer as a means of recentralizing managerial decision-making. He finds decentralization both economically and socially desirable and predicts a bright future for it.

Counter to many arguments, the anticipated advances in information technology, in my opinion, can *strengthen* decentralization in those businesses that have adopted it and will encourage *more* managements to experiment and to operate in accordance with the decentralization philosophy.[16]

There is nothing in the following account of the computer's impact at Westinghouse that indicates whether the locus of decision-making has changed, and if so, how.

On the eighth working day of every month, "come rain or shine," Francis E. Dalton, vice-president and controller of Westinghouse Electric Corp., carries a set of forecasts into the 23rd floor office of President D. C. Burnham in the company's Pittsburgh headquarters.

These forecasts for the month have been submitted by Westinghouse's 69 divisions via the company's now highly developed tele-computer system. After an hour or so consultation with Dalton, President Burnham calls in other executives for a thorough going-over of the forecasts at group and divisional levels.

Until a year ago, when computerization was extended into this area, such a review could be held only "spasmodically." Top management was never able to compare

15 Gardner M. Jones, "Organizational Consequences of E.D.P.," *Business Topics*, 7:no. 4, 25 (Autumn, 1959).

16 John F. Burlingame, "Information Technology and Decentralization," *Harvard Business Review*, 39:no. 6, 124 (November-December, 1961).

164   THE ADVANCE AGAINST PAPERWORK

forecast against performance and corporate objectives on a regular month-to-month basis.[17]
The example cited above can be interpreted to support either decentralization or centralization of top management decision-making.[18] Certainly the quoted statements are essentially valid for the state of computerization found in the surveyed firms.

A third view appears to be developing regarding the impact of computerization on managerial decision-making. Morse examined the trend toward centralization of management control and concluded that it was not irreversible.

> Foes of centralization sometimes intimate that the computer is to blame for the trend. Actually, the computer's role is a neutral one. It can work for either side.[19]

According to Morse management has used the computer as a means of conquering problems of information processing and has espoused a central direction and control philosophy. The former was a matter of economics, and the latter was a matter of choice.

It is evident that generally computerization may affect managerial decision-making and control it in four ways. It may centralize it, decentralize it, do both, or do neither. The data in both the literature and my surveys indicate that computer impact will vary among firms depending upon the particular circumstances that control a firm's decisions. Axsmith points out that

> In the years ahead, general patterns of centralization-decentralization will be matters not of technical necessity, but of management decision. In fact, management's freedom to implement either philosophy will be considerably advanced.[20]

---

[17]"How Computers Liven a Management's Ways," *Business Week*, 1926: 112 (June 25, 1966).

[18]It is reported in the article that all managers have new decision-making roles and that they are extensive. However no evidence to substantiate the point is offered. *Ibid.*, p. 116.

[19]Gerry E. Morse, "Pendulum of Management Control," *Harvard Business Review*, 43:no. 3, 164 (May-June, 1965).

[20]Douglas J. Axsmith, "A Management Look at Data Processing: Promise, Problem, and Profit," Alan D. Meacham and Van B. Thompson, eds., *Total Systems* (Detroit: American Data Processing, Incorporated, 1962), 14.

One significant question is, "What is actually done with the improved decision-information, even if we assume that present applications on the computer are able to generate it?"

Computers and Decision-making: Where Do We Stand?: The exact effects of the computer on top management decision-making are not yet clear. The current contribution of the computer to the decision process, providing more timely and comprehensive information, need not necessarily alter the process significantly. If the assumption is true that decision-information is generated presently in a form and manner which enable the firm to change the decision process drastically, an assumption which is often expressed but not adequately documented, it need not follow that the decision-information is so used.

In none of the firms surveyed in 1959-61 did top management *ask* for specific outputs from the computer programs to facilitate the making of decisions relative to its top management responsibilities. Typically the systems analysts determined the type of data to be generated by the computer and the form in which it was to be presented to management. The systems analysts frequently "peddled" reports. Further, in some conflict situations the determination of what data were to be produced, in what form, and for whom, was made on a political basis. The following statement fairly describes the early phase in the surveyed firms:

> The accuracy of management information has been improved, often (but not always) speed, and at times value of content. Most top managers (and the second and third echelons as well) would probably state, however, that their responsibilities and their work have been little affected by the installation of E.D.P. equipment for commercial data processing.[21]

One top manager accurately assessed the impact of the computer — both in 1961 and for the future:

> Computers in a company play a star's role in many of

---

[21] B. Conway, J. Gibbons, and D. E. Watts, *Business Experience with Electronic Computers* (New York: Controllers Institute Research Foundation, Incorporated, 1959), 175.

these decisions (major top management decisions). Even more important, they alter the decision making process itself. They make it possible to work with broader and deeper facts and figures. They cut the time lag on reporting so sharply that we are going to be able to detect and analyze changes in our business virtually as they occur. They provide the tools to implement mathematical models which can actually make a host of minor decisions for us — *if* we understand what they can do and set ourselves up to make full use of them. In other words, they are going to change the kinds of decisions we make, and the timing and bases of those decisions.

Thus the computer has affected the decision-making process by altering the quantity, quality, and speed of information flows. In addition the new tool holds out the promise of handling routine decisions as well.

Simon divides decisions into two categories: 1) programmed decisions, i.e., routine and repetitive decisions, and 2) unprogrammed decisions, i.e., nonrecurring, ill-structured, novel, and policy decisions.[22] He then summarizes the impact of computerization upon these two types of decisions:

1) The electronic computer is bringing about, with unexpected speed, a high level of automation in the routine programmed decision making and data processing that were formerly the province of clerks.
2) The area of programmed decision making is being rapidly extended as we find ways to apply tools of operations research to types of decisions that have up to now been regarded as judgmental — particularly, but not exclusively, middle-management decisions in the area of manufacturing and warehousing.
3) The computer has extended the capability of the mathematical techniques to problems far too large to be handled by less automatic computing devices, and has further extended the range of programmable decisions by contributing the new technique of simulation.
4) Companies are just beginning to discover ways of

---

[22] Herbert A. Simon, *The Shape of Automation* (New York: Harper and Row, 1965), 62.

bringing together the first two of these developments: of combining the mathematical techniques for making decisions about aggregative middle-management variables with the data-processing techniques for implementing these decisions in detail at clerical levels.[23]

Simon's comments on what he calls "the revolution in programmed decision making," although originally made in 1960, accurately characterize the state of affairs in my surveyed firms in 1965. They continue to implement computer applications which program routine, lower echelon management decision-making. Also, at least three firms are working on computer simulations; several others are experimenting with various mathematical analysis and operations research techniques. These latter projects, which are directly related to top management decision-making, have not become operational as yet.

There is a tendency to think that the quantity of data and the speed at which they are made available alter the decision process within a firm. It is fashionable to equate these data processing capabilities with more efficient decision-making. However, the outpouring of data may actually distract top management and turn a president or vice-president into an information expediter. The managerial need for adequate and timely information can be exaggerated:

> Levels of a business each "pulse" with a characteristic rate. Thus, the information needs of top management typically have a monthly, even an annual quality about them. At the division level, the pulse may be monthly or weekly. Further down among department heads it becomes weekly or daily.[24]

The implications of this analysis for real time or instantaneous information systems are provocative. A former systems manager, now an "administrative assistant," said his firm plans to implement an I.B.M. System/360. It will be an unnecessary waste in his judgment. In fact it is difficult to predict the future significance of third generation computers for manage-

---

[23] *Ibid.*, p. 75.
[24] "Real-Time, On-Time and Realism," *Administrative Management*, 27:no. 1, 15 (January, 1966).

ment. In its current stage computerization is affecting middle management directly.

MIDDLE MANAGEMENT

The predicted demise of middle management has not occurred. Almost from the time computers were first used in business data processing, the programming of administrative decision-making was supposed to displace many middle managers. It was said that those managers lucky enough to remain on the payroll would handle routine matters and would no longer be required to interpret policies.

Leavitt and Whisler predicted in 1958 that "information technology is likely to have its greatest impact on middle and top management."[25] "There will be many fewer middle managers, and most of those who remain are likely to be routine technicians rather than thinkers."[26] Michael concurred, predicting in 1962 that "growing numbers of middle managers will find themselves displaced."[27] In 1965 Burck evaluated the Leavitt and Whisler predictions. He found that: 1) "The number of middle-management jobs relative to output appears to be declining...."[28] 2) "The prediction that many middle-management positions would be routinized or degraded does not seem to be coming off, at least not yet."[29]

Whisler has taken a second look at his and Leavitt's original predictions. He believes that developments in the interim have produced evidence supporting their earlier forecast that information technology would 1) flatten the organizational structure, and 2) recentralize organizational control.[30] However, ...(O)n a third prediction I now have some doubts.

---

[25] Leavitt and Whisler, *op. cit.*, p. 41.

[26] *Ibid.*, p. 44.

[27] Donald N. Michael, *Cybernation: The Silent Conquest* (Santa Barbara: Center for the Study of Democratic Institutions, The Fund for the Republic, Incorporated, 1962), 19.

[28] Gilbert Burck, *et. al.*, eds., *The Computer Age* (New York: Harper and Row, 1965), 115.

[29] *Ibid.*, p. 116.

[30] Thomas L. Whisler, "The Manager and the Computer," *The Journal of Accountancy*, 119:no. 1, 28-29 (January, 1965).

The prediction was that information technology would routinize many of the middle management positions in the reorganized structure.[31]

In a recent study entitled "Automation and the Middle Manager," the major conclusion reached was that computers have not yet affected middle management only because of social lag.[32] There is no doubt that company policies, employee resistance, and good times tend to delay the displacement of computer-caused obsolescent managers. Further, it is extremely difficult to determine the extent to which this redundancy exists in private businesses. Nevertheless, there is evidence to suggest that the computer may have exactly the opposite effect.

Unexpectedly, the computer itself has been a major reason for this robust growth of middle management. Technical change, in both production and office, has created a base for rapid corporate expansion. Advances in data processing have not only spawned groups of computer and systems experts, but have created pressure all over the company, in areas such as marketing, finance, personnel, and production. Growing sophistication has created a need for more middlemen of competence.[33]

Although there may be little slackening of demand for middle managers, this does not mean that particular managers are not affected adversely. Lee reports that the computerization of three line departments in a shoe manufacturing firm from 1955 to 1963 resulted in: 1) a 35.5 percent reduction in the total number of employees, 2) an 11.1 percent reduction in managerial-technical employees, and 3) a 41.3 percent reduction in clerical employees. The effect, however, was to increase the *proportion* of managerial-technical and reduce the *proportion* of clerical employees to the entire work force.[34]

---

[31] *Ibid.*, p. 29.

[32] This study, conducted by the Foundation on Automation and Employment, Incorporated, a labor-management-sponsored group, was reported on in the *New York Times.* "Automation Seen Affecting Bosses," *New York Times,* CXV: no. 39,517, 29 (April 4, 1966).

[33] "A Boost for the Man in the Middle," *Business Week,* 1899:85 (January 22, 1966).

[34] H. C. Lee, Electronic Data Processing and Skill Requirements," *Personnel Administration,* 29:no. 3, 51 (May-June, 1966).

In another article Lee reported a significant increase in data processing personnel from 1955 to 1962 in the same firm.

In the Data Processing Department as a whole, managerial personnel increased both in number (from 10 to 24) and proportion (from 21.7% to 26.4%)....[35]

What has happened to middle management in the surveyed firms under computerization?

Organization

The organizational changes resulting from E.D.P. have not altered middle management structure significantly. The line departments and/or sections served by centralized machine rooms, and, also, later by the computer center, underwent change and in some instances were moved from one function to another. All these actions have required transfer and reassignment of middle managers.

Naturally some functions and responsibilities have been augmented and some have been narrowed as a result of E.D.P. Yet the formal organizational structure of the middle management area has remained surprisingly untouched. There has been no general movement upward or downward of *classes* of middle management jobs. Some individuals, e.g., systems analysts, have advanced rapidly to the middle management level, while the status of others, e.g., actuaries, has probably declined relatively.

In a few instances E.D.P. has led to a reduction in the number of administrative layers in middle management.[36] The proliferation of "assistant-manager" positions in these same firms, however, merits further inquiry as to the degree of flatness of the present organization structure. It may very well be that it

---

[35] Hak Chong Lee, "On Information Technology and Organization Structure," *Academy of Management Journal*, 7:no. 1, 209 (September, 1964).

[36] This conflicts with Woodward's finding that with increasing levels of technology the number of levels of authority within the management hierarchy *increased*. She considers manufacturing production processes rather than information processing, but whether or not this is enough of a difference to explain the conflict is not clear. Joan Woodward, *Management and Technology* (London: Department of Scientific and Industrial Research, 1958), 14, Fig. 2.

is flatter; and that the assistant positions reflect the firm's social consciousness.

Finally departmentalization has remained unchanged, except for a rearrangement of work sections and the minor changes at the lower levels mentioned. This follows from the limited ability of organizations to utilize the computer creatively in their operations. The systems approaches and type of applications in the surveyed firms preclude more drastic structural change at this point.

Responsibilities

Middle management structure has not changed radically, but management responsibilities in those departments affected by computerization have changed. The closer the manager is to the paper work process the more valid this statement is.

Middle management decision-making need not be absorbed by the computer, information technologists, or top management. There is some evidence that the possible range of middle management decisions is diverse and dynamic. The interview data suggest that as middle management responsibilities change with computerization, the type of decisions made may change also.

Middle managers are able to give more attention to planning responsibilities because of E.D.P. A line manager said that he has more time to think, to look further ahead, and to react more quickly to changes. He found that he communicates more with *both* supervisors and subordinates and has greater involvement with other department managers. "One half of my job now is planning where we're going, how to get there, and relating to other people," he said.

The greater necessity for the middle manager to "relate," i.e., to coordinate with his co-managers under computerization, is described by Atwood:

> For a considerable time, there has been no room in our organization for a salesman engineer, or purchasing agent who wanted to keep his own records and run his own show. I think the RAMAC has simply accentu-

ated this fact, in the sense that the fellow who does want to keep his own records is not being told what he has to know to do so. Only RAMAC has that information; therefore he is forced to go to RAMAC for it and, furthermore, to realize that he must give the necessary information to RAMAC in order to get results.[37]

Freeing the middle manager from operating details enables him to spend more time on personnel administration in addition to planning, communication, and coordination. Several middle managers interviewed indicated that they now are able to give more attention to personnel matters and to work more closely with their supervisors.[38] The possibility that line managers may become primarily personnel administrators is a provocative thought. As far as management of the work itself, the increased standardization of the process does affect the middle manager's responsibility.

One result of this rationalization of work is management by exception. Hoos comments on the implications of this for middle managers:

> At present ... much of middle management's function in private industry is devoted to monitoring for errors before information reaches the E.D.P. machine, and handling those exceptions not covered by the program. With few opportunities for the exercise of initiative or judgment, such work is neither challenging nor rewarding, nor does it have the prestige which must compensate ambitious young men in their gradual upward climb.[39]

The above statement probably is more accurate the lower within the organization that it is applied. Certainly management by exception does involve some tedious checking by clerks. But the process also presents a challenge to lower

---

[37] Seth G. Atwood, "The Atwood Vacuum Machine Company," George Shultz and Thomas Whisler, eds., *Management Organization and the Computer* (Glencoe, Illinois: The Free Press of Glencoe, 1960), 234.

[38] There is some evidence, according to the latest business textbooks, that the distinction between general management and personnel management is fading. This seems to be true also in practice, particularly under advanced systems, increasingly designed, altered, and maintained by technical specialists.

[39] Ida Russakoff Hoos, "When the Computer Takes Over the Office," *Harvard Business Review*, 38:no. 4, 107 (July-August, 1960).

managers to find the cause for the exception. In several of the surveyed firms staff specialists have been appointed to coordinate the activities of line departments and systems and machine centers. These staff managers not only take care of the exception, but also try to revise the system, if it is at fault, to prevent a similar error.

Another result of standardization of the work process is cited by Uris as having drastic impact on the middle management level. According to him "communications screening" is no longer required of middle managers because of E.D.P.[40] Whether or not the communications function of middle management is changing to relate more to people and organization than to the work process is not clear.

In the foregoing several of the changes predicted in middle management responsibilities have been discussed; some data from the surveyed firms have been included in support or modification of these predictions. The reactions of middle managers to their positions under computerization offer another dimension with which to evaluate E.D.P.'s impact.

Reactions

The reactions of middle managers, recorded below, illustrate the general significance of E.D.P. for them.

One manager said that under the old system the work had been divided on a monthly schedule, that scheduling was simple, and that a lost day's work was easily made up. Prior planning and careful judgment were not important aspects of his job.

Under the new system the production cycle is determined and the work of the department is closely scheduled in order to conserve the allotted computer time. If the schedule is not met the operations of the machine center and other departments are disrupted. Thus over-all planning, he said, is more critical to successful operations.

This manager finds his job more interesting and rewarding.

---

[40] Auren Uris, "Fitting Today's New Specialist into Your Plant Organization," *Factory*, 117:no. 9, 232 (September, 1959).

He has more contacts with people in other departments and communicates more with his peers. He was "forced to learn a lot of new things" to be an active manager and to progress. Also he is consulted a great deal more by top management.

Another middle manager feels that no appreciable management job changes resulted from the computerization of his department, nor has his job changed so far. He, unlike the other manager, is not close to the developments the computer has brought about in his department. He did not have or request special training, nor did he become involved with the minor details of conversion.

After this manager had stated that his job was not changed, he had an interesting conversation with the staff specialist in charge of the conversion and operation of the new procedure.

Staff Specialist: Your job *has* changed!

Manager: We have given you and ——— complete responsibility in this automation.

Staff Specialist: You have new tools, for example, reports.

Manager: Yes, reports have changed our operations. But you're getting more and more into operations because of your knowledge.

The dialogue is significant for several reasons. First, it illustrates the line-staff problem in the implementation and administration of computerized systems. Second, the manager's reluctance to take an active part in operations or to prepare himself through retraining to meet his changing job requirements better was reflected in his refusal to acknowledge that changes had occurred.

In the early stages of computerization this type of behavior is condoned by top management. Obviously if good management practices are to prevail, some changes are necessary. In the meantime a younger manager who is perhaps a staff specialist, as in the example above, must assume these new responsibilities.

Middle management foot-dragging has existed for some time, but it is becoming impossible to conceal. As one manager said, "our performance is now immediately pinpointed under data processing." For example, in one firm several middle managers find themselves in the spotlight. They have direct contact with clients and perform a highly specialized function which involves the exercise of judgment. The computer treats their clients indiscriminately. Exceptions and special treatment, not always in the best interest of the company, went unnoticed under the old system. Now the computer flags these exceptions, advertises the circumstances and the manager involved, and demands justification for the special treatment.

The reactions and comments of middle managers reflect the fact that planning, coordinating, and communicating presently take more of their time, and that their job responsibilities are changing.

Middle managers in the surveyed firms reported the following job changes:

1) There is a general increase in both the quantity and quality of planning they do. They are able to devote more time to planning because of the new accuracy, depth, and timeliness of management information.

2) There is a decrease in the amount of time these managers spend in controlling operations, while the quality of their control activities has increased tremendously.

3) There is no clear pattern of change in the middle management responsibilities for directing, organizing, and assembling of resources. In practice middle managers experienced slight increases, slight decreases, or no change in these responsibilities.

4) In general, the middle managers' scope of job responsibilities expanded under computerization basically because of better planning and control capabilities. They are not only doing more work, but doing it better. These job changes have taken place even though managers now may supervise fewer employees.

These conclusions are in general conformance with Shaul's study of middle managers and the impact of computerization upon their job functions.[41] He found

---

[41] Donald A. Shaul, "What's Really Ahead for Middle Management?," *Personnel,* 41:no. 6, 10-12 (November-December, 1964).

In short, the experience of the managers I interviewed has not borne out the prediction that E.D.P. would bring about basic changes in the nature of the middle-management job.[42]

Shaul concluded that the scope of middle managers' jobs also expanded under computerization. Middle managers have assumed new responsibilities, conduct better evaluations, and devote more time to planning.[43] Has the supervisor fared as well as the middle manager under computerization?

LOWER MANAGEMENT

Many of the comments made in the literature about middle management are made also about lower management. For instance, Shultz and Whisler predicted that with operations computerized fewer supervisors and fewer levels of supervision will be needed. Coordination problems will diminish in importance, and the content of the job will change: there will be more communication downward, less upward, less attention to motivation, and less perception of the immediate environment.[44]

Job Changes

Faunce studied the impact of automation on workers and supervisors in the automobile industry. He cites the increasing pressure on supervisors to meet production schedules, and notes that as a result the supervisor has no time to bother with human relations or to use his conventional technical skills.[45]

Similarly Bright finds that new demands are placed on lower management by automation. The supervisor, Bright says, must be better acquainted with a wider portion of the production

---

[42] Ibid., p. 12.

[43] Ibid.

[44] Thomas Whisler and George Shultz, "Information Technology and Management Organization," George Shultz and Thomas Whisler, eds., Management Organization and the Computer (Glencoe, Illinois: The Free Press of Glencoe, 1960), 16.

[45] William A. Faunce, "Automation in the Automobile Industry: Some Consequences for In-Plant Social Structure," American Sociological Review, 23:no. 4, 406 (August, 1958).

process of which his section is a part. In the case of manufacturing automation, which is the focus of his study, the supervisor must be machinery-oriented to insure sustained production. The supervisor must be more flexible, to accept rapid change, more imaginative, to meet new problems.[46]

Shultz and Whisler also deal with this topic, addressing themselves specifically to the meaning of information technology for lower management.

> The supervisor's job involves a number of activities which we call planning — such things as scheduling men to jobs, establishing sequence of operations for a given job, and so on. These activities oriented toward work accomplishment, are much the same whether in manufacturing operations or service operations. Planning of this kind in an organization of any size raises problems of coordination with others outside the area within which the supervisor has jurisdiction. In addition to planning activities, most supervisors spend a substantial amount of their time worrying about the problems of motivating employees, dealing with their personal problems, and clearly communicating the demands of the organization on them.
>
> The integrative effects of information technology, the emphasis upon systematization and development of rules, and the increase in volume and speed of information circulation all lead to the conclusion that a great deal more programming of lower- and middle-level supervisor jobs is to be expected....[47]

The logical impact of these developments on supervisory job responsibilities is described by Hoos:

> As a group, supervisors are hard hit, because when functions are taken over by the computer, they are left without a *raison dêtre* in the organization. With

[46] James R. Bright, *Automation and Management* (Boston: Division of Research, Harvard University Graduate School of Business Administration, 1958), 209.

[47] Thomas Whisler and George Shultz, "Information Technology and Management Organization," George Shultz and Thomas Whisler, eds., *Management Organization and the Computer, op. cit.*, p. 15.

decreased labor loads and fewer persons under their supervision, the need for supervisors shrinks.[48]

This group as a whole has been affected by computerization more than any other within the management hierarchy since this is the level where the impact of computers on operations has been greatest. The jobs of first and second line supervisors have been changed, and in some cases their jobs have been eliminated. Computers are beginning to influence production line supervisory jobs as well.

The Survey Data: The interviews confirmed that there have been major changes in lower management jobs. At this level planning, controlling, and directing are important job functions, while organizing and assembling resources are of minimal relevance. Computerization changed supervisory job responsibilities in the surveyed firms in general. Planning and controlling responsibilities increased. About half the supervisors experienced an increase in their directing responsibilities and half experienced a decrease.

Although supervisory responsibilities are changing with E.D.P., there are strong indications that supervisors will continue to play an important role in the management hierarchy. Two supervisors exemplify the major job changes that have occurred in supervisory responsibilities in the surveyed firms.

The first supervisor performs in a staff and line capacity. He considers himself a trouble shooter, and stated that he has "no regular responsibilities." The duties he performs include tracing each discrepancy to its source and directing the appropriate employee or lower supervisor 1) to correct the error, and 2) to take action to change the conditions which led to the error. Corrections in a procedure usually involve deliberations with other departments, the systems group, and the machine center personnel.

This supervisor maintained that his duties now require a wider knowledge of operations to enable him to answer many specific and minute questions. The job also requires more formal training, e.g., attendance at computer school, and per-

---

[48] Hoos, *op. cit.,* p. 106.

mits more time for personnel matters, less for details. When he first joined the department fifteen years ago, "there were no bosses around." Now he often sees and sometimes talks with middle and top managers. Some of his clerks now have more supervisory duties also. Senior clerks may be sent for supervisory training and participate in personnel decisions. Thus, although the computer determines the pace and the order of work, closer contact with and better knowledge of each employee is now possible.

The second supervisor, who is also representative of the supervisors affected by computerization, simply enumerated the changes in his job. He maintained that his major duty is personnel administration. He cited organizing, or the moving around of people to get the production out, as another important aspect of his job. The nature of the work process has made absences a troublesome manpower problem, as is the balancing of work teams through careful allocation of employees. This supervisor recognized that the routine of supervisory work has decreased considerably, "and the importance of handling personnel problems with regard to getting the most from each individual on the job comes to the forefront."

The emphasis on personnel administration by these lower managers is an interesting trend, consistent with Uris' description:

> True, the foreman is "in charge" of the employees. He schedules their work, keeps track of attendance, listens to complaints of a shortage in pay, or arranges for a few hours off when requested.[49]

The fluid state that exists under computerization at the lower levels of the management hierarchy is reflected by the data presented above. In addition to the job changes cited, organizational charts from the surveyed firms show that the number of supervisors has not decreased. The number of lower management levels has been increased in several firms by senior clerks being given higher status and more supervisory duties.

---

49 Uris, *op. cit.*, p. 226.

Supervisory Reactions to Computerization

The work process changes and new requirements necessitated by computerization have created strong feelings of insecurity and difficult personnel problems among supervisors. The major problem is probably that of the older, male supervisor who cannot or does not wish to adapt to the changing dimensions of his job.

One such supervisor unburdened himself in an interview. He said that his job is increasingly technical, and that the new system is very complicated. Even though there may actually be less to do the problems are different. He now has to determine "what happened" in terms not only of individuals but of the computer as well. "There is always an unknown quantity when you work with the computer." The supervisor, he continued, needs more technical knowledge in order to evaluate the inputs to the computer. Errors are always difficult and sometimes impossible to identify.

Supervisors were the most susceptible to transfer and reassignment to new duties following computerization in the surveyed firms. Sometimes their jobs disappeared. What to do with these supervisors is a current problem in some of these firms. The highly rated clerk somehow has been absorbed, and the younger clerks usually have not suffered because of high turnover in their ranks, but the plight of the older supervisor still has not been resolved adequately.

One manifestation of the insecurity experienced by these supervisors was described by a methods manager. He said that certain supervisors were dragging their feet, impairing the progress of the E.D.P. program. In addition, deliberate as well as unintentional errors were made in the preparation of input to the computer. The methods manager felt that the older supervisors had been most vociferous in disparaging the new systems and were probably instrumental in deterring computerization.

Uris states the problem of supervisory insecurity succinctly:

The supervisor whose job has caved in under the weight of technological changes sometimes becomes fretful and discontented. He's a deposed monarch. He yearns for his past glory and dislikes the new ways.[50]

The picture that emerges is one of major changes in lower management. The supervisor feels the pressures generated by the need for new leadership skills, by the complex job duties, by the emphasis on ability, and by the requisites of flexibility and progressive attitudes. It is not surprising that some supervisors, especially the older ones, find the pressures overwhelming.

The foregoing data and evaluation of computerization's impact on line management are not conclusive. There is much evidence, however, to support the view that middle management has not and possibly will not be altered as radically as predicted by some observers. Nonetheless, numerous noteworthy managerial, organizational, and operational changes have occurred under computerization. The management of these innovations is discussed in the next chapter.

---

[50] *Ibid.*, p. 228.

Chapter VIII

SOME LESSONS IN THE MANAGEMENT OF CHANGE

Through improvement management, executives may find a new future, a new look, and a new approach to their future responsibilities. They may find the way to live successfully with uncertainty.

— LEO B. MOORE

Managers must continually adapt organizational resources and structure to rapidly changing technological advances.[1] This is particularly true of office innovations that accompany the introduction of computer technology. Until recently the managerial problems generated by organizational change have been handled in an off-hand manner. Today managers recognize not only that change is inevitable but that it can be dealt with systematically. Three topics are related to the question of how these changes may be better effectuated: 1) manpower and organizational planning, 2) the approach of labor unions to the problems of organizational change, and 3) the personnel administration function and the management of change.

PLANNING FOR INNOVATION[2]

Manpower and organization planning are essential manage-

---

[1] This chapter is based, in part, upon my article, "The Dynamics of Organizational Innovation," *Industrial Management Review*, 5:no. 1, 3-16 (Fall, 1963).

[2] Recently several books have been published on the management of change. These include an excellent book of readings by Warren G. Bennis, Kenneth D. Beene, and Robert Chin. eds., *The Planning of Change* (New York: Holt, Rinehart and Winston, 1961); a preliminary report on studies of managerial interpersonal competence and innovation by Chris Argyris, *Organization and Innovation* (Homewood, Illinois: Richard D. Irwin, Incorporated, 1965); and a book on trends in the development of organizations and how change agents may contribute to organizational change by Warren G. Bennis, *Changing Organizations* (New York: McGraw-Hill Book Company, Incorporated, 1966).

ment responsibilities if problems of computerization innovations are to be met successfully by a firm. Expedient solutions are of little value to a management which anticipates continuous change. Under these conditions the ability to adapt requires flexibility on the part of management, employees, and unions. Expediency should not be allowed to dissipate existing or latent cooperative attitudes.

The capability of a manager to control future events and to make effective and timely decisions is a function of the planning he has done beforehand. Planners, of course, cannot foresee all eventualities; but plans can provide a framework within which *some* problems may be predicted. Because it is a continuing process, planning also uncovers new factors relevant to a firm and allows for quicker accommodation to them. Thus although manpower and organization planning is not a panacea, it does afford a firm an opportunity to minimize the costs of uncertainty when systems changes are in the offing.

The products of planning are company objectives, policies, procedures, programs, and budgets, all of which contribute to the effective management of the enterprise. The guidance and direction which planning affords the firm are determinants of over-all organizational efficiency. The general importance of planning, and of manpower and organization planning in particular, is highlighted by computerization.

General Lack of Planning Noted

Manpower: Although the need has existed, manpower planning as a top management responsibility is not operative in any Greater Boston Area firm surveyed. There is no evidence that top management has concerned itself with *anticipating* changing manpower requirements under computerization. The characteristics of individual company work forces and changes in them over time have played no appreciable part in top management decision-making. Further, no statistics are being generated within these firms to indicate, for example, future manpower needs, the types of employees to recruit, the skills that should be developed, or future training needs. The

Bureau of Labor Statistics predicts major changes in the labor force with resultant implications for the staffing process, but even the large corporations are not now planning to meet changed internal and labor market conditions. Organization planning in these firms is neglected also.

In general, organization planning pertains to 1) the development of structure, 2) the delegation of responsibility and authority, and 3) the establishment of policies and procedures to guide and regulate working relationships in the pursuit of joint objectives. The paucity in the survey firms of formal organization charts, job descriptions, and policy and procedure manuals attests to the bad job being done in organization planning.

Organization Structure: Two of eleven firms surveyed maintain organization manuals which include formal organization charts. In another firm the numbers in its telephone directory are arranged by function and the hierarchical position indicated by indenting the names. The farther the indentation, the lower the employee's position within the hierarchy. Although formally distributed organization charts are scarce, many informal charts are maintained but discreetly kept hidden at the middle and higher levels of management.

Every manager responsible for a sizeable group of employees has at least an off-the-record chart of his organization. This chart is not open to scrutiny by his subordinates, but aids the manager somewhat in his reporting duties to his boss. Its design usually violates the logical principles of organization. Typically such a chart would be produced only after persistent inquiry.

The managers used stock arguments to justify their failure to develop and freely communicate organization charts. They felt, in general, that formal charts restricted initiative, cultivated provincialism, retarded the broadening of skills by easy transfer of duties, and tended to harden an organization, leaving it inflexible in the face of changing needs.

There is, of course, some merit in all of the above criticisms of organization charts. They should not be considered inviolate documents on scientifically efficient structures. Bize's warning is appropriate:

The perfecting of new methods and new organizations constitutes a hard and permanent problem. We generally tend too much to think that all the questions are solved when we have traced the colored lines of a theoretic organigram.[3]

The practitioners' reservations and Bize's admonition notwithstanding, the need for the primitive stage of organization planning exemplified by organization charts is particularly relevant for management organization during periods of change. A particular informal organizational structure, supported by the working relationships between various levels, may suffice as long as the firm is functioning well within a traditional pattern. But in a situation wherein technology, for instance, is changing rapidly, strong pressures for organizational change are generated. These charts are then important aids to the process of organization because they facilitate the attainment of changed company objectives and work activities, as well as the assignment of new or changed job responsibilities, and thereby the designation of commensurate authority.

Delegation: The second aspect of organization planning, the formal delegation of responsibility and authority, also is not handled adequately by the firms in the survey. In none of the companies did managerial personnel have position descriptions which adequately designated organizational relationships, position duties and degree of responsibility, or position requirements. One firm was "working on it," while another firm designated major functional responsibilities on the organization chart. Most of the companies, however, have had some form of job description for their non-managerial employees.

Policies and Procedures: The third feature of organization planning, policies and practices guiding and controlling working relationships, is found most widely in the surveyed firms. The emphasis, however, is upon directives and procedures

---

[3] Pierre Bize, "Automation and the Scientific Management of Enterprises," *Views on Automation* (Paris: Organisation for European Economic Cooperation, 1957), 28.

rather than policies. All the firms surveyed had elaborate procedures, although the degree to which these were formalized and communicated varied from firm to firm. In one instance operating procedures before computerization were not written down, but retained only in employees' memories. On the other extreme, procedures in some firms were elaborately committed to paper.

Need for Planning Evident

The foregoing suggests that at present, at least in the firms visited, organizational planning has not been effectuated. The nonchalance that this indicates on the part of mangement is beginning to be dissipated. Computerization has forced management to feel some discomfort from this lack of manpower and organization planning. The managers closest to and most favorably affected by electronic data processing, the systems analysts, are keenly aware of the organizational problems caused by a lack of planning. Unfortunately their comments suggest that the organizational problems raised by their activities have been dealt with after, not before the fact.

A methods manager indicated that he had made changes in the organizational structure of his firm but that no one else appeared concerned over some serious implications thereof. Another systems manager said that to his knowledge there was virtually no planning for change in his company. He had related to his boss what he felt was the departmental impact of his activities on organization and management; that was the last he heard of it. Finally, a third systems manager said that no policy guidance or coordinated effort was being made with regard to organizational planning. He said:

I worry about it, but everyone understands that no one will be fired or laid off. The most probable reason for lack of concern is that no one will be hurt financially. Training is being neglected, and no one is preparing for the future needs of the new systems.

One result of this lack of interest in organizational planning is that the predicted efficiencies accruing from computerization seldom materialize in the time allotted. What is even more dis-

couraging is that the expected organizational changes and reduction in manpower may be delayed indefinitely. A systems
manager, who is also responsible for machine operations and
the two line departments serviced by the computer, complained
of such a situation. The work process had been designed efficiently, but for expediency the organization had not been
revised, nor had the personnel reductions been made. The
manager commented that management inertia had resulted in
duplication of work and organization by personality.

This idea, that the personality of the manager, not the work
process, is the major determinant of organization structure and
delegation of responsibility and authority, is a potent one in
all the firms studied. As one manager said, "The personal outlook and drive of the manager is still the most important force
in shaping the organization."

The importance of individual personalities and abilities to
the development of enterprises is recognized. The surprising
fact is that computerization and organization by personality
can coexist. This does not imply that the personalities of top
managers are not crucial variables in establishing the climate
or general structure for the firm. A proper climate and adequate structure are essential if the policies of the firm are to
be implemented effectively by lower levels of management.
An example illustrates the problem.

One top manager of a firm is entrusted technically with
organization planning. Instead of creating a conducive climate,
developing appropriate plans, and implementing policies, the
manager works underground to bring about organization
change. When he could not directly overcome the resistance
of the home organization to accept a procedural change, he
convinced the field organization that the system he desired
would work more efficiently. The field then brought pressure
to bear upon the home organization to effectuate the desired
changes. The manager thus overcame the resistance of the
home organization department to his system, at least temporarily. It is this type of maneuvering which tends to drain
the cooperative energies of a firm and reduces the opportunity

to achieve efficiencies from improved methods employing advanced technologies.

Organization planning, like manpower planning, in summary, is not being taken seriously in most firms in the sample. Even the minimum requirements, formal organization charts and meaningful job descriptions, do not exist. In the firms examined there were no policies that offered guidelines to managers on organization planning. The major activity in this area was carried out by middle managers who by *ad hoc* means attempted to fill the void. After E.D.P. was installed these middle managers attempted to modify the structure, reassign duties, and transfer employees as best they could. These activities, of course, indicate that some organization planning does exist on an informal basis. In addition haphazard grooming of replacements and performance evaluations occur. Training and development programs and rotation and transfer policies exist to varying extents. The point is that these policies and programs are uncoordinated and are not used in planning. Hence, they are of little or no help in meeting the stresses of technological change.

THE EMPLOYEE VIEWS CHANGE

The traditional view of the employee as unalterably opposed to any change in his work environment is slowly being refuted by objective research. The preoccupation of many managers with the idea that employees resist all change, especially technological change, regardless of the long-range results, tends to obscure the realities of the situation.

Further, the predominant concern of management has been with the hourly-paid or blue collar workers' reaction to change. At higher technological levels of production the fact has been illustrated that *all* levels of the organization are susceptible to the difficulty of adapting to work-oriented change. The stereotype of the blue collar, organized, and unskilled or semi-skilled worker as the enemy of economic progress should be discarded as not the general case in fact.

Organizational change also places managers in a fluid and

often fast-changing environment. As such, the organization provides not only new opportunities, but also the possibilities of obsolescence of skills and threats to security. *Sub rosa* rivalries often become overt and may erupt into open hostilities. Questions of relative status, the distribution of power, future opportunities, and even continuance with the firm must be anticipated and answered carefully by top management.

It is not surprising that managers, too, may resent innovations. And not only supervisors, but top and middle managers sometimes sabotage change. In this regard, one top manager's comments on the introduction of a computerized procedure is characteristic of the subtle resistance of this management level:

> My point simply is — we haven't done it yet. They tell us we can. I think I see some problems that look real to me, for all the system's capabilities. If we can do all this successfully — swell. I just don't know yet that we can.[4]

Fiock graphically cites several reasons why computerizing may be an extremely traumatic experience for a middle manager.

> For middle management, moving to a computer operation is like moving into a glass house. Here is why. One reel of computer tape can contain information equivalent to a normal file cabinet. On a fully integrated network, a few reels of tape may contain all of the operating information pertinent to an entire department or division. The tapes are maintained and stored in an area geographically removed from the department. It is conceivable that the tapes could be read on orders from upper management without the knowledge of the departmental manager. In fact, a few reels of tape portraying the status of an entire functional area could fit easily into a briefcase and could be read on other machines at other locations.[5]

The implications for the security of a middle manager are

---

[4] "A Steel Company's Date with a Data Machine," *Business Week*, 1757:146 (May 4, 1963).

[5] L. R. Fiock, Jr., "Seven Deadly Dangers in E.D.P.," *Harvard Business Review*, 40:no. 3, 92 (May-June, 1962).

clear. His feeling of vulnerability before top management can be crushing. He may not have time to screen reports, to correct or camouflage them, or to intervene in a bad situation. A middle manager may become unsettled over these worries and fearful that systems specialists will create a job for him in which he will fail.[6]

Management must attempt to curtail effectively or at least to minimize the threatening aspects of change, and at the same time engage in an active effort to emphasize the opportunities inherent in change.

There is a basic assumption which management must accept before it can attempt convincingly to minimize negative factors and maximize positive factors of change.[7] That is, of course, acceptance of a statement similar to Lawrence's: " ... (P)eople do *not* resist technical change as such and ... most of this resistance which does occur is unnecessary."[8]

Research Findings

Several investigations have found attitudes of employees to be generally favorable toward technological change. In commenting upon a research study statement "I think the firm should put in new machinery," 51 percent of production workers, 64 percent of maintenance workers, and 86 percent of staff (including all but senior executives) agreed.[9]

A question asked in the same study was " 'Do you think you are better off after change?' ... Only a small minority found

---

[6] *Ibid.*

[7] Bright's discussion of negative worker attitudes toward automation and worker benefits from automation provides a good summary of the negative and positive characteristics of technological change. James R. Bright, *Automation and Management* (Boston: Division of Research, Harvard University Graduate School of Business Administration, 1958), 129-202.

[8] Paul R. Lawrence, "How to Deal with Resistance to Change," *Harvard Business Review*, 32:no. 3, 49 (May-June, 1954). According to Neuloh, German workers refer to an obsolete plant as a "worm-eaten joint." Cetto Neuloh, "Paving the Way for Technological Change," *Personnel*, 34:no. 5, 23 (March-April, 1958).

[9] *Men, Steel and Technical Change* (London: Department of Scientific and Industrial Research, 1956), 21.

any changes unfavorable on the whole...."[10] Another question asked was "Do you think you are better off after the latest change?" The contrast with the first attitude reported above is interesting: 60 percent of production workers, 52 percent of maintenance workers, and 64 percent of staff answered affirmatively.[11]

In another study Stieber reports that "An overwhelming proportion of the employees questioned thought that technological change in general was desirable."[12] Moreover:

> Interestingly enough, a substantial number of employees (about 40 percent on the whole) felt that during the past year their jobs had become more secure, more interesting, and more responsible, required greater skill and accuracy, and were more varied.[13]

Hardin did a follow-up investigation of earlier research done by the Labor and Industrial Relations Center at Michigan State University. He concludes:

> The results of the study indicate that the installation of the computer by the insurance company affected the work environment of a number of employees in several respects, that most of its effects were those that employees desired, and that the computer installation was liked more often than disliked.[14]

Finally, Lee studied how employees felt about the impact of computerization on work. He found that:

> All employees expressed increased satisfaction with their work. The managerial employees as a whole were relatively more content with the work conditions after the computer installation than the clerical.[15]

---

[10] *Ibid.*, p. 26.

[11] *Ibid.*

[12] Jack Stieber, "Automation and the White-Collar Worker," *Personnel*, 34:no. 3, 15 (November-December, 1957).

[13] *Ibid.*

[14] Einar Hardin, "The Reactions of Employees to Office Automation," *Monthly Labor Review*, 83:no. 9, 932 (Washington, D.C.: United States Government Printing Office, September, 1960). For a comparison of attitudes toward technical change in six countries see *Steel Workers and Technical Progress* (Paris: European Productivity Agency of the Organisation for European Economic Cooperation, June, 1959), Chapter IV.

[15] H. C. Lee, "Do Workers Really Want Flexibility on the Job?," *Personnel*, 42:no. 2, 77 (March-April, 1965).

These references do not offer conclusive proof of every employee's complete enthusiasm for all change. The data do suggest, however, that the traditional view of employee resistance to change should be modified to reflect changed attitudes based upon the altered political, social, and economic factors affecting the work environment. Individual employees should not be viewed categorically as hindrances to progress. Employees no more desire to maintain the *status quo* than any person in any other role in society. Non-managerial employees are receptive to innovations. The real challenge is in its effective management. "People do not resist change or resent criticism; they do resist *being* changed and do resent *being* criticized."[16] What procedures does management use in furthering its objectives in managing change?

THE MEANS OF IMPLEMENTATION

The job of building employee understanding, acceptance, and cooperation in regard to change is not an easy one.[17] Inept attempts to facilitate adaption to change may aggravate the situation. "It is clear...that the motivational and the communication techniques used by the manager have as much impact as the character of the change itself."[18] Perhaps Moore has overstated the point, but the importance of the warning may merit some exaggeration.

Communication

The benefits of two-way communication are generally acknowledged.[19] Most managements have come to recognize,

---

16 Leo B. Moore, "How to Manage Improvement," *Harvard Business Review*, 36:no. 4, 77 (July-August, 1958).

17 For a discussion of a ten-point top management program to facilitate organizational change, see Patrick H. Irwin and Frank W. Langham, Jr., "The Change Seekers," *Harvard Business Review*, 44:no. 1, 81-91 (January-February, 1966).

18 Moore, *op. cit.*, p. 78.

19 Through experience with computerization, managers have refined some useful guides for implementing a communications program to promote employee understanding of the need for technological change. See Richard A. Beaumont and Ray B. Helfgott, "Management, Automation, and People," *Industrial Relations Monograph Number 24* (New York: Industrial Relations Counselors, 1964), 278-282.

some through difficult experiences, the value of exchanging information with employees on matters which are of direct mutual concern. Changes that result from technical innovation are especially appropriate topics for information exchange.

A sound, managerial two-way communications program, according to Mumford, rests upon the recognition of diverse group interests in an organization.

> This leads to the conclusion that when an organization sees innovation as essential to the attainment of its economic goals and wishes to get change fully and rapidly accepted by employees, it is not sufficient merely to adopt public relations techniques of "selling." A more fundamental approach is necessary which will involve, firstly, an understanding of the nature of social relationships within the firm; secondly an identification of employee goals and a recognition that these will differ according to such variables as age, sex, job status and the norms of the work and special groups to which the employees belong. With this knowledge, a plan for organizing and implementing change must be designed so that innovation assists and is *seen* to assist the furtherance of as many individual and group goals as possible, or, negatively, that it hinders the attainment of as few as possible.[20]

Mumford studied two firms' communications policies regarding computerization and described the clerks' reactions. In the first firm *no* information regarding the introduction of the computer was given to the clerks. In the second firm there was no attempt at secrecy, and information was shared well before the computer arrived. On the basis of the reactions, Mumford concludes "...that change is only resisted if it is seen as conflicting with personal goals and aspirations."[21]

> This leads to the conclusion that when devising a strategy for change an important preliminary is an identification of these goals together with an analysis of the effects of the proposed innovation upon them. Communication will always be an important part of the

---

[20] Enid Mumford, "Clerks and Computers; A Study of the Introduction of Technical Change," *Journal of Management Studies*, 2:no. 2, 140 (May, 1965).
[21] *Ibid.*, p. 151.

change process. If personal goals can be furthered by change this should be made explicit. Similarly, if the change is unlikely to either help or hinder the attainment of goals, communication of this fact will allay unnecessary anxiety. If, on the contrary, change is likely to damage the interests of a group, communication can increase hostility by making the group aware of the threat. In this situation the withholding of information or the giving of reassuring information would be unethical as staff have a right to know what is going to happen to them, but mechanisms other than communication will have to be adopted to secure the acceptance of change. These might include procedures to minimize hardship, compensation, or even an alteration of organization goals so that they no longer conflict with the goals of groups or individuals.[22]

Serious communications gaps in a firm may occur for a variety of reasons. Gray cites three that he discovered in studying the social aspects of computerization. First, sometimes managers think organizational changes are so minor, i.e., reasonable and routine, that they fail to communicate them to employees. Second, top management may not comprehend the full significance of a particular change, and therefore fails to communicate adequately. Third, managers who are effectuating technical changes often forget that new procedures may shatter office traditions and social patterns, and disrupt employee security.[23]

These types of communications gaps, as well as other communications problems, abounded in the surveyed firms.

One surveyed firm had undergone extreme difficulty in changing over from a manual to a mechanized system. A top management official indicated that "things had fallen apart," and it looked as if "somebody had carefully sabotaged our program." In analyzing the reasons for this period of extreme confusion, the manager said he felt that the employees had not understood the reasons for the conversion and what was going to happen to them. Management had made no attempt

---

[22] Ibid.
[23] Arlen Gray, "Problems of Adjustment in the Automated Office," *Personnel*, 41:no. 4, 45-46 (July-August, 1965).

to communicate with them. Later, when this firm converted to computerized operations, it had an extensive communications program.

In general, the firms surveyed communicate freely and openly with their employees.[24] For instance, in one firm eight months before the computer was delivered, an article in the company paper told of the rental of the computer, and assured the employees that no one would lose his job. A month later a picture of the president signing the order for the machine was printed along with a summary of the computer's strengths and weaknesses. Later numerous articles appeared describing various aspects of preparing for the computer, its installation, and initial operations. Finally, a scale model of the installation was exhibited with recorded comments; and the local newspapers publicized the first operations of the computer.

A top management official of another firm described his firm's communications program:

1) We keep the employees fully informed of what we are doing; no editorials, we give them only the facts.
2) We brought the employees as quickly as possible into contact with the computer and its operations.
3) We emphasized the importance of employees and their duties in the overall computer operations.

While there is much formal communication with respect to computerization, two important qualifications need to be mentioned: first, not *all* firms subscribe with equal vigor to communicating with employees about relevant changes; and second, the *content* of what is communicated may be censored severely.

One firm gave no advance notice that a feasibility study had been made, or that a computer had been rented. The employees learned about the computerization plans through their

[24]For a detailed discussion of methods used in informing employees about computerization, see "Adjustments to the Introduction of Office Automation," *Bureau of Labor Statistics Bulletin Number 1276* (Washington, D.C.: United States Department of Labor, May, 1960), Chapter VI. Also, for an excellent summary of the kinds of information communicated to various levels in the organization and to affected and unaffected employees, see B. Conway, J. Gibbons, and D. E. Watts, *Business Experience with Electronic Computers* (New York: Controllers Institute Research Foundation, Incorporated, 1959), 75.

union. In fact, the union leadership and rank-and-file employees knew about computerization before many members of lower management.

The content of communications in the surveyed firms was general, except for the provision that no one would lose his job, and in some instances, that existing salaries would be maintained.[25] Typically communications would include commentary on the timetable of installation, a description of the equipment and job changes. Specific changes in manpower requirements, skills, or organization were not communicated. This reflects both the lack of planning in this regard and the conscious withholding of information. That information may be withheld even at the highest levels of an organization is revealed by interview notes with a top management official of a large firm:

> Top management (in reality, a select few) knows the direction in which the organization is going, and is planning accordingly. Not all members of management can be told of expected organizational changes that result from computerization. If we told them what the organization is going to look like five years from now, chaos would result. Next June, watch for some announcements of major changes in our organizational structure.

Karsh and Siegman reported on a study of the introduction of a computer into a bureaucratic setting. They, too, observed how "people deliberately attempt to keep others ignorant and how ignorance functions to protect existing statuses."[26]

In summary, there is much communication in connection with E.D.P. in the firms of the survey. As cited, some firms refuse to communicate even the barest essentials of impending changes. There is also much evidence to support the thesis that most communication is fairly general, with few or no references to specific organizational changes to be expected. Participation of persons interested in or affected by technical changes, and especially E.D.P., is limited also.

---

25 In the case of unionized firms, no such specific statements were made.

26 Bernard Karsh and Jack Siegman, "Functions of Ignorance in Introducing Automation," *Social Problems,* 12:no. 2, 141 (Fall, 1964).

Participation

At the higher levels of the organization, there is generally an E.D.P. committee which supervises the computerization process within the firm or the independent administrative unit.

> With the rapid growth in procurement and use of computers, the company has created several important committees which should be mentioned here. The first of these is the Systems Development and Coordination Committee, made up of key representatives from the fields of data processing, technical computing, and operations research. It also has a representative from employee relations because of the present and potential impact of these techniques on such problems as personnel displacement, employee and management training, etc.[27]

Rush's comments do not typify the E.D.P. committees of the surveyed firms. These committees were less representative of the areas affected by E.D.P., did not have a personnel department representative, declined in influence after the feasibility study, and were usually run by one manager who frequently used the committee to rubber-stamp his decisions.

There was virtually no consultation with non-managerial employees during and after computerization. Employees played no part in organizational changes; they did not contribute their ideas or suggestions to the line managers or to the systems analysts. Personnel transfers and assignment of job duties, as well as all other changes resulting from the introduction of E.D.P., were accomplished without consideration of employee sentiments. One manager, who is notably not representative, indicated picturesquely how he felt about the management of change, with particular reference to consultative management.

An Uneasy Look at One Manager's Philosophy

Manager X is a piquant New Englander, a maverick, self-confident, and one of the leaders in his technical specialty.

---

[27] Carl H. Rush, "Standard Oil Company (N.J.): Organizational Development," George P. Shultz and Thomas L. Whisler, eds., *Management Organization and the Computer* (Glencoe, Illinois: The Free Press of Glencoe, 1960), 196.

Manager X is also dynamic and seemingly unafraid of taking organizational risks. He is very vocal on the topic of current management practices.

Manager X is disenchanted with human relations and his company's "sociological" principles of organization, the proliferation of quasi-managers, over-decentralization of authority, and philosophy on management development. For him management development based on a philosophy that management is an art in itself, and that a manager need not understand in depth the technical aspects of his job is nonsense. Manager X maintains that a manager must manage something, and it is this "verb content" that must be reinserted in the concept of management.

How would Manager X implement his management philosophy? He believes 10 percent of the employee population are capable. Therefore, the system should be built around this nucleus. About 80 percent of the employees are cows who will do as they are told. The remaining 10 percent of the employees are incompetent and should be fired. The system should be developed with as little communication as possible. He favors telling top and middle managers of big, general changes, but would not tell lower levels of management or employees anything. The system itself should be designed to prevent interference by the employees. He would outwit the employees by knowing the tricks they pull, and by designing the system to inhibit their sabotage.

The excesses of any prevailing wisdom or fad are always subject to ridicule, often by capable and gifted observers. Tolerance and a good sense of humor notwithstanding, the above approach to leadership and change is not the most balanced. Current research on the management of change suggests that a management approach including the maximum useful communication with the employee and his meaningful participation in matters that directly affect him is more likely to attain organization objectives.

THE UNION RESPONSE

Trade union policies toward technological change have been evolving to meet membership needs and interests. Unions have long been concerned with maintaining the skills of and preventing reduction in their membership. Research during the 1930s focused on the unions' policies toward technological change emphasizing the protection of job opportunities, income, and working conditions. Researchers found that unions were placing less reliance on obstruction and competition as viable policies toward technological change, and were turning more toward regulation, control, and alleviation of the effects of technological change.

Currently, most unions do not oppose technological change steadfastly, *per se*. The unions do insist that workers share in the gains from increased productivity, that change be implemented with a minimum of cost to the worker, and that the major social and economic costs incurred be borne by management and government.

Collective bargaining has been used by workers to protect their interests in the face of technological change.[28] The ways in which specific contests between labor and management have been resolved have varied.[29] One ameliorative device, the automation fund, has been developed to provide displaced employees with financial support.[30]

The government has also been drawn more deeply into the problem of worker adjustment to technological change. As a measure of its concern, the first report of the President's Ad-

[28] For an excellent discussion of collective bargaining as a means to reconcile labor-management conflict over automation, see George W. Taylor, "Collective Bargaining," John T. Dunlop, ed., *Automation and Technological Change* (Englewood Cliffs. N.J.: Prentice Hall, Incorporated, for The American Assembly, 1962).

[29] Six different industry approaches to technological change are discussed by Charles C. Killingsworth, "Cooperative Approaches to Problems of Technological Change," Gerald G. Somers, *et. al.*, eds., *Adjusting to Technological Change* (New York: Harper and Row, 1963).

[30] Seven union-management funds designed to compensate displaced workers and reduce resistance to change of the remaining work force are explored by Thomas Kennedy, *Automation Funds and Displaced Workers* (Boston: Harvard University Press, 1962).

visory Committee on Labor-Management Policy, issued in 1962, was devoted to benefits and problems relating to technological change. Legislative measures were undertaken as well. The Manpower Development and Training Act of 1962 was enacted to help retrain workers displaced by automation. Late in 1964, the United States held the first international conference on automation in Washington, D.C. These are examples of growing government interest in meeting automation problems.

Union reliance on management and government to bear the costs of change does not mean unions will not have to face their own organizational problems resulting from innovation. Such matters as union structure, jurisdiction, classification, and size of membership will offer strong challenges to the unions' leadership.[31]

The leadership of most unions, like the institution itself, faces many problems during rapid technological change. It is extremely difficult for a union leader to retain the image of "labor statesman" while remaining responsive to minority membership interests. As Walter Reuther has commented:

> In its day-to-day activities the U.A.W. has had to face up to these questions of job displacement, not as academic issues, but as stern realities which vitally affect the lives of hundreds of thousands of its members.[32]

Computerization and the Unions

The implications of the technological changes confronting clerical bargaining units have not been as vast as those faced

---

[31] "Automation in the Metal Trades," *Report II* (Geneva: International Labour Office, 1956), 49-50. See also "Impact on Union Size, Structure and Function," *Automation and Major Technological Change, Publication Number 19* (Washington, D.C.: The Industrial Union Department, AFL-CIO, April 22, 1958) and "Collective Bargaining Problems," *Automation and Major Technological Change, Publication Number 18* (Washington, D.C.: The Industrial Union Department, AFL-CIO, April 22, 1958).

[32] Walter P. Reuther, "Statement to Subcommittee on Automation and Energy Resources," *New Views on Automation* (Washington, D.C.: United States Government Printing Office, 1960), 551. See also Alain Touraine, *et. al.,* "Workers' Attitudes to Technical Change: an Integrated Survey of Research," *Industrial Relations Aspects of Manpower Policy* (Paris: Organisation for Economic Co-operation and Development, 1965).

by the United Auto Workers, and the union programs designed to protect the membership have not been as comprehensive. On the contrary, unionized (as well as non-unionized) firms in the survey sample have been able to accommodate E.D.P. without drastic changes in the original employer-employee relationship. This finding is consistent with that of a study conducted by the International Labour Organisation:

> The fundamental changes entailed in the introduction of mechanised or electronic data-processing systems in offices, — changes in work organisation and methods, job classification and occupational structure, and in the size and distribution of staff, — appear to have had so far surprisingly little effect on the traditional pattern of labour-management relations in the undertakings concerned. The problems of adjustment to new situations have apparently not over-taxed the existing relationships between clerical employees and their employers, since there is little evidence indicating that unusual difficulties have been encountered in the field.[33]

The probable reasons that E.D.P has not disrupted traditional relationships, methods of dealing with divergent interests, and personnel policies and practices are: 1) the existing relationships, methods, and policies had been reviewed and revised, and, therefore, did not undergo drastic change, and 2) labor market conditions and labor force characteristics of clerical workers facilitated the required changes. The latter, labor market and labor force conditions and characteristics, were cited often by managers as factors mitigating against union and/or employee resistance to technological change.

The general shortage of clerical workers, particularly those with scarce skills, has eased the unemployment effect of technological change. Firms have been able to transfer and thus retrain displaced employees. Turnover among clerical workers is especially high; for instance, in several of the firms visited, there had been a complete change in the clerical work force in about three years. The clerical work force is primarily

---

[33] Effects of Mechanisation and Automation in Offices," Report III (Geneva: International Labour Office, 1959), 105.

female, and has an uncertain and uneven commitment to the labor force. Many of the clerical employees are young; a large proportion of them are recent high school graduates. Many (often those most drastically affected by E.D.P.) can be transferred easily and retrained with a minimum of effort and time. Finally, the most drastic impact of E.D.P. may be on future job opportunities within the firm, an impact with which the present employee is not and the union may not be concerned.

These, then, are some of the factors at work to moderate the disruptive impact of E.D.P. on the clerical employee. Primarily because of these factors, the three organized firms in the survey experienced very little pressure from the unions because of E.D.P.

Only one contract provision in the surveyed firms definitely derives from E.D.P. The clause states that "no employee in the bargaining unit who has five (5) or more years of continuous service...will be laid off or reduced in pay for lack of work." A supplemental memorandum of understanding in the same firm provides that for one and one-half years all clerical additions to the staff would be on a temporary basis.

A union's ability to strike successfully against a firm to force salary increases is another matter, however.

Computers and Strike Effectiveness: In two surveyed firms, the computer played a key role in breaking a strike. In the first instance, labor and management were locked in a bitter conflict over job security. Production and maintenance employees demanded a clause prohibiting subcontracting of work, and clerical employees asked for a stronger no-layoff clause. The parties could not agree, and the union called the first strike in the company's history.

The computer helped break the strike. Managers were able to maintain computerized operations. An executive indicated that without computerized procedures the entire paperwork process would have ground to a halt.

In the second case, a production and maintenance union went out on strike. Two other unions, including the one for clerical employees, refused to cross the picket line and stayed home. Management, with computerized operations, was able to sustain the paperwork flow; this helped substantially to break the strike.

In both the cases discussed above, production and maintenance work as well as office work are highly automated. This allowed management to cover all phases of work adequately, thereby lessening significantly the strikes' effectiveness.

Union participation in E.D.P. was not studied intensively in this research. Union representatives were not consulted, nor were direct union matters discussed with bargaining unit employees. The following summation, therefore, is based upon limited data.

A few of the firms in the survey are unionized. Generally the unions have had little or no effect on the rate or cost of computerization. No formal grievances have arisen over E.D.P. The restrictions placed upon management are similar to those that have been developed in the non-union firms. There have been no significant formal union demands pertaining to E.D.P., nor is there any evidence to suggest that the unions have attempted, in any way, to prevent technological change itself.

THE PERSONNEL FUNCTION AS CHANGE AGENT

The existence of a personnel department is taken for granted in most firms today. Almost every medium- or large-sized firm has designated someone to handle personnel matters. Theoretically a personnel administrator is an expert in handling personnel problems, in diagnosing organizational health, in building and maintaining an efficient work force, in administering salaries, wages, services, and programs, and in dealing with unions.

In the management of personnel problems connected with technological change, the personnel staff can contribute much to the efficient utilization of human resources within the firm.[34] Given the function, role, and interest in the management of change, this question naturally follows: To what extent does the personnel staff participate in the management of change?

Odiorne has assessed the responsibilities of the personnel department in firms experiencing change, and emphasizes the need for innovation in manpower and organization planning. He finds that personnel administrators are not meeting these needs, and are ineffective in this role.[35] The survey data are consistent with this evaluation. Personnel administrators and their departments have made only peripheral contributions to solving the organizational problems caused by E.D.P. The reasons for this disappointing performance are found at least in part in the organization, programs, and status of the personnel function.

Organization of the Personnel Function

Each of the companies studied maintains a central personnel department. These departments are unable to perform effectively because of several organizational practices.

In one firm the responsibility for the personnel administration function is divided badly. The essential activities are supervised by two managers, each of whom reports to a different boss. Manager X is responsible for management recruitment, training, administration of fringe benefits, the operation of the cafeteria and the hospital, safety, hygiene, social and recreational activities, employee counseling, and factory employment. Manager Y supervises clerical employment, office space, layout and equipment, form design and control, and paperwork routines, and serves as mediator and coordinator between departments and as counselor to employees. Manage-

---

34 For a discussion of the kinds of challenges automation thrusts at personnel managers see Russell J. Cooney, "Manpower Planning for Automation," *Public Personnel Review*, 26:no. 3, 151-155 (July, 1965). Several procedures which enhance the personnel specialist's role as change agent are discussed by Lawrence E. Schlesinger, "Personnel Specialists and Change, Monks or Missionaries?," *Personnel Administration*, 28:no. 4, 3-5f (July-August, 1965).

35 George S. Odiorne, "Company Growth and Personnel Administration," *Personnel*, 37:no. 1, 33 (January-February, 1960).

ment and clerical wage administration are handled by committee action, while hourly wage administration in this non-union firm is handled by Manager Z, who reports to the same boss as Manager Y.

Decentralization of the personnel function within the *same* independent administrative unit is the second reason for ineffectiveness. This is not the familiar problem created by the existence of central- and plant-staff personnel groups. Firm A illustrates the consequences of a function, such as sales, maintaining its own personnel staff.

Mr. X is on the sales vice-president's staff. He is responsible for hiring and firing employees, salary administration, placement, counseling, transfers, and promotions. In his view the personnel department acts as liaison between the operating departments (e.g., sales) and the personnel committee. Therefore, Manager X funnels requests for information and unique problems to the personnel department. Also, if a decision made in Manager X's department affects other departments, or if he wishes to know what other departments have done in a similar situation, he will check with the personnel department. The final decision, nevertheless, rests with Mr. X.

Mr. X also has taken the initiative on several occasions. He has persuaded the managers he serves to allow the first line supervisor to make salary recommendations. He also has recommended that all supervisors, as well as their bosses, have a copy of the administrative personnel manual. Lastly, Mr. X is disregarding a company personnel policy which he considers unfair. Mr. X, in summary, disregards the personnel department except for routine checks or to use it to pressure the personnel committee to institute changes.

A similar situation, complicated by other considerations, exists in firm B. In this instance the ineffectiveness has resulted not from the duplication of responsibilities nor the provincialism of several personnel staffs in one location, but rather from a line manager's abdication of his personnel duties by, in effect, designating his secretary as personnel assistant.

In firm B the secretary to the manager of a subdivision within the controller's department (referred to by her boss as an administrative assistant) is for all purposes the personnel officer for this unit. She maintains all records, handles discipline, promotion, personal problems and gripes, hires employees, and runs the office in the absence of the manager. The secretary's boss, when asked what relation his department had to the personnel department, answered: "Personnel handles salary administration."

A third reason why personnel departments are ineffective is that bad organization results from incompetent line managers being retained by their companies. The exact amount of "deadwood" being carried by the companies surveyed cannot be ascertained. Stated and implicit policies, conservative systems revision approaches, the lack of organizational shakeups, and my general impressions suggest that a significant number of managers are being carried by the companies. One manager said that he handled his boss's line responsibilities, that his boss was "63 and working it out," and was primarily entrusted with "personnel matters."

In another firm an ineffective manager said: "The personnel department more and more is letting the line handle personnel administration." This line manager refers to himself as a counselor. One of his subordinates said: "Mr. X is responsible for personnel matters."

The practice of maintaining ineffective, displaced, or older managers in positions which are devoid of content except for "personnel matters" impedes the proper utilization of personnel administration as a staff function and line responsibility.

The fourth and final organizational reason for ineffective personnel administration in the management of change results from its downgrading in unionized firms. This is illustrated in one firm with a militant union. The labor relations function is handled extremely well, but personnel administration suffers as a result. In this particular unit of the company the major department maintains a manager whose primary responsibilities are for management personnel administration, representation on the training staff, arrangement of leaves of absence, and the formulation and administration of budgets. The need for a personnel program, separate from budget formulation and administration, is not recognized.

The strong influence of labor relations on manpower and organization matters is exemplified also in another unionized firm. A top management representative said that "the small bite" approach necessitated by the union has been good, because it allows the organization to adapt and react to change without great instability. The labor relations manager of this firm views his job in easing the impact of E.D.P. as entailing activities such as new job evaluations after installation of the computer.

Manpower and organization planning in the unionized firms discussed herein consists of formal negotiation of contractual problems raised by E.D. P. Such areas include manning requirements, training and retraining needs and opportunities, transferring employees, and hiring temporary personnel.

The reason for mentioning this fourth factor, the emphasis on labor relations, is not to say that this is bad necessarily. In many firms it may be the only attempt to facilitate change within the organization. The danger is that these labor relations activities, in themselves, may be thought to meet the requirements for an active personnel administration program in unionized firms.

In summary, organizational practices such as divided responsibilities, profusion of personnel staffs, use of ineffective managers for personnel matters, and emphasis on industrial relations in unionized firms have limited the contribution of the personnel function to the management of change. The preoccupation of the personnel department with "housekeeping" activities also interferes with the fulfillment of its major responsibilities especially when change, such as computerization, is afoot.

Activities under the Personnel Function

The personnel departments in the surveyed firms play a

disappointing role in the management of change, although in several of the firms a personnel representative does participate in discussions about reorganization. One methods manager commented that personnel participates by receiving advance communications about coming changes and "working things out."

One personnel manager felt that the small size of his company allowed for planning to be carried on "informally." He also felt that there was no need to modify personnel policies because of computerization. This manager added that his dealings with E.D.P. personnel were informal and that the only impact, so far, was the need to hire programmers from outside the company.

Another methods manager, referring to the activities of the firm's personnel department, lamented the fact that "it participated in E.D.P. only to the extent of inquiring why the predicted personnel cuts were not made. It voiced no concern when management refused to communicate to employees about the coming introduction of the computer."

Finally, a personnel manager complained that a big organizational change was on the way, but that he was not supposed to know about it. "The controller runs the show, but I heard about the change through the grapevine." The nature of the activities of the personnel departments in some measure explains their failure to participate in manpower and organizational planning.

The personnel department typically is burdened with the odds and ends duties in a firm. Attention to these tends to distort the image of the department, to dissipate the energies of the staff, and to isolate it from the mainstream of the company.

Activities in two surveyed firms illustrate this. The over-all responsibility of one personnel department is for developing and administering the personnel program. This includes a telephone exchange, a travel reservation service, and a sales promotion section. The other personnel department supervises employee loans, a thrift plan, internal charity, drives, floaters, pages, secretarial services, executive assistants, and trainees.

Status of the Personnel Function

Line management's evaluation of the personnel department affects its ability to participate actively in the management of change. The standing of the personnel function and its representatives in the firms of the survey generally is not high. This position inhibits, to some extent, the personnel function's contribution to the management of change.

The implications of computerization were discussed with a top management official in a large company. He said:

> The personnel department is not in top level management counsels. I don't want them. I check, on a limited basis, with them as a matter of courtesy. I wouldn't be where I am today if I weren't personnel-minded.

Some organizational and functional reasons contributing to this low status for personnel administration have already been suggested. Whatever other reasons may contribute to this situation, it is clear that line managers, as a group, hold the personnel function and staff in low regard. The following comments on a particular personnel department visited are presented hopefully to offer some insights into this situation.

The director of personnel felt that the introduction of E.D.P. had not resulted in any significant changes in his firm. He seemed surprised that I wished to continue my research in his firm nevertheless, was reluctant to make appointments, and wanted assurances that any further inquiries would be made through his office.

An interview with a subordinate personnel representative was equally negative. He was somewhat belligerent and very suspicious. He repeatedly asked, "Why do you ask that?," or "Why discuss the old way?" He wanted to know if he could "check" my notes for accuracy.

Apparently the major reason the members of this personnel department behaved in this manner lies in their ignorance of and lack of participation in the personnel problems raised by E.D.P. My impression, both from discussions with the members of the personnel department *and* the line, is that the prestige of the department is low. The line neither seeks advice and counsel, nor nurtures the line-staff relationship. The line-staff principle does not apply to many typical personnel procedures because the personnel department does not participate in those procedures.

In short, this department is not active in a role consistent with current theory *or* past practice. Even in the more routine personnel areas the department accumulates rather than applies data creatively. With regard to computerization this department is not planning in any way for the new technology, nor does it perceive the implications which, in its isolation, it claims do not exist.

These comments on the status of one personnel department are not exhaustive, nor may they be applied to personnel departments in general. They do offer at least a clue to explain the bad performance of the personnel departments visited.

PART III
ENCOUNTER AFTERMATH

Chapter IX

THE CHANGING FACE OF OFFICE WORK

The computer is revolutionizing the American office. It is changing office systems, altering the nature of office work, increasing labor productivity, upgrading the structure of the labor force, and changing its sex composition.

— Roy B. Helfgott

Changes in the nature and the form of information processing have been brought about by computerization. Four features of the work process — integration, formalization, standardization, and social context — are considered in order to assess the impact of computerization upon them. Data from the surveyed firms are compared with the literature, and some conclusions are drawn. Lastly, the narrowing distinction between plant and office work is examined. Throughout the chapter, the emphasis is upon input generation in the procedures for computerized operations.[1]

THE MACHINE-PACED CLERICALS

With computerization information processing is becoming more orderly and rational. Characteristically increasing mech-

---

[1] Prospects are excellent that new developments in optical scanning equipment may revolutionize data input in computerized programs.

The applications for optical scanning have grown rapidly in recent years. The reason for this growth is that this system has provided the "missing link" in the data processing flow. That is, it automatically prepares input data at high speeds, thus eliminating the time-consuming manual preparation of cards and tape. Jobs with high-speed and accuracy requirements are particularly well-suited to optical scanning procedures used today. From "An Updated Look at Optical Scanning and Its Uses," *Administrative Management*, 27:no. 2, 27 (February, 1966). See also "From One Machine: 100 Days' Work in 8 Hours," *U.S. News and World Report*, XLI:no 8, 11 (August 22, 1966).

anization of the work process has resulted in tighter integration of operations through the elimination of intermediate steps. There is a more even or continuous flow through the various work stages from raw material (input) to finished product (output). Intergration also implies that movement is in one direction. Back and forth movement of intermediate or unfinished products between the same stages of the work process is eliminated.

Increasing mechanization also leads to more rigid formalization of the work process. An emphasis on systems results in more routine. Scheduling and deadlines become more important. More activities are programmed through the establishment and enforcement of procedures, rules, and regulations. Coffee breaks and quitting time in the machine paced office are now policed by a buzzer which signals the start or end of the day, lunch period, and coffee breaks. Not an autocratic boss, but an implacable machine demands such discipline.

The work task itself is altered by technological advance. Work becomes more standardized and thus can be measured more precisely. Consolidation of similar work functions facilitates concentration of employees performing the same tasks. Consolidation also makes greater specialization or subdivision of tasks more feasible. Operational problems, such as errors, are recognized, the cause noted, and corrections expedited.

Finally, some social aspects of the job undergo change. Superior-subordinate relations are altered as the individual employee's work pace becomes impersonally established and controlled by "it" (a machine) rather than by "him" (a boss, once removed). Personal differences between employees of relatively equal standing are reduced. With increasing rationalization some petty status symbols tend to disappear. Under more advanced technologies it has become more difficult for employees to assume the reflected status of the supervisor that they tend to apply to themselves and their job.

The implications of this increasing rationalization of the work process are specifically relevant under computerization. The results of research conducted by the International Labour

Organisation indicate that a computerized work process is more highly integrated:

> Even a cursory examination...shows that office automation is a movement of much more profound significance than earlier forms of mechanisation, whose effects were, on the whole, limited to the simplification and speeding up of routine clerical work. The integration of clerical procedures in one continuous work flow, and the suppression of intermediate steps, which were glimpsed under advanced forms of mechanisation, are pushed with automation to greater and greater extremes.[2]

In regard to work tasks and social changes under computerization, Mann and Williams found that:

> The new and more highly integrated work process allowed less autonomy for setting the work pace for both individual employees and work groups. Work could not be held over from one day to the next. Each group had to process a specific number of accounts every day or perform specific functions. Deadlines had to be met, regardless of how the job had been going or how personnel and equipment were performing. Absences and tardiness became increasingly important because they interferred with the group's ability to complete its portion of the job.[3]

THE ALTERED PROCESS OF CLERICAL WORK

Strategies for deploying computers have affected the work process appreciably.[4] Each specific feature of the work process, i.e., integration, formalization, standardization, and social context, has not been changed to the same degree.

Integration

Integration—continuous flow—of the work process probably has been the least altered by computerization. The major

[2] "Effects of Mechanisation and Automation in Offices: I," *International Labour Review*, 81:no. 2, 163 (February, 1960).

[3] Floyd C. Mann and Lawrence K. Williams, "Observations of the Dynamics of a Change to Electronic Data-Processing Equipment," *Administrative Science Quarterly*, 5:no. 2, 251 (September, 1960).

[4] Work process is defined to include all tasks performed by clerical workers either before or after the actual processing of information in the machine center.

reason for the lack of impact is the lack of integration among the computerized procedures. This often results when manual work flows into computer programs without a significant alteration of systems. The prospects for innovative systems implementation are good, and no doubt integration will progress accordingly.

The survey data indicate, nevertheless, that some elements of integration have been extended under E.D.P. The shuffling of punched cards back and forth between the input and machine processing groups has been eliminated where magnetic drum or tape installations exist. This did not occur in installations which had a card input and output to the computer, or where two machine centers were involved in a single computerized procedure.

In one case, a rearrangement of functions has led to a smoother functioning of the information work process. Punched paper tapes are prepared in the line department rather than as before, when cards were keypunched by the machine center. In another instance the further rationalization of a payroll program has eliminated the need for overtime and the problems created by crises situations generated by work tieups, vacations, and plant shutdowns.

The warehousing example in Chapter III illustrated how the time factor, crucial to the order-delivery cycle, was improved upon with the result being greater over-all efficiency of operations. The centralization of warehousing operations was facilitated by the introduction of E.D.P. In the near future the warehouse will be tied in more closely with the manufacturing plants through an improved computerized system of production planning.

Formalization

Evidence indicates that computerized procedures lead to a more formal emphasis on systems, routines, schedules, procedures, rules and regulations, and time control. The nature and use of schedules, manuals, and codes indicate the degree to which formalization has increased in the surveyed firms.

The need to coordinate work activities among related departments becomes apparent under E.D.P. Three organizational units' activities for a given payroll procedure were bound closely by an agreed upon schedule, to within a half-hour of work time. In one case the schedule covered the activities of an operating department for an entire month.

Conway, Gibbons, and Watts describe the meaning of such a schedule for a machine center:

> The short-term operating plan or schedule usually covers the current day's work. The console operator works directly from it. It is in complete detail and shows, by quarter- or half-hour divisions, the work that will be performed during the day. It reflects any changes that have occurred in the long-range program, and also indicates the "reserve" applications which are to be processed, if for any reason, it becomes impossible to process scheduled work.[5]

There is evidence of more rules and regulations. The use of a manual with codes in one large firm, and the more general use of codes to direct the actions of clerks was noted. In offices with large groups of clerks, work, coffee breaks, and lunch time typically are regulated by a buzzer. Computerization has reinforced the need to control employee activities because of the greater interdependence of functions and dependence upon hardware.

In their study Mann and Williams summarize the generally greater degree of formalization following the introduction of a computer in an insurance firm:

> A change-over to E.D.P. appears to accelerate the level of formalization within the organization. The organization of work is further rationalized; rules and regulations are substituted for individual decision making. Programming itself is a large step in this direction. Decisions formerly left to individual employees to handle within the spirit of a general statement of policy are programmed into the machine.[6]

---

[5] B. Conway, J. Gibbons, and D. E. Watts, *Business Experience with Electronic Computers* (New York: Controllers Institute Research Foundation, Incorporated, 1959), 149.

[6] Mann and Williams, *op. cit.*, p. 251.

Mann and Williams may overstate the degree to which the clerks previously had used policy guides. The authors probably use policy in a rather loose sense. Their comments are otherwise consistent with the data from our surveyed firms.

Standardization

The standardization that results from computerized work procedures takes the form of further subdivision of work functions, the consolidation of related job functions, more precise measurement of work performed, and stricter error control.

The survey data suggest that movement in regard to specialization of job duties may be in two opposite directions. Specialization and functionalization work toward smaller tasks, but also may lead to "job enlargement;" combining related elements of the job may permit more variety. In one computerized procedure in a surveyed firm, the bookkeeper's job was fractionalized into very small segments. Some of the former duties have been absorbed by the computer, e.g., posting the ledger, while others have been broken down and are handled piecemeal by clerks in assembly line fashion.

Other examples indicate that the most menial tasks and job classifications have been eliminated by computerization. Clerks perform only the more demanding aspects of the old jobs. Further, more variety, control, and analysis are involved in the new clerk jobs. In fact, some clerks feel insecure because their new jobs are less routine.

In another case a team organization of responsibilities instead of individual functional specialization has been used following computerization. This system allows for more variety and is an excellent means for training new clerks. A similar form of organizing clerical functions is described by Mann and Williams:

> The work of the non-mechanized accounting groups responsible for the steps preparatory to the machine handling of the customer's account was completely reorganized. The specialized tasks previously done in five separate sections were consolidated into a "station arrangement," and each member of a station was trained

to handle all five operations as part of a new, enlarged job. . . . The members of each team gained considerable job satisfaction from helping train others in their own specialty. Problems, where they did occur, were most prevalent among older employees.[7]

It was also found that job duties are subject to more precise description under computerization. The corollary, of course, is that measurement of performance also becomes more precise.[8] Procedures built into the computer allow the mass of information processing to be accomplished with little or no judgment being exercised by the clerks. Even most exceptions to the procedure which the computer returns for individual attention may be handled in a prescribed manner. As Mehl points out:

> Control can then be exercised, not on questions of form, but on essential problems, efficiency of decisions taken, reaction of persons concerned, regulation problems, human relations, etc.[9]

This new precision under computerization allows for quicker error detection, for designation of the individual responsible for the error, and for correction at an earlier stage of information processing. These observations, based upon data from the surveyed firms, are consistent with Mann's and Williams' findings:

---

[7] *Ibid.*, p. 253. The answer to the question of whether employees actually prefer job enlargement is usually assumed to be affirmative. That this may not be valid is suggested by the fact, mentioned above, that less routine has bred insecurity in some employees. Kilbridge also comments on this possibility:

> . . . 104 workers, roughly half the sample, showed a preference for smaller assembly tasks; 74, or about 37 per cent, seemed indifferent to the size of the task; and 24, or about 12 per cent, preferred larger tasks.

From M. E. Kilbridge, "Do Workers Prefer Larger Jobs?," *Personnel*, 37:no 5, 48 (September-October, 1960). For an excellent study of the economic, technological, and behavioral aspects of a job enlargement program in a manufacturing firm, see Eaton H. Conant and Maurice D. Kilbridge, "An Interdisciplinary Analysis of Job Enlargement: Technology, Costs, and Behavioral Implications," *Industrial and Labor Relations Review*, 18:no. 3, 377-397 (April, 1955).

[8] There is ample evidence that work measurement and standards techniques, long applied to the production floor, are being modified for application to office work. Computers are playing a key role in this important development by pinpointing employee performance and establishing new standards. "Desk Work Gets Faster Countdown," *Business Week*, 1887:91 (October 30, 1965).

[9] Lucien Mehl, "Automation in Public Administration," *Views on Automation* (Paris: Organisation for European Economic Cooperation, 1956), 15.

Under the old system,...a number of individuals shared responsibility for a given phase of the process and a number of check points were relied upon to eliminate errors or to pin-point the responsibility for a given error. Under the new system, however, errors were immediately detected within the processing system and responsibility for the error readily traced. Such changes allowed the development of tighter standards of performance, and the increasing cost of errors augmented concern for standards.[10]

Social Context

Specifically noted among the changes effectuated in the social system aspect of the work process was the impersonality of establishing the pace of work and the narrowing of status differences among jobs. The literature contains polar views on the impact on social factors of increasing mechanization of clerical work. Mills finds that many of the social characteristics which distinguish the office from the factory are disappearing.

> The new office is rationalized: machines are used, employees become machine attendants; the work, as in the factory, is collective for interchangeable, quickly replaceable clerks; it is specialized to the point of automatization.[11]

He goes on to say:

> Mechanized and standardized work, the decline of any chance for the employee to see and understand the whole operation, the loss of any chance, save for a few, for private contact with those in authority — these form the model of the future. At present, status complications inside the office and store are still often quite important in the psychology of the employee; but in the main drift, technical and economic factors and the authoritative line-up will gain ascendency over such status factors as now interfere with the rationalization of the white-collar hierarchy.[12]

---

[10] Mann and Wiliams, *op. cit.*, p. 254.

[11] C. Wright Mills, *White Collar* (New York: Oxford University Press, 1951), 209.

[12] *Ibid.*, p. 212.

Lockwood, at the other extreme, feels that the modern office is not subject to the depersonalizing effects of mass production as in manufacturing.

There is no radical break between management and clerks corresponding to that between the "office" and the "works." ... The rationalization and routinization of work and the disciplined impersonality of the superordinate and subordinate relationship go together. Office work is most frequently not of the character that can be subjected to factory-work rhythm, and office relations form a social system in which work has traditionally been maximized by personal, rather than by impersonal command. . . .

Not only are clerical staffs separated physically to to a great extent among departments and thrown together into small working groups with managers and supervisors, but they also tend to be separated individually from each other by the authority and status hierarchy of the company.[13]

The survey data indicate that under computerization Mills' view is probably more accurate although somewhat overstated. Work status differentials are being narrowed, with the higher rated jobs being fractionalized and the lower rated jobs eliminated. The team form of organization tends, also, to make minor job differences less significant.

The pace and control of work tend to be determined impersonally.[14] The use of schedules, manuals, procedures, and codes, for example, relieves the supervisor of giving numerous direct orders to his subordinates. Woodward comments on this impersonalization of the control function in another context.

At the top of the scale the exercise of control was so mechanical and exact that pressure on people was again at a minimum. Productivity was related only indirectly to human effort; on the whole, people were hard-pressed only when things went wrong. Moreover, the plant

[13] David Lockwood, *The Blackcoated Worker* (London: George Allen and Unwin, Limited, 1958), 79.

[14] The changes in superior-subordinate relationships that occur as a result are described by Arlen Gray in "Problems of Adjustment in the Automated Office," *Personnel,* 41:no. 4, 48 (July-August, 1965).

itself constituted a framework of discipline and control. Any demands on the operators were in fact made by the process rather than by supervision. Most of those interviewed seemed to resent authority less when exercised over them by the process than by a superior.[15]

The centralization tendencies made possible by computerization allowed at least one manager to exert closer "visual control" over his subordinates. This decrease in dispersion — in Moore's phrase, "social spatial dispersion"[16] — may have a personalizing or depersonalizing effect, depending upon how it is used.

Finally, the question of whether or not clerical employees will be able to identify upward with their managers to the same degree as before computerization is not answered by the survey data. There is some evidence to suggest that the organization of work is as important as standardization and specialization in determining the size of the work group with which a clerical employee becomes acquainted.

Employee attitudes toward computerization were not studied in the surveyed firms. However, the reaction of employees to computerization and its impact on their work environment in a shoe manufacturing firm was studied by Lee. He found that:

   1. All employees, both managerial and clerical, felt that the computer installation had imposed an increased number of deadlines on their jobs. They also felt that their work required an increased amount of cooperation with other departments.

   2. Both employee groups thought that their freedom and flexibility in adopting their own work methods had been reduced because of the computers. On the other hand, they thought that the variety of tasks in their jobs had been increased. The magnitude of these changes was comparatively small, however.

   3. The clerical employees felt that there had been a marked decrease in their ability to control the pace

15 Joan Woodward, *Management and Technology* (London: Department of Scientific and Industrial Research, 1958), 29.

16 Leo B. Moore, "How to Manage Improvement," *Harvard Business Review*, 36:no. 4, 146 (July-August, 1958).

and sequence of their work, whereas the managerial employees felt only a slight decrease in this respect.

4. All employees expressed increased satisfaction with their work. The managerial employees as a whole were relatively more content with the work conditions after the computer installation than the clerical.[17]

Aspects of the work environment which merit special consideration are the traditional social and economic distinctions which delineate plant and office work. In the next section these plant-office differences are discussed as they are influenced by computerization.

E.D.P. AND PLANT-OFFICE DIFFERENCES

The introduction of computerized office operations has tended to eliminate the technical and social barriers which separate white collar from blue collar operations. Further mechanization in the factory has had the same effect. This trend is noted both in the literature and in the survey firms.

Diebold comments that with increasing mechanization of offices and plants, the new emphasis will be on the business as a whole rather than on its separate parts.

Automation is going to change the traditional distinction between plant and office, linking them together as a single interconnected system. Up until now, there has been little real consideration of the plant and the office as essential and fundamental parts of the whole.[18]

Mills' observation on the implications of increasing mechanization in offices stresses the lessening of social differences between the plant and the office.

In the office, as we have seen, white-collar technology and social rationalization have definitely lessened technical differences between white-collar and factory work.[19]

17 H. C. Lee, "Do Workers Really Want Flexibility on the Job?," *Personnel*, 42:no. 2, 76 (March-April, 1965).

18 John Diebold, "Automation as a Management Problem," Jacobson, Boone, and Roucels, eds., *Automation and Society* (New York: Philosphical Library, 1959), 319.

19 Mills, *op. cit.*, p. 245. In this connection, it is interesting to note that the proportion of men in a firm's office work force has grown under computerization. See Roy B. Helfgott, "EDP and the Office Work Force," *Industrial and Labor Relations Review*, 19:no. 4, 510-512 (July, 1966).

Finally, Bright states that the linking of office and plant technologies is the foremost accomplishment of current technological changes.

In my opinion, the most significant trend in mechanization is the merging of data-processing systems with production machinery. Five years ago the process engineer and the production manager had, we thought, little mechanization interest in common with the accountant and the treasurer. Factory and office automation were separate fields. Such an approach and philosophy would be wrong today. Indeed, the trend is in exactly the opposite direction.[20]

These statements in the literature indicate that there are forces working in the plant and in the office to remove technical and social distinctions which have grown over the last half century.

Extension of E.D.P. into the Plant

The extension of E.D.P. into the plant was observed in two manufacturing firms in the survey sample. In both of these, stresses were generated between two functional groups because each felt that control of E.D.P. should rest with itself.

Finance versus Industrial Engineering: The systems manager in the controller's department decided to computerize. This decision extended to information procedures in the manufacturing departments of the firm. A conflict arose with the engineering department which was responsible for clerical and industrial procedures in these operating departments.

A compromise was negotiated by these two competing groups: the controller's systems group was to be responsible for programming, coding, and computer operation, plus systems work *in the office alone;* the industrial engineering group was to handle all the other systems activities. However, this "gentleman's agreement" was broken; the industrial engineers did not move ahead with plant clerical systems, primarily be-

---

[20] James R. Bright. "Are We Falling Behind in Mechanization?," *Harvard Business Review,* 38:no. 6, 103 (November-December, 1960).

cause their major interests were in the industrial rather than the clerical procedures.

The controller's systems group brought the issue to a head by submitting a carefully documented E.D.P. proposal to top management. Top management approval established the indisputable authority of the controller's systems group to systematize and computerize clerical procedures in all areas of the firm.

A new disagreement is now developing in this firm. As E.D.P. reaches deeper and deeper into manufacturing areas, the controller and the manufacturing manager are beginning to lock horns over who should control the new systems and the machine center. This issue was more clearly defined in another surveyed firm.

Finance versus Manufacturing: The manufacturing manager of this firm feels that current activities extending E.D.P. into his area of responsibility will, in a matter of time, eliminate distinctions between engineering, cost accounting, and finance. Therefore, he considers a fight between the finance manager and himself for control of the new system to be inevitable.

For his part the finance manager agrees that a showdown is approaching. Consolidation of machine room functions and the desire of each of these men to control activities which are crucial to their operations emphasize the need for top management organization planning. For the time being each of these managers is waiting to see what direction the extension of E.D.P. will take. The objectives of the systems now being implemented and the comments of the two managers indicate that changes now taking place are altering plant-office functions and responsibilities in this firm. The creation of new job responsibilities and the elimination of old ones are changing the internal job structures within all computerized firms.

CHANGING JOB HIERARCHIES

Altered work processes are reflected also by changes in a firm's internal labor force. In his study of computerization, Burack attempted to define those organizational characteristics that led to significant dislocations of managerial personnel. He found that the banks and insurance companies in his survey, where the severest impact was felt, had these features in common:

Information Features:
— large volume of activities,
— standardized procedures which were programmable.

Organization Features:
— important activities built around transactions or computation,
— large clerical and staff groups (in routine work) characterized by high turnover who are difficult to hire and retain,
— large middle management groups committed to many routine activities.[21]

These characteristics must affect clerical personnel greatly in order to be significant as indicators of managerial dislocation. There have been several recent reports on significant changes in occupational structures under computerization.

Hill reported on job changes in a large, investor-owned gas and electric utility. Computerization of the customer accounting department brought these changes: there were 28 job types before and 32 job types after E.D.P. was introduced; 8 job types underwent no change: those closely tied to customer service, and those related to the unique demands of individual supervisors; 11 types of jobs were eliminated: jobs entailing the recording, checking, or filing of data; 9 of the original 28 job types were revised under E.D.P., i.e., they served the same purpose but required a different manner of performance; and finally, 15 new job types were created, most being involved with input preparation and equipment operation.[22]

---

[21] Elmer H. Burack, "The Impact of the Computer on Business Management," *The Business Quarterly*, 31:no. 1, 43 (Spring, 1966).

[22] Walter A. Hill, "The Impact of E.D.P. Systems on Office Employees: Some Empirical Conclusions," *Academy of Management Journal*, 9:no. 1, 13-15 (March, 1966).

Based upon his analysis of these job changes, Hill concludes in part:

The types of jobs which tend to be eliminated as a result of the installation of an EDP system are generally jobs such as posting, checking records, computing, filing, sorting, and tabulating, which are clerical in nature, relatively repetitive, and not related directly to customer contacts.

The new jobs which are created tend to be jobs which are concerned directly with either the computer "hardware" or the transformation of data into a form acceptable to the computer.[23]

Lee documents such job changes in the data processing department of the shoe firm mentioned previously. Employment increased from 46 in 1955 to 91 in 1962. Additional personnel were required for systems, programming, equipment operation, and keypunch jobs.[24]

In another report on the shoe firm, Lee summarized his findings with regard to the impact of the computer on job skill. He collected data on three line departments that were affected by computerized procedures and determined the degree of job changes on skilled and unskilled employee classifications. Lee found that:

1. The total number of employees in the three departments decreased from 186 to 120, a 35.5 percent reduction, between 1955 and 1963.

2. There was no increase in the number of skilled jobs. The managerial-technical employees decreased from 36 to 32 for an 11.1 percent reduction, and clerical personnel decreased from 150 to 88 for a 41.3 percent reduction.

3. The proportion of the skilled managerial-technical employees increased from 19.4 percent of the entire work force in the three affected departments in 1955 to 26.7 percent in 1963, while the proportion of the unskilled clerical employees decreased from 80.6 to 70.3 per cent during the same period.[25]

23 Ibid., p. 18.
24 Hak Chong Lee, "On Information Technology and Organization Structure," Academy of Management Journal, 7:no. 1, 208 (September, 1964).
25 H. C. Lee, "Electronic Data Processing and Skill Requirements," Personnel Administration, 29:no. 3, 51 (May-June, 1966).

The most comprehensive and detailed analysis of the computer's impact on job structure was reported recently by Delehanty. He attempted to measure occupational changes in several large clerical operations.[26] One firm in his survey, firm A, provided the most extensive data and was characteristic of the other firms as well. A detailed analysis of job structure changes for the period 1952-1964 is shown in Table 1.

The table records some very striking changes. They are indicated by comparing total yearly employment measured against data for 1953 as the base year. There was a 29 percent relative *decline* in beginning or low skill entry jobs by 1964. All other job categories experienced a relative *increase* as follows: middle clerical — 24 percent, upper clerical — 21 percent, technical — 11 percent, managerial specialists — 50 percent, junior officers — 38 percent, and senior officers — 25 percent increases.[27] These data indicate a general upgrading of the work force, especially at the middle clerical and middle management levels of the organization. It is these groups which enjoyed the greatest increase in the number of people employed during the 1953-1964 period.[28]

What, in summary, do these research reports on job structure tell us about changes in office work? Computerized work procedures have been accompanied by a sharp increase in the relative proportion of employees in managerial and technical groups. There is also a reduction in the number of low level clerical employees and an increase in the number of high level clerical employees. Finally, there is a greater proportion of managerial to clerical employees in the studies reported upon. Such developments in work processes and jobs are of vital concern to a firm in determining its manpower requirements. This topic is explored in the next chapter.

---

[26] George E. Delehanty, "Office Automation and the Occupation Structure," *Industrial Management Review*, 7:no. 2, 99-109 (Spring, 1966).
[27] *Ibid.*, p. 103.
[28] *Ibid.*, p. 104.

Table 1

Company A: Home Office Work Force Distribution by Type of Job, December, 1952, to December, 1964

	1952	1953	1954	1955	1956	1957	1958	1959	1960	1961	1962	1963	1964
BEGINNING JOBS Typist and mail and file clerks	60.4	54.1	53.8	50.8	48.7	47.8	46.8	45.5	45.0	42.8	39.4	39.3	38.4
MIDDLE CLERICAL Clerk stenographers, Junior secretaries	19.6	24.2	24.7	26.3	27.5	27.7	28.0	28.7	28.4	29.5	30.6	30.6	31.7
UPPER CLERICAL Senior secretaries, first level of supervision	6.9	8.1	7.6	8.0	8.1	8.5	8.9	9.0	9.2	9.6	10.3	10.5	10.2
TECHNICAL JOBS Assistant managers	5.8	6.6	6.6	6.9	7.1	7.0	6.9	7.2	7.3	7.6	8.1	7.8	7.4
MANAGERIAL SPECIALISTS High-level staff, professional	4.1	3.3	3.9	4.1	4.3	4.7	4.7	4.9	5.2	5.3	6.2	6.2	6.6
JUNIOR OFFICERS	2.5	2.8	2.5	3.0	3.3	3.4	3.7	3.8	3.9	3.9	4.1	4.4	4.5
SENIOR OFFICERS	0.7	0.9	0.9	0.9	1.0	0.9	1.0	1.0	1.0	1.3	1.3	1.2	1.2

Source: George E. Delehanty, "Office Automation and the Occupation Structure," Industrial Management Review, 7:no. 2, 103 (Spring, 1966).

Chapter X

THE NEW WHITE COLLAR JOB MARKET

We can all agree that the need for machine operators, computer programmers, and systems personnel is acute and becoming worse. I know companies that will hire, on the spot, anyone that has seen a computer or who has an uncle that has taught him the word "modular" or "binary." The thinking is that, "This person is not completely ignorant of machines and therefore he can be trained." But, can he be or should he be?
— HARVEY W. PROTZEL

Management attention has been focused upon the staffing process under computerization.[1] With electronic data processing, the availability of skills often determines the rate at which the new technology may be exploited. Computerized firms have more and tougher staffing problems as the human factor of production rather than technology has been recognized as a major bottleneck retarding progress. This general staffing problem has several facets. The attraction of suitable job applicants to the firm is more difficult. Clerical and machine operator (worker) problems are unlike management and technical (professional) problems in this regard. Changes in promotion from within policies are also apparent. Selection procedures and selection criteria are not the same after the computer arrives. Placement, replacement, and transfer procedures differ. Involuntary separations may occur because of computerization. Let's look at each in more detail.

RECRUITMENT

Computerization affects the manner in which a firm finds and

[1] This chapter is based, in part, upon my article, "The Staffing Process and the Computer," *Management of Personnel Quarterly*, 1:no. 5, 32-36 (Autumn-Winter, 1962).

attracts potential employees. Increasing mechanization of office work affects the kinds of experience and skill required of as well as the sources for qualified manpower. Statements in the literature and data from the surveyed firms suggest that recruitment policies and procedures are changing to meet these new requirements. The implications for clerical, machine operator, and managerial recruitment are discussed separately because of important differences.

Clerical and Machine Operator Recruitment

Requirements: Computerization eliminates the most menial and the most highly skilled jobs of clerks. For example, some filing and posting clerks' jobs in the lower job classifications, and accounting and bookkeeping clerks' jobs in the higher job classifications have been eliminated. The middle classifications have been bolstered by increasing demands for coders, control clerks, and clerks whose jobs include a wider variety of smaller tasks.[2]

The growth of the machine center has increased its requirements for keypunch operators, machine attendants, and console operators. Some of these jobs, e.g., the punching of paper tape, have been transferred to operating departments. The maintenance of E.D.P. equipment does not create a major new skill need.

Maintenance of E.D.P. equipment is a small work element in the computerization process. If the computer is purchased, the manufacturer is responsible for upkeep during the trial period. After satisfactory performance levels are reached and any malfunctions corrected, a firm usually has three options: 1) to

---

2 These changes correspond with the findings of a study conducted by the Bureau of Labor Statistics:

A little over 80 percent of the employees affected by the change were in jobs involving posting, checking, and maintaining records, filing, computing, or tabulating, keypunch, and related machine operations. Most of the remainder were in administrative, supervisory, and accounting work. Only a little over 4 per cent were engaged in the less routine clerical jobs such as correspondence, stenographic, and secretarial work.

From "Adjustments to the Introduction of Office Automation," *Bureau of Labor Statistics Bulletin Number 1276* (Washington, D.C.: United States Government Printing Office, United States Department of Labor, May, 1960), 3.

purchase equipment servicing from the manufacturer, 2) to hire company staff to perform maintenance, or 3) to contract out the responsibility to someone other than the manufacturer. Typically the equipment is rented; the rental charge includes the cost of upkeep.

Potential Applicants: The quality of applicants for clerical and machine operator jobs in the surveyed firms has remained about the same or, perhaps, has risen slightly. Their major recruiting effort continues to be directed at recent high school graduates. But the requirements for machine room employees often include training beyond high school. For example, tabulating clerks typically must have attended classes to familiarize them with office equipment. Console operators, too, must have thorough training in the operating techniques of the extremely complicated computer controls. Applicants often must demonstrate their typing proficiency in order to qualify as trainees for keypunch operator positions.

Present Employees: Computerization reduces the number of employees in the affected departments. The Bureau of Labor Statistics reports that employment in these affected departments decreased 25 percent on the average.[3]

Lee reports on the computer's impact on employment in four departments in a shoe firm:

> Combining all three operating departments and the Data Processing Department, the total number of employees declined from 232 to 211 from 1955 to 1962. While clerical manpower was decreased by 31 (from 186 to 155), managerial manpower was increased by 10 (from 46 to 56) over the same period. In 1955, before the installation of computers, the total employment was divided into 19.8% managerial and 80.2% clerical. However, in 1962, after the installation of computers, managerial personnel constituted 26.5% and clerical 73.5% of the total work force. There was an increase of 6.7% in the proportion of managerial work force to the total over the seven year period. This increase was primarily due to the displacement of clerical workers and the expansion in managerial work

[3] *Ibid.*

because of computer applications. Obviously, this increase in managerial responsibilities was for technical activities rather than additional human resources.[4]

It is not surprising, then, that a manager in one of the surveyed firms feels that since there are fewer employees in his computerized department, he requires better people. A supervisor in this manager's department commented that since his section was computerized, better qualified employees have been recruited.

The demand for clerical labor in computerized firms has grown less rapidly than has that for office employment in general. For example, the B. L. S. found:

Over the 4 years from December 1953 to December 1957, total office employment at 17 of the offices studied increased an average of 7 per cent. This increase, however, was less than the 15 per cent rise reported for clerical and kindred workers in the Nation as a whole.[5]

In a later B.L.S. study it is reported that the growth rate of office personnel for the more advanced computerized firm is less than that for its less technologically advanced competitors. For the 207 insurance firms surveyed it was found that:

After the initial conversion to E.D.P. was completed, the annual rate of growth in office employment in surveyed companies declined from 4.2 percent to 2.4 percent a year. Those responding companies which had more recently installed computers experienced a constant rate of increase in office employment. The comparison indicates that after an initial adjustment period (and perhaps after attrition has begun to affect growth), E.D.P. begins to break the rapid growth in office staff otherwise experienced by many insurance companies.[6]

Upgrading and elimination of the most menial clerical jobs also tend to raise applicant requirements. Several personnel departments place the most gifted new employees in the

[4] Hak Chong Lee, "On Information Technology and Organization Structure," *Academy of Management Journal*, 7:no. 1, 209 (September, 1964).

[5] "Adjustments to the Introduction of Office Automation," *op. cit.,* p. 4.

[6] "Impact of Office Automation in the Insurance Industry," *Bureau of Labor Statistics Bulletin Number 1468* (Washington, D.C.: United States Government Printing Office, United States Department of Labor, 1966), 5.

machine and computerized clerical areas. This is because the demands of the jobs are greatest in those areas and provide the greatest opportunity for advancement.

One top manager interviewed holds the opinion that the recruitment policy of his firm should be revised drastically to take full advantage of the new computerized systems. He is thinking seriously of restricting hiring to males only.[7] The goal is to recruit and to develop a more stable, better educated work force with a higher potential for growth. He recognizes that salaries will have to be raised but thinks that the resultant efficiencies, including less turnover, would more than offset the increased salary costs.

In general, the recruitment of an adequate clerical and machine operator work force in computerized firms has not created any major problems. The managerial manpower needs of the computerized firms, on the other hand, have not been met as easily.

Management and Technical Recruitment

Computerization has created a demand for new, high level skills that relate to the administration of, conversion to, and operation of E.D.P. systems. Recruiting qualified or potential systems analysts, programmers, and computer operators is the most critical manpower problem faced by the surveyed firms.[8] These new skills are related to systems analysis and machine operations. The number of personnel so involved, it should be emphasized, is minute compared to the total employee population of a firm. The B. L. S. found that there were in these positions an average of twenty-nine employees in each of twenty private industry offices operating large computers.[9]

---

[7] This opinion was expressed prior to the passage of legislation prohibiting discrimination in hiring based upon sex.

[8] In his survey of eleven firms in the Minneapolis-St. Paul area, Vergin found that "In these firms the major unforeseen and, in many instances, still unconquered problem was that of building an expert E.D.P. staff." From Roger C. Vergin, "Staffing of Computer Departments," *Personnel Administration*, 28:no. 4, 6 (July-August, 1965). For suggestions on how recruiters can do a better job in this regard see W. H. Griffin, "Staffing an E.D.P. Installation," *Personnel*, 42:no. 3, 60-66 (May-June, 1965).

[9] "Adjustments to the Introduction of Office Automation," *op. cit.*, p. 4.

Close to 7 out of 10 persons in electronic data-processing work were in programming and planning positions,
about a quarter were engaged in operating the equipment, and 8 per cent of the group were in administrative and supervisory positions.[10]
According to statistics provided by Richi and Alli, 3,742
employees held similar positions at 238 government installations. The average number of such employees at each installation was 16, well below the B. L. S. figure of 29; 8 percent
were in administration, 16.4 percent were management analysts, 47.4 percent were programmers, 2.2 percent were electronics technicians, 16.6 percent were computer systems operators, and 9.3 percent operated peripheral equipment.[11]
In a B. L. S. survey of 206 insurance firms, it is reported that
employment in E.D.P. units climbed from about 600 in 1954
to about 15,000 in 1963. The average number of employees per
unit was 74, with a range of 5 to 1,391 employees. The occupational breakdown for the E.D.P. units is as follows: input
personnel—37.0 percent; supporting clerical workers—22.5 percent; systems analysts, planners, and programmers—21.6 percent; computer operators—14.6 per cent; supervisors—3.9 percent; and computer maintenance engineers—0.5 percent.[12]
The increase in total E.D.P. unit employment probably is
due in part to the centralization of machine operation and input
preparation tasks. This also explains in some measure the
relative decrease of systems analysts and programmer personnel
to total unit employment. The job applicant sources and qualifications as well as the recruitment pattern for these new E.D.P.
positions have changed over time in the surveyed firms.

Recruitment: Inside or Outside the Firm?

The computer feasibility study committee provides a nucleus
for future systems and machine operations managers. The major
recruitment effort actually is required after the committee has

10 *Ibid.*
11 Richard W. Riche and William E. Alli, "Office Automation in the Federal
Government," *Monthly Labor Review*, 83:no. 9, 937 (Washington, D.C.: United
States Government Printing Office, September, 1960).
12 "Impact of Office Automation in the Insurance Industry," *op. cit.*, pp. 25-27.

recommended the purchase or rental of a computer, and top management has approved it. At this point the recruitment of a professional and technical staff to exploit computerization becomes vital for future success.

The Initial Approach: The initial effort to recruit a staff in the surveyed firms was generally not well organized. In several of these firms a promotion from within policy and informal adherance to seniority required that new openings be filled by company applicants.[13]

In one firm systems analysts and programmers were "hand picked by the systems manager after scouting around the company." In another firm bad economic conditions forced a cutback in operations. Displaced managerial personnel were assigned to the E.D.P. department. In another company a memorandum was circulated asking department managers to recommend likely candidates for E.D.P. positions. The department managers, many of whom were antagonistic toward E.D.P. anyway, used this as a signal to unload their least competent managers and supervisors. One manager admitted that he faced a difficult problem in recruiting the best qualified applicants from the various departments. He complained, "I needed the complete support of the senior vice president to finally dislodge them."

The difficulties associated with recruiting qualified applicants forced many a company to go outside the firm to obtain high caliber people. The line departments, at the same time, stopped recommending applicants when, as in one instance, seven out of nine failed to pass training tests and were returned to their old departments. Failures on the part of the computer installations to meet conversion schedules and increasing pressure to move ahead more quickly finally hastened the decision to recruit applicants from outside the company as well.

The Revised Approach: At present, with two exceptions, the

---

[13] In the B. L. S. report based on 35 returns from insurance firms, it is shown that about 72 percent of the E.D.P. staff were selected from within the company. *Ibid.,* p. 30. Vergin also found that most of the eleven firms in his survey depended entirely on developing programmers from their own personnel. Vergin, *op. cit.,* p. 8.

systems and computer staffs in the surveyed firms contain some mixture of personnel recruited both from within and from without. The employees who have been recruited outside the company, with few exceptions, are recent college graduates. They do programming work primarily. Several companies have hired computer manufacturing representatives to do systems work or to manage computer operations.

For example, one firm has three systems analyst-programmer men who have been promoted from within, and nine new, young employees, six of whom are recent college graduates. The systems manager related how he had staffed his group.

> An effort was made to secure competent, trained men for the Data Processing staff from within the company. We were able to secure the release of only three men, one from each of the following departments: Sales Engineering, Planning, and Auditing. The Personnel Department gave us excellent cooperation by undertaking an active recruiting program. Soon we had recruited the nine new men we needed.

One of the most important contributions to the computerization effort made by personnel departments in all the surveyed firms was recruiting applicants for positions on the systems and computer staff. Many of these firms previously had very rarely gone to the labor market to bring in specialized skills, such as a knowledge of computers, and in the case of programmers, potential, as indicated by a college degree.

In the next section the process is explored by which the most promising E.D.P. job candidates are screened out from the many who are made available by both internal and external recruitment.

SELECTION

In discussing the selection process for positions affected by E.D.P., it is important to reiterate that a relatively small group of employees in a firm is involved. For instance, the B. L. S. found that an average of only 5 percent of total office employees in twenty firms studied were affected directly by computerization.[14] The group of employees, then, who designs the systems, programs them, and operates the computer and its peripheral equipment constitutes considerably less than 5 percent of total office employment. In the insurance study the B. L. S. found that about 4 percent of the total office staff were E.D.P. unit employees.[15]

Another clarifying statement is in order before discussing the E.D.P. personnel selection process in detail. The major employee component as measured by numerical strength in this group, programming personnel, represents the chief selection problem, just as was true with recruitment. Selection procedures for clerical positions in computerized operations have remained basically unchanged by the introduction of E.D.P. Therefore, the following discussion of selection is relevant primarily to a small group of new positions created by E.D.P.

Development of Procedures

Consistent with the initial policy of recruitment from within, the firms tended to overemphasize company experience as a requirement for success in the E.D.P. occupations. The firms that sought to abide by their commitment to promote from within whenever possible also thought that knowledge of the particular business was an essential job requirement. This initial approach to selection for E.D.P. positions is characterized below:

> The pattern that emerges when one carefully studies the recruitment and selection practices that were reported is one of a high degree of informality in such practices as systematic evaluation of experience and training, standardization of the oral interview practices and means of making and recording the results of supervisory evaluations. Further, the written test appears to be spottily used and rather casual use seems to be made of the training processes as a selection device. Finally, there is a great deal of conflict of opinion on

[14] "Adjustments to the Introduction of Office Automation," *op. cit.*, p. 4.
[15] "Impact of Office Automation in the Insurance Industry," *op. cit.*, p. 4.

the relative values of promotion from "within" versus recruitment from "without" in selecting A.D.P. (automatic data processing) personnel.[16]

Examples from the surveyed firms illustrate how these rather informal procedures affected the selection process. One department head said he had selected five young men "who had imagination, intelligence, and were not tied up" for analyst-programmer training. Another manager selected analyst-programmers on the basis of personality, since he felt this was important in dealing with line managers in systems activities.

In one firm the financial vice-president and the three other members of the computer feasibility study group "selected twelve young men, all college graduates, and with an average of three years of seniority" to fill programming positions. It is worth emphasizing that these twelve men did not volunteer for or evince interest in any of these openings in any formal manner.

Finally, the following criteria for selection of managers for systems and computer operations were characteristic for all the surveyed firms during the early stages of computerization. In one firm a manager was selected because he had participated in the feasibility study, another because he had knowledge of the line areas which would be immediately affected by E.D.P.; a third manager did not know why he had been chosen.[17]

It Paid Off to Speak Up: A young manager explained how he had become an analyst-programmer. He had begun his career in the firm performing routine clerical work in a branch office. He became dissatisfied, threatened to leave and join a competitor, and "fussed." As a result of these expressions of dissatisfaction he was transferred to a department in the home office of

[16]"Use of Electronic Data-Processing Equipment," *Hearings before the Subcommittee on Census and Government Statistics of the Committee on Post Office and Civil Service, House of Representatives* (Washington, D.C.: United States Government Printing Office, 1959), 133. For a detailed list of methods used to select employees for E.D.P. positions in twenty firms, see also pp. 213-244.

[17]Vergin reports that during computerization's pioneering days the eleven firms in his study relied primarily upon the personal qualities projected by prospective programmers in the selection process. More recently the firms have relied upon the Programmers Aptitude Test (P.A.T.), Vergin, *op. cit.,* p. 8.

the firm as a trainee for a higher position in a branch office. While waiting for the training program to start, he was "selected" by the home office department head to represent his department as an analyst-programmer trainee.

At first the E.D.P. managers were unhappy about the choice. The future analyst-programmer was unhappy also. He did not know what the job would entail and had no interest in E.D.P., but was "persuaded" by his department head and the personnel department to accept the assignment. The strenuous objections of the E.D.P. managers were overruled also.

He and four other analyst-programmer trainees were assigned to the E.D.P. department. He said at that time, "No one knew what it was all about." After he had spent a "miserable three months" at the work, he began to like it, and today he is a successful analyst-programmer. He has progressed rapidly, which is unusual in this firm, and is grateful for the rather unorthodox selection procedure by which he embarked upon his present career.

Refinement of Procedures: Only after making the initial selection of personnel for E.D.P. positions did management become aware of the need to establish better criteria for selection. E.D.P. managers formulated more accurate ideas about the type of experience and education to look for in applicants for subordinate positions. The need for standard prerequisites rather than dependence upon a manager's intuition had become painfully evident. The refinement of selection techniques was recognized by E.D.P. managers as a necessary concomitant of increasing office mechanization. Managerial requirements change as the technological level of the firm's productive activities rises. Increasingly higher levels of technology demand, in turn, managers with greater specialized knowledge.

Criteria: One change brought about by the new emphasis on the technical requirements of the new E.D.P. positions in the surveyed firms was the downgrading of company experience as as a requisite for success. Slater is representative of those who go even further in this regard:

In operation we have found that an aptitude for computer methods and a concern with systems to be more important than an understanding of the company's routines as such.[18]

The time probably has passed when nineteen out of twenty positions in computer operations, as reported in one study, will be filled from within the firm.[19]

Actually work experience has not been an important consideration when selecting from among applicants recruited outside the firm. Most new employees hired for E.D.P. positions have been assigned to programming activities. These positions, by and large, have been filled by recent college graduates with little or no business experience. Occasionally a seasoned systems analyst is hired from the outside; in such a case experience is an important consideration. Finally, computer operators also have been recruited from outside the firm in limited numbers, and again, previous experience is relevant. Very often employees of the computer manufacturer have provided firms with a source for the latter two types of jobs.

A general statement which describes current selection criteria is quoted below:

> The selection criteria established for the new jobs were experience, proficiency in mathematics, and college training, if any. The latter criterion was considered desirable but not essential, and some of those finally selected were not college graduates.[20]

The educational background of the new programmers varied considerably. For instance, in one systems group the programmers had degrees in mechanical engineering, engineering and business, industrial management, naval architecture, architec-

---

[18] Robert F. Slater, "Thinking Ahead: How Near Is the Automatic Office?," *Harvard Business Review*, 36:no. 2, 168 (March-April, 1958).

Protzel maintains that many people in E.D.P. should not be in the field. He thinks that beside a knowledge of computers and systems, "extensive and diversified business experience" is essential. Harvey W. Protzel, "Personnel Problems in Data Processing Systems: The Approach of Top Management," *Computers and Automation*, 14:no. 8, 16-17 (August, 1965).

[19] "The Introduction of an Electronic Computer in a Large Insurance Company," *Bureau of Labor Statistics Report Number 2, Studies of Automatic Technology* (Washington, D.C.: United States Government Printing Office, United States Department of Labor, 1955), 8.

[20] *Ibid.*

ture, electrical engineering, business administration, and education.

Another criterion appears to be increasingly important for at least the higher managerial positions connected with computerization. This criterion is the ability to abstract and use symbols.

Testing: The use of aptitude tests to predict success in E.D.P. positions is common. It is reported that 73 percent, or 94 out of 129 government agencies surveyed use written tests in selecting E.D.P. personnel. Fifteen of those agencies, or 12 percent, use these tests as a rejection factor, while 79, or 61 percent, use these tests mainly for their prognostic value.[21] That these practices are comparable to those used in private industry is noted in the same report:

> The similarity of selection practices in use in private industry to those used in Government is striking. The so-called I.B.M. aptitude test is the standard test in business even by users of other hardware. There is the same mixed experience with it, the same variation in practice as to use for rejection versus prognostic purposes and the same implicit decision that on balance it is better than nothing.[22]

One survey firm manager who uses the standard I.B.M. test said that "it seems reliable." This firm, which hires E.D.P. personnel only from within, administers the test to applicants from the engineering and finance departments. The manager indicated that his company is "attempting to validate the test by administering it to all types, ages, etc.," and that he found the test "a useful tool."

Another surveyed firm uses a test originally designed for freshmen entering college. The test has two sections, one with mathematical, the other with verbal questions. This test is used in selecting programmers.

Finally, another surveyed firm also uses the latter test for selection purposes. This firm had attempted to recruit all of its

---

21 "Use of Electronic Data-Processing Equipment," *op. cit.,* p. 101, Exhibit 13.

22 *Ibid.* For a detailed analysis of testing procedures in twenty offices studied by the B. L. S., see "Adjustments to the Introduction of Office Automation," *op. cit.,* pp. 45-46.

E.D.P. personnel from within. When a call went out for all interested employees to take this test, over two hundred employees responded. Those selected were: 1) the applicants who scored highest, and 2) those who had not tested well, but had had long company service, or who were being displaced by the computerized operations. Hiring from within failed, and the firm has been forced to seek applicants from outside the company.

The tests administered, their purposes, and their final use varied greatly in the surveyed firms. The supposition made by these firms is that testing applicants for E.D.P. jobs is helpful in making better selections.[23]

New Problems

The new positions created by E.D.P., namely systems analyst, programmer, and computer operator jobs, are highly specialized, yet the skills required to fill them are easily transferable from one firm to another. The long-standing policy of promotion from within, at least for these jobs, has been broken, and, according to Leavitt and Whisler, ". . . multiple entry points into the organization will become increasingly common."[24]

Some of the surveyed firms have begun to notice higher turnover rates among their E.D.P. personnel than among their other employees. In fact some managers are concerned that the newer E.D.P. personnel have not exhibited a strong loyalty to or identity with the company. As their new skills are in short supply, strong labor market pressures are being felt high in the organization, in some firms for the first time.

Lack of loyalty and identity are only two manifestations of the problem of managing technical and professional personnel in business enterprises. The increasing need for improved utilization of these types of employees in office operations under computerization no doubt will arouse the concern and interest

---

[23] Vergin reports success in using psychological tests to aid his clients in the selection of E.D.P. personnel. Vergin, *op. cit.*, p. 17.

[24] Harold J. Leavitt and Thomas L. Whisler, "Management in the 1980's," *Harvard Business Review*, 36:no. 6, 47 (November-December, 1958).

of management to develop more effective personnel policies and practices.

Selection and the Union

The three unionized firms in the Boston survey have not been unduly hampered in selecting employees for E.D.P. jobs in the bargaining unit.[25] As is customary in unionized offices, notices of the E.D.P. jobs to be filled are posted on a bulletin board, so that qualified union members (employees) may apply for them. All union contracts in the surveyed firms provide that selection is to be made on the basis of ability, and only when two applicants are equally qualified will the senior employee get preferential treatment. Thus employees of a firm are given an opportunity to fill the new jobs first, but the firm is perfectly free to set the requirements and to recruit outside the firm if it chooses to do so.

Union contracts apply generally to computer and peripheral equipment operators. The existing contract clauses and the machinery to handle selection of employees for transfer and promotion have sufficed. No special problems have arisen in the surveyed firms, and no issues have been raised by the unions in regard to selection procedures.

PLACEMENT-DISPLACEMENT

Computerization has had little or no effect on the placement of new employees, replacement transfers have created some difficult problems, and the number of separations has been inconsequential in the surveyed firms.

Placement

The placement of new employees in the surveyed firms presented no new problems. In fact, in those companies that organized work on computerized procedures on a team basis, the induction, training, and orientation of new employees were

---

[25] The survey data on unions and their effects on selection of E.D.P. personnel are similar to those found in the B. L. S. survey. See "Adjustments to the Introduction of Office Automation," *op. cit.*, pp. 42 and 45.

improved. The placement of new management or technical employees also was facilitated by computerization. The process of accommodation was enhanced by the emphasis on their technical knowledge or potential rather than on learning the workings of a specific business. Often these new managers and technical personnel received extensive training before they were expected to perform on the job.

Placement in some positions was temporary until the employee proved that he could perform the duties of his job satisfactorily. This aspect of placement is more important than before in many of the surveyed firms. Employees placed in highly sensitive E.D.P. positions must demonstrate their ability and capacity to perform at higher levels than before, because hiring and placement mistakes have more serious consequences for a computerized firm.

Replacement Transfers

The transfer of displaced employees is one of the most exacting problems management faces in dealing with the manpower consequences of E.D.P. Evidently management in the surveyed firms has not planned carefully enough in this regard. Nor is this a small problem in terms of the number of people affected. For instance,

> Within 1 year after the installation of the computer, about one-third of the approximately 2,800 employees in units whose work was directly affected had been reassigned to other positions, either within the same unit or elsewhere in the office.[26]

In a study of ten government agencies employing 1,325,000 persons, it was reported that 1,628 employees were affected by E.D.P. for the years 1961 through 1963.[27]

> Seventy-seven percent of actions affecting the displaced employees were reassignments of which —

[26] *Ibid.*, p. 3.

[27] *A Study of the Impact of Automation on Federal Employees.* Prepared by the United States Civil Service Commission and referred to the Subcommittee on Census and Government Statistics of the Committee on Post Office and Civil Service, House of Representatives, Eighty-Eighth Congress, Second Session (Washington, D.C.: United States Government Printing Office, August, 1964), 11.

8   percent were to higher grades;
86   percent were to the same grades; and
6   percent were to lower grades but only
1.5 percent also involved a loss in salary.[28]

Finally, Hill reports on the job status of transferred employees in his study of utilities. He says that 59 percent of the total number of employees (223) experienced a position change: transferred to other units—34 percent; transferred to computer unit—5 percent; and reassigned within the same work unit—20 percent. These changes took place one year after the introduction of a computer. Eleven percent of the employees experienced no change in position.[29]

In the non-union firms surveyed, policies state that no one will be laid off; and although salaries are not guaranteed, in none of these firms has a job transfer involved a salary decrease. In the unionized firms there are no guarantees of continued employment or maintenance of salary, and in a few instances the bump-back procedure has resulted in a reduction in salary.

Managers in the surveyed firms felt that, on the whole, the impact of computerization on job duties has been greatest for first-line supervision and for the next one or two higher levels in the management hierarchy. The stickiest problem mentioned regarding replacement transfers is the plight of the older supervisor whose specialty no longer has value because of computerization. The section head who no longer can manage his group but is retained in his position, functioning as a "personnel manager," presents a similar problem, though a less common one.

A Lack of Planning: Very little attention has been given to the problem of transferring employees affected by computerization. One firm surveyed does maintain a pool of open requisitions to avoid layoffs and to facilitate efficient replacement transfer of employees. Generally a line department manager transfers a displaced employee to meet changed needs for

---

[28] *Ibid.*
[29] Walter A. Hill, "The Impact of E.D.P. Systems on Office Employees: Some Empirical Conclusions," *Academy of Management Journal*, 9:no. 1, 16 (March, 1966).

manpower in his own department; or an employee is transferred by the personnel manager to another area of the company.

For instance, in one surveyed firm the highest rated clerical classification was for bookkeepers. As the ledger work was put on magnetic tape, bookkeepers were transferred to coding or to paper tape punching jobs, two of the most menial and least skilled jobs in a computerized office. There was much discontent, even though the transferred bookkeepers continued to receive the same salaries while working side by side with newly-hired clerks paid considerably less for performance of the same duties. The bookkeepers who had not yet been transferred morosely awaited the day.

Involuntary Separations

Layoffs from a firm because of computerization are relatively rare. Ginder reports on the findings of a survey to determine the degree of displacement:

> When asked what had happened to the personnel whose jobs were replaced by the machine, the responses from the 219 companies that answered the question were: no jobs replaced—42 per cent; integrated to (*sic*) other departments—36 per cent; integrated into data processing departments—19 per cent; laid off—2.7 per cent; transferred to new location—less than 1 per cent.
>
> The number of employees involved in the loss, transfer, or integration of their jobs totaled 2,552. Of the 6 companies (2.7 per cent) that laid off personnel, only 19 employees, or less than 1 per cent, of the 2,552 affected were laid off.[30]

The B. L. S. reports that separation is a minor part of the total impact of computerization on manpower. Only 19 out of 2,800 employees affected by E.D.P. were laid off.[31] A significant number of voluntary separations (quits), as well as some early retirements and leaves of absence, may have been brought about by E.D.P. These tend to obscure the number of sepa-

---

[30] Charles E. Ginder, "Why Automation?," *Office Executive*, 34:no. 10, 12 (October, 1959).

[31] "Adjustments to the Introduction of Office Automation," *op. cit.*, p. 3.

rations caused by computerization. Nevertheless, these two studies indicate that undisguised involuntary separation from firms because of E.D.P. is rare.

In the 1964 government study discussed before, of the 1,628 employees affected by E.D.P. in the agencies from 1961 through 1963,

> Nine percent of the actions were declinations of re-assignment offers. Only 2 percent of the actions were separations by reduction in force, 6 percent resignations, and 6 percent separations for other reasons, including retirement and refusal to accept reassignment.[32]

Finally, in Hill's study referred to above, resignations, lay-offs, and other separations accounted for 30 percent, or 68 job status changes one year after the introduction of E.D.P. Of these, the majority left for maternity and personal reasons, while 2 percent, or 4 were laid off, and one-half percent, or one was discharged for cause.[33]

The surveyed firms had no relevant statistics on separations because of E.D.P. In no instance were layoffs mentioned as having been necessitated by E.D.P.

Two interesting hiring policies in the surveyed firms, in addition to those already mentioned, related to manpower requirements and possible separation at a later date.

Non-unionized Firm: According to the financial manager of a surveyed firm, all newly hired employees in the E.D.P. and the general accounting departments were told when they were hired that there was a possibility of their being laid off as a result of further computerization. These new employees were considered permanent employees. The objectives of this policy were: 1) not to jeopardize relationships with the community where the firm is located, and 2) not to encourage a job applicant to leave a good job to come to this firm without first knowing the risks involved.

Unionized Firm: Computerization involved running parallel procedures during the de-bugging stage of conversion in one unionized firm. In order to protect the jobs of permanently

---

[32] *A Study of the Impact of Automation on Federal Employees, op. cit.,* p. 11.
[33] Hill, *op. cit.,* p. 16.

employed union members, management and the union worked
out a special employment arrangement. A supplemental agreement to the contract was negotiated authorizing the company
to hire only temporary employees to meet all new manpower
requirements.

The agreement was to be in effect for one and one-half years.
Then, unless these new employees had been terminated by the
company, they would become permanent members of the union
and employees of the company.

At the expiration of the supplemental contract agreement,
all temporary employees were fired, then rehired and placed
on customary six-month probation. Thus, although these former
temporary employees retained their seniority for all benefits, the firm could still fire them at will until the six-month
probation expired.[34]

The major concern which had prompted this special agreement never materialized. The large cutback in manpower fore-
casted by the E.D.P. department did not occur after computerization. When the parallel operating system was
discontinued, the temporary employees were transferred to
other duties.

Enlightened personnel management emphasizes that a firm
must attempt to minimize the impact of change on employees.
Few personnel problems present a greater challenge to a firm
than that of redundant managers.

Managerial Obsolescence

In one surveyed firm thirty-two managers recently were
retired. They were fifty-five years of age and over, but below
normal retirement age. This was a unique experience in the
firm. Early retirement had never been used prior to this time.
The affected managers, in about equal numbers, came from
middle and lower management ranks.

These managers were let go because they had been resistant
to change. It was estimated that about half of these managers

------

[34] If they remained on the firm's payroll for the next five years under the contract, they then could not be laid off for *any* reason.

were affected directly by computerization. They fought to preserve the *status quo* and lost their jobs instead.

An E.D.P. executive noted that top management was less vulnerable. Computerization and other innovations "go around them," and "they are carried" by more dynamic middle managers. Undoubtedly this problem of obsolescence will grow more serious with the extension of computerization and its accelerating impact on the management hierarchy.[35]

---

[35] For a provocative discussion of four methods to attack the problem of managerial obsolescence, see Harold J. Leavitt, "Dealing with Management Obsolescence," in "Computer-Based Management for Information and Control," *American Management Association Bulletin 30* (New York: American Management Association, 1963), 51-52.

Chapter XI

SALARIES, HOURS, AND CONDITIONS OF WORK

The task of wage theory is to specify the factors that determine compensation, the manner in which they do so, and the relative and absolute importance of each.

— David W. Belcher

The managerial policies that determine what an employee is paid, what hours he works, and the environmental conditions in which he works have been relatively unchanged by computerization. The changes that have occurred, although accommodated by existing personnel policies, have nevertheless received special attention. Of particular note, in this regard, are the weights assigned factors for evaluating changed or newly created positions, the impact of the computer on job skills and upgrading, the question of increased shift work, and the implications of machine-paced work in the office environment. These and related matters are treated in this chapter in order to ascertain the impact of computerization on all elements of the employee compensation package.

REMUNERATION

The payment process for office positions has not been altered greatly by computerization. Even in some jobs directly related to electronic data processing, the degree of change has been slight. Data from the surveyed firms indicate that modifications have become necessary in such areas as job analysis, job evaluation, and collective bargaining contracts. The personnel policies regarding remuneration of employees in the surveyed firms have sufficed, but computerization has generated needs and pressures which require some revision and adaptation in the remuneration procedures of these firms.

Job Analysis and Evaluation

Job description and analysis procedures have remained the same under E.D.P., but the relative weight placed on the job factors has changed. A wage and salary administrator indicated that skill, mental capacity, and accountability are still valid factors with which to describe and to analyze clerical jobs for salary evaluation. However, for clerical jobs in computerized departments skill requirements have been deemphasized, accountability has been stressed, and the mental capacity factor has received the same consideration as before. The increasing standardization and routinization of the work process, the greater significance of clerical errors, and the fact that fewer employees are needed under E.D.P. led to the changes.

After the introduction of the computer the firms moved very slowly in changing job descriptions. In fact relatively few jobs have been changed formally. In the non-unionized surveyed firms, the pressures for change are not strong because the employees have no formal means to articulate any dissatifaction occasioned by working at new jobs which have not been analyzed or evaluated for long periods of time after change. The managements of these firms do not wish to analyze or to evaluate these jobs until they are "firmed up." This transition period may take years, since the computerization process is a long term project averaging five years from the time the feasibility study is made till normal operations are achieved.

The unionized firms' experience with job description and analysis has not varied greatly from the above pattern. The unionized firms have been forced to acknowledge job changes faster. One firm negotiated a special agreement with the union to handle job changes.

As originally understood, all temporary upgradings of permanent employees in the Revenue Accounting Department made necessary because of the conversion will not become permanent and will terminate when conversion is completed and the employees will return to their regular pay grades with seniority rights for training and re-adjustment on their permanent roster.

In the two other unionized firms the problem of job description and evaluation is not great. In both of these firms job changes were slight, so that there has been little need to undertake a major reevaluation of clerical jobs. Most of the existing descriptions are broad enough to absorb the amount of change occasioned by E.D.P. Also, the unions involved are not in a position to force the issue militantly, or for other reasons have chosen not to do so.

The surveyed firms, therefore, have not been under strong pressures to revise job descriptions or to reevaluate them immediately following computerization. The problem of over-evaluation of clerical jobs because of miscalculation, therefore, did not occur in the surveyed firms. Bright found overevaluation to be a mistake on management's part in his survey of automation in manufacturing.

> In many cases, the job evaluation analysis will indicate, "This automated job is worth less than the former job." Then the "fair" answer is likely to yield a difficult administrative situation. Shall the job evaluation answer be applied or ignored? If the purpose of job evaluation is considered to be to rate jobs relative to each other and not against some concept of absolute contribution, then it would seem that job evaluation still is feasible although we may have to weigh factors differently or add new ones.[1]

In the surveyed firms new jobs which have required analysis and evaluation fit well within the existing salary structure. Since on the whole no new skills are involved, comparisons with similar jobs in other areas of the firm are possible. Within computerized departments, however, the job hierarchy has been affected.

Management job analysis and evaluation procedures have not been affected by computerization either. When job changes did take place, they have been ignored or they have been recognized by promoting the employees. Jobs of managers

---

[1] James R. Bright, *Automation and Management* (Boston: Division of Research, Harvard University Graduate School of Business Administration, 1958), 208.

whose responsibilities were diluted greatly by E.D.P. have
not been reevaluated; and replacement transfers have been
made with no reduction in these managers' salaries. Promotion
for lower and middle managers often has entailed the same
delay in reevaluation experienced by clerical workers. The
recognition of new responsibilities by higher remuneration
often has been delayed. The one exception in the management
ranks involves programmers.

Programming Positions Are an Exception: Just as the recruitment of programmers is a unique problem for the surveyed
firms, determining programmers' salaries has also received
special consideration. Programmers acquired new skills, training, and status in assuming their responsibilities. While new
clerical jobs can be compared with elements of other jobs
within a firm, the elements of programmer jobs are not comparable. The fact that programmer skills have been in short
supply has made management very sensitive to the relative
proficiencies and salaries of programmers as determined by
market forces.

Job analysis and description vary according to the duties of
programmers in individual firms. The duties have been determined primarily by the level of mechanization and the systems
approach taken by a firm. Job evaluation or payment, on the
other hand, has been determined largely by what other firms
pay for similar positions or "the going rate."[2]

One surveyed firm considers salary determination for its
programmers to be "a special problem." A salary administrator
traveled to several states to talk with personnel managers in
his industry. He asked, "What should we be paying these
people?" The salary administrator brought back job descriptions and salary ranges to compare with those developed by
his firm's systems manager. The salary administrator compared 1) the data collected on his trip, 2) the systems mana-

[2] See, for example, a survey of 2,324 computer users covering 92,000 employees
in 427 cities in "Eighth Annual Report on E.D.P Salaries," *Business Automation,*
13:no. 6, 36-47f (June, 1966).

ger's recommendations, and 3) the salaries for other jobs within the firm.

After considering all the relevant facts, job descriptions and salary ranges were established competitive with the labor market. The salary administrator felt that "the extra effort paid off, since programmers would leave and use their skills in another firm if they were not properly paid."

Obviously, other jobs connected with computerization, both clerical and managerial, have not been subject to the same attention. This same salary administrator said he hadn't "set up job descriptions and evaluations for the clerical employees because the jobs were not as yet firmed up. The procedure is to let the job jell before taking action." It appears that labor market forces are not as pressing for these clerical positions.

Job Skills and Upgrading

It is difficult to generalize about the impact of E.D.P. on job skills and the degree to which upgrading represents changes in job skills. Yet the following general comments provide some insight into what has happened to date in the surveyed firms. The findings of one Bureau of Labor Statistics survey support my observations except with regard to downgrading.

> A little over two-thirds of the employees who remained with the company during the 18 months covered by the study were in positions classified at the same grade as at the beginning of the period; nearly a third had been promoted to higher grade positions; and only a little over 1 per cent had been downgraded.[3]

Salary grades may not accurately reflect skill changes, however, depending upon the manner in which job analysis and evaluation have been handled. Even doing the same type of work in the same grade may entail less skill. New E.D.P. job requirements other than skill may merit the same salary. A firm also may choose to ease the transition to E.D.P. by limiting

---

[3] "Adjustments to the Introduction of Office Automation," *Bureau of Labor Statistics Bulletin Number 1276* (Washington, D.C.: United States Government Printing Office, United States Department of Labor, May, 1960), 33. In this connection it is noteworthy that of these promotions, four out of five people transferred to machine room jobs were ungraded. *Ibid.*, p. 55.

downgrading as a matter of policy. In no instance did a surveyed firm downgrade an employee affected by E.D.P. Changes in the job classification structure as a result of computerization are evident.[4]

Job Classification Structure

In the B. L. S. study referred to above, it is reported that the average job grade has been altered only slightly in the survey sample.

> The introduction of electronic data processing raised the average grade or skill of office occupations, but only to a slight extent. Routine low paid jobs becoming vacant during the transition period were eliminated, which resulted in the higher paid group making up a larger proportion of the total in the affected group. The classification of electronic data processing positions at the top of the office pay structure also tended to upgrade the pattern. Since the newly created positions constituted a small proportion of total office employment, however, the net effect on the structure of an entire office was small.[5]

Mann and Williams refine the B. L. S. statement quoted above in line with the findings of my own survey sample. They find that: 1) some higher clerical jobs have been eliminated, as well as the lowest ones, 2) the complexity of computerized clerical positions has been overrated generally, and 3) programmers should be excluded from the discussion since they are members of management.

> Toward the end of the conversion, an extensive job evaluation and analysis was undertaken by wage analysts and, with the exception of the programming area, there was no significant change in the average job grade. The least interesting and the most menial types of jobs had

---

[4] Bright argues against the popular belief that automation raises the level of work force skills. He claims that with few exceptions the work force in manufacturing will not require higher skills. Bright asserts that the evidence he has seen points to a reduction of skill requirements, and that the unskilled worker will continue to be needed in manufacturing. See James R. Bright, "Does Automation Raise Skill Requirements?," *Harvard Business Review*, 36:no. 4, 85-87 (July-August, 1958).

[5] "Adjustments to the Introduction of Office Automation," *op. cit.*, p. 5.

been eliminated, but so had a number of high-level non-supervisory jobs. Certain previous job grades in the accounting division had been somewhat higher than similar jobs in other parts of the organization, and for the first time in a number of years it was possible to bring these jobs into line with the rest of the company. Moreover, as might be expected, nearly everyone had at the outset overestimated the complexity of the new jobs because there had been no experience with them.[6]

The B. S. L. assessment is further qualified by relevant data from the firms I surveyed. First, not *all* of the lowest classifications have been eliminated, although employees in these classifications are fewer in number. Second, job grade is not necessarily the equivalent of skill level on computerized clerical jobs. Replacement transferees may retain their classification and salary, but their new jobs may require a good deal less skill. Third, as pointed out by Mann and Williams, programmers should not be included in the clerical unit; but if they are, it should be recognized that the upgrading effect of their presence may decrease over time. As more procedures are placed on the computer, the systems analysts and programming staff will not increase proportionally. In fact there is some evidence to suggest that these E.D.P. positions will decrease in number as experience with E.D.P. systems grows and computer languages are developed further.

There is an interesting sidelight to the fact that there are fewer employees in the lowest salary classifications. In one surveyed firm, for example, promotion velocity has increased. According to a personnel representative, employees in grades 1 and 2 used to remain at those grades for an average of two years. Now the average employee remains in classifications 1 and 2 only six months. Since there are fewer employees in the lower grades, their chances for promotion are much greater. This is true, although annual turnover in this particular firm has dropped from 25 to 20 percent under computerization.

This fact of faster promotion itself has some side effects.

[6] Floyd C. Mann and Lawrence K. Williams, "Observations of the Dynamics of a Change to Electronic Data-Processing Equipment," *Administrative Science Quarterly*, 5:no. 2, 246 (September, 1960).

Recruitment is curtailed, but a better qualified applicant with greater potential is sought. The brightest prospects recruited among the June high school graduates are steered into the areas where procedures have been computerized.

Pay Grade Changes

In two recent studies salary grade changes under computerization are documented. Based on these studies the following analysis of changing salary classes provides data which complement the previous discussion of occupational changes. Thus the general upgrading noted before is also confirmed by the following empirical data.

Delehanty's data on the structure of salary grades over time in firm A are depicted in Table 1. Delehanty interprets Table 1, which excludes junior and senior officer salary grades, and the salary movements which accompanied distribution changes as follows:

> In terms of the salary structure underlying these classes, there appears to have been a slight narrowing of various wage differentials. In terms of the minimums of the salary ranges, from 1954-1964, the increase in the minimum for Grade 1 was the greatest of all the grades, and considerably greater than those for Grades 15 and 16.
>
> Considering average salaries, the greatest increases were in Grades 1, 5, and 7, and the smallest were in Grades 9, 11, 13, and 15. For all grades, 1-16, the increase in average salary was about 55%. This reflects the general upgrading of the occupation structure, since the greatest of the increases by grades, that for Level 1, was only about 45%. The standard hiring rate, that for a female high school graduate with no experience, also rose by about 45% from 1954-1964.
>
> While there is some dispersion in the rates of increase in salaries among the various grades, the pay grade structure clearly appears similar enough over the period to justify the assumption made earlier that it is a reasonable basis for measuring the occupational structure.[7]

---

[7] George E. Delehanty, "Office Automation and the Occupation Structure," *Industrial Management Review*, 7:no. 2, 104 (Spring, 1966).

Table 1

Company A: Home Office Work Force

Distribution by Job Grade

Percent of Population by Year

Job Grade	1952	1953	1957	1958	1963	1964
1	14.6	9.4	5.6	5.6	4.0	3.7
2	21.3	22.2	21.4	21.1	18.5	14.9
3	24.2	23.4	19.6	18.6	17.0	17.9
4	11.9	13.9	16.5	15.2	16.6	17.6
5	4.2	6.1	7.3	8.6	9.3	9.7
6	4.2	5.2	5.2	5.6	6.5	6.4
7	2.8	2.7	3.4	3.3	3.4	3.0
8	1.9	2.8	3.1	3.3	3.9	4.0
9	2.5	2.8	2.4	2.7	3.8	3.8
10	2.4	2.7	2.9	2.9	3.3	3.1
11	2.1	2.5	2.6	2.5	2.5	2.5
12	1.5	1.7	1.8	1.8	2.4	2.2
13	0.9	0.9	1.4	1.4	2.0	2.0
14	1.9	1.3	1.4	1.4	2.0	2.0
15	0.7	0.6	1.1	1.1	1.4	1.5
16	0.2	0.3	0.3	0.4	0.7	0.8
20[a]	2.4	0.9	3.3	3.8	2.1	4.3
22[b]	0.5	0.5	0.8	0.7	0.5	0.7

[a]Unclassified jobs likely to be in Grade 11 or below are placed in this class.
[b]Jobs in special categories in the range between Grades 12 and 16 are placed in this class.
Source: George E. Delehanty, "Office Automation and the Occupation Structure," *Industrial Management Review*, 7:no. 2, 103 (Spring, 1966).

These general findings are supported by another empirical study. Helfgott, reporting on computerization in seven offices, also found that an upgrading of the work force has taken place. This development in a large insurance firm is depicted in Table 2.

Table 2

Employment, by Salary Grades, in the Home Office,
Large Insurance Company
(Fourth quarters of 1960 and 1964)

Types of Jobs and Salary Grades	1960		1964		Change	
	Number	Percent	Number	Percent	Number	Percent
Clerical	4,475	66.9	3,872	60.2	−603	−13.5
Grades 1 and 2	2,570	38.4	2,156	33.5	−616	−16.1
Grades 3 and 4	1,905	28.5	1,716	26.7	−189	− 9.9
Supervisory and technical	1,812	27.1	2,087	32.4	+275	+ 15.2
Grades 5 and 6	1,025	15.3	1,059	16.5	+ 34	+ 3.3
Grades 7 through 10	787	11.8	1,028	16.0	+241	+ 30.6
Managerial	399	6.0	477	7.4	+ 78	+ 19.5
TOTAL	6,686	100.0	6,436	100.0	−250	− 3.7

Source: Roy B. Helfgott, "E.D.P. and the Office Work Force," *Industrial and Labor Relations Review*, 19:no. 4, 508 (July, 1966).

Helfgott determined that during the period 1960-1964 the median home office salary grade increased from 2.7 to 3.1. He feels this has resulted from the reduction of clerical and increase of high-level jobs.[8] He reports that, in general, salary grades were raised by E.D.P. in these ways:

...(T)he new jobs which emerged tended to be rated higher than those they replaced; the simplest clerical jobs were wiped out; a whole new group of analytical jobs centering around the computer emerged. A fourth factor could also be involved. There appears to be a shift in the performance of certain clerical tasks from clerical workers to administrative personnel as the nature of the work becomes less quantitative and more qualitative.[9]

[8] Roy B. Helfgott, "E.D.P. and the Office Work Force," *Industrial and Labor Relations Review*, 19:no. 4, 509 (July, 1966).
[9] *Ibid.*

The empirical data just presented must be interpreted with care. Broad generalizations, based on these reports, should not be generated. Nevertheless, the data are indicative of the salary grade changes precipitated by the computer. How has computerization affected the manner in which salaries are determined?

Method of Payment

Like most clerical and management employees affected by computerization those in the surveyed firms are paid a salary. Hence, what is being said in the literature concerning the need to revise the method of payment from hourly or piecework rates to a salaried status does not have relevance for office personnel. The following paraphrase of Bright's remarks before the American Bar Asssociation is more relevant to automation in manufacturing:

> Among the results of increasing automation is the outmoding of traditional methods of compensating employees for time spent at work. Bright lists a dozen criteria on which pay has been based: physical effort, mental effort, dexterity, "general" skill, education, experience, exposure to hazards, acceptance of undesirable job conditions, responsibility related to safety of equipment or people, decision making, the worker's direct influence on productivity, and seniority.
>
> Among these, only seniority remains unaffected by the degree of automation with which an operator or maintenance man may be involved. In general, the needs among the other criteria grow less stringent with "automaticity."[10]

Goodman also comments on revision of the method of payment under automation. He emphasizes the team nature of the new jobs and the increased need to keep the machinery running.

> With automation the operator does not directly control his output, which is determined by the management. He works as part of a team and it will not usually

---

[10] "Increasing Automation Usually Cuts Needs for Skilled Men, Bright Says," *Daily Labor Report*, 196:A-8 (August 30, 1960).

be possible to separate his contribution from that of others. Thus piecework and automation are not compatible. With the high output of automatic processes, utilization of machinery is important, so this may well form a basic factor in methods of payment.

Here, again, research is necessary. Even today, wages, salaries, and status are too often fixed by intuition rather than by rational inquiry.... New jobs will require evaluation, and techniques like merit-rating, job evaluation, or time-span of discretion may prove to be the basis for payment. Suffice it to say that even today the old criteria for comparing jobs just do not work.[11]

Bright's and Goodman's analyses argue against the future effectiveness of piecework and incentive systems of wage payment in manufacturing under advanced forms of mechanization. It is interesting to note that although no form of incentive payment system exists in the surveyed firms, the productivity on computerized jobs is more capable of measurement, and the establishment of standards is now more feasible. In the discussion of work process changes, it was indicated that at the present level of office mechanization several jobs can be placed on an incentive method of payment.

The only incentive system for information processing office employees which I have seen in operation was not in a surveyed firm but in the United States Treasury Department. The purpose of the program is quoted below:

The purpose of this memorandum is to announce that a Special Incentive Awards Program has been initiated in the Northeast Service Center. This program is considerably broader than any plan used in this office heretofore. Cash awards will be made for sustained superior work performance and while quantity of production will be an element of major consideration, satisfactory quality of production must also be maintained. Moreover, such factors as dependability and conduct

[11] L. Landon Goodman, *Man and Automation* (Baltimore: Penguin Books, 1957), 163.

must be fully satisfactory in order that an employee may
be entitled to an award under the program.[12]

Like many incentive systems, however, the program did not
appear to motivate employees effectively. Few employees received cash awards.

The Union Contract

The remuneration provisions of the union contracts in the
three unionized firms in the survey have not been modified as
a result of computerization. Just as the existing transfer and
reclassification procedures have met the needs of both labor
and management, the existing classification and evaluation
procedures have sufficed in regard to the new E.D.P. positions
within the bargaining unit.

The new positions are covered under a representative contract clause such as the one quoted below from a surveyed
firm contract.

> It is recognized that changing circumstances such as
> the introduction of new machinery, equipment, systems, operations or procedures during the life of the
> Agreement may require new Job Specifications or
> changes in the revised Job Specifications..., and it is
> therefore agreed that if such changes do occur the
> Company agrees to negotiate with the Union, changes in
> Job Specifications or the creation of new Job Specifications and the pay rates for the same. If no agreement
> is reached the Company may establish and put into effect
> said changed Job Specifications or newly created Job
> Specifications and if the Local believes that the Job
> Specifications do not accurately describe the duties or
> qualifications required by the Company for the job or
> the rates of pay, the Company agrees that it will arbitrate the question of accurate description of the duties
> or qualifications required by the Company for the job,
> and the rates of pay.

This common clause has been sufficient to classify and to

---

[12] *Memorandum Number 18-11* (Lawrence, Massachusetts: United States
Treasury Department, Internal Revenue Service, Northeast Service Center, March
27, 1958), 1. (Mimeographed.)

evaluate the new E.D.P. positions and to reach agreement without resort to arbitration.

HOURS

The introduction of the computer has had little or no effect upon the hours of work except for a few groups of employees in the surveyed firms. At present the scheduling of computerized information processing has not altered basic white collar work patterns significantly. In some ways the observed lack of shift work as a result of computerization is surprising.

In theory higher levels of mechanization tend to require greater utilization of equipment to offset the increased capital costs of production. Thus in manufacturing such continuous process plants as are found in petroleum refining are highly capital intensive, and are operated continuously twenty-four hours a day and seven days a week. With increasing mechanization in other industries, researchers have tended to overgeneralize that these plants would also be operated continuously. For instance, Canter notes that:

> Automation is a 24-hour-a-day proposition, seven days a week, in most instances. Now in some cases, it will be possible to have only two shifts because the third will be involved almost entirely with maintenance activity.[13]

The capital costs of highly mechanized production processes are also increased because a new technological change may more quickly make obsolete a plant which is highly automatic. Thus capital intensive plants may have a shorter life span, especially in industries subject to rapid innovation. Under these circumstances, as Goodman points out, management must make quick, optimum use of the plant.

> As the working life (in years) of the plant is liable to be short, the only way to extend its useful life (in hours) is shift-working and this would appear to be an essential corollary to automation.[14]

In order to evaluate the extent to which E.D.P. has affected

---

[13] Ralph R. Canter, "Automation's Impact on Future Personnel Policies," *Proceedings of the First Conference, Research Development in Personnel Management* (Los Angeles: University of California, 1957), 17.

[14] Goodman, *op. cit.*, p. 164.

office work hours, the following discussion is divided into two parts: 1) the impact on management and the general clerical employees, and 2) the impact on machine room employees.

Management and General Clerical Employees

Shift work for managerial and general clerical employees is not even contemplated in the surveyed firms. No pressure or need has been cited as working in the direction of shift work. In fact evidence indicates that *fewer* total hours of work will be required under computerization. The following findings of the B. L. S. study are applicable to several of the surveyed firms:

> Several offices reported that after the installation of electronic computers, the need for overtime for data processing had been reduced, hiring cut back, and part-time employment curtailed.[15]

One exception to regularity of hours is the case when a computer program being run in the machine room breaks down during the night. At such a time it is not uncommon for the systems analyst or programmer who developed the procedure to be telephoned, either to answer some questions or to go to the machine room to straighten things out. Problems of this nature are more likely to occur during the de-bugging stage of procedure computerization, but they have occurred after a procedure had been operational for several years.

Machine Room Employees

Computer centers, cited in another B. L. S. study, have experienced an increased demand for multishift services. In the B. L. S. survey of 206 insurance companies, it was shown that over half were operating more than one shift; 25 percent were on a two-shift basis, and 30 percent were on a three-shift basis. It is important to recognize, however, that in about 70 percent of these multishift companies, only E.D.P. unit em-

---

[15] "Adjustments to the Introduction of Office Automation," *op. cit.*, p. 37.

ployees — not general clerical employees — worked on the second and third shifts.[16]

The scheduling of machine center operations in some of the surveyed firms has been affected by the introduction of the computer. In most of the firms, however, the machine room typically has two shifts, with a third shift occasionally being added during specific periods of increased information processing requirements.

The number of people involved in machine room second and third shift operations is very small. The crew typically consists of a night supervisor, a console operator, and three or four other equipment operators. Some of the larger firms which process great quantities of data may have a larger crew and, in addition, employees who run more peripheral equipment and do some preparation of input for the computer. Generally, however, input generation is handled on the main production shift during the day.

When the responsibility for input preparation and processing rests with one manager, there tend to be: 1) fewer peripheral machines; 2) fewer input preparation employees on the day shift; and 3) more multiple shift input preparation. Such operations would require lower rental or capital costs, since fewer machines are required; but whether this saving would exceed increased costs because of shift differentials is unknown.

Multiple shift operations may affect more employees, including managers and non-machine room clerical employees, as E.D.P. is extended. The conversion of additional procedures and refinements of them may require fewer employees and higher capital investment. Should this be the case, the probability that additional employees would work on multiple shifts in the office undoubtedly would increase.

CONDITIONS OF WORK

The conditions of work for office employees have not received as much attention as that directed at non-office opera-

---

[16]"The Impact of Office Automation in the Insurance Industry," *Bureau of Labor Statistics Bulletin Number 1468* (Washington, D.C.: United States Government Printing Office, United States Department of Labor, 1966), 32.

tions. Most offices in the surveyed firms are relatively pleasant places in which to work.

The computerized office has been brought closer to the plant in terms of working conditions. Researchers are concerned about nervous tension, fatigue, and work discipline as parts of the new work environment of office employees. Row upon row of office machines bear a striking resemblance to light manufacturing operations. These facts, as well as the increasing rationalization of the work process, are heightening the interest of social scientists and managements.

The International Labour Review rightly points out that the office was undergoing transition in this direction before computerization.

> Long before the computer appeared it was recoznized that the introduction of machinery in offices created an entirely different atmosphere from that which prevailed before....A certain amount of dust and grease is inevitable when machines are involved; the noise of the machines in constant operation is a source of strain; the speed at which they function imposes a rapid working rhythm comparable to assembly-line production, which again creates increased nervous tension for employees; while the routine mechanical operations involved are often more monotonous, if less arduous, than former manual methods of work. The widespread attention that has been devoted during the last few decades to the creation of an agreeable physical environment in offices has been to a great extent an attempt to attenuate the harmful effects of mechanisation on the physical and mental health of employees.[17]

The offices of the surveyed firms were well lighted and heated, clean, and pleasantly painted. It is, rather, the work conditions relating directly to the job which produce undesirable side effects. Fatigue, as maintained in the I.L.R., is a more important factor in mechanized office operations.

> Fatigue induced by increased speed of output which the machines imposed is difficult to evaluate. It is beyond doubt, however, that the gains in facility through

[17] "Effects of Mechanisation and Automation in Offices: II," *International Labour Review*, 81:no. 4, 351 (April, 1960).

mechanical as opposed to manual methods of work were largely imposed by a more rapid working pace. The experience of factory workers who found themselves obliged to adapt the speed of their movements in handling materials or parts to the increased speed of the machines has been duplicated to some extent in offices — in feeding the cards, for instance, to keep machines operating continuously.[18]

It is important to note that employees need not be in the machine room or engaged in input preparation in the line departments to be subject to the stresses outlined above. Managers' and other clerical employees' activities also are affected by the pace and rhythm of computerized operations. Ultimately the scheduling process should affect even the chief executive of the organization. Managers and clerical employees not working directly with the machines, but nearby, may be affected merely by their noise.

It is reported further in the I.L.R. that nervous strain may be a concomitant of office mechanization. The comments relevant to machine operators are in some ways just as applicable to managers and other clerical employees.

> The uniformity and excessive simplification of work of many machine operators, the extreme subdivision of functions which further limits their area of activity, can induce in employees the feeling of being simply an unimportant cog in the machine. . . .
>
> For these workers no physical strain or high-speed operations are involved; noise and dust are absent; but a considerable amount of mental tension may be engendered by the exactitude required of programming work, the responsibility for the functioning of delicate mechanisms, and the urgency of avoiding interruptions in the work through errors or malfunctioning, because of the high cost of "down time."[19]

Comments on the impact on individual employees of job changes caused by computerization are beyond the scope of

---

[18] *Ibid.*, p. 352.
[19] *Ibid.*, pp. 354-355.

this study.[20] Observations and supporting data on changes in the work process nevertheless indicate that some office workers, both managerial and clerical, do and, perhaps, many more will work under conditions very similar to those existing in some areas of manufacturing.

Reorganization of a Department after Computerization

Under the punched card system each operation was functionally organized, and each section operated relatively independently of the others in the department. The work process was similar to a pipe line operation, with the work carried from one section to another until completion.

Punched card cabinets containing information necessary for operations were interspersed in the functional sections, obscuring visibility and blocking air circulation. As one supervisor said, "When I looked up, I could only see the back wall."

Under the computerized system a team form of work organization supplanted the functional or pipe line system. Many functions of the department were consolidated and handled by small groups of employees.

The punched card files were eliminated; records were placed on magnetic tapes. The air conditioning system worked more efficiently; and the supervisor had better visual control over his subordinates and the work flow. The small group form of organization also facilitated supervision of employees' activities.

Finally, new files, containing information from the computerized system, were located along the walls of the department's work space. These files enabled the department to function without recourse to the far more numerous punched card files. The new files were placed so that all department members would have access to them.

In this example, therefore, both positive and negative elements with regard to work conditions were precipitated by the

---

[20] For a discussion of employee attitudes toward their computerized jobs, see H. C. Lee, "Do Workers Really Want Flexibility on the Job?," *Personnel,* 42:no. 2, 175-177 (March-April, 1965).

computer. There was improvement in work organization, lighting and, ventilation. However, a great deal more walking and bending was necessary with the new operations.

Chapter XII

LEARNING TO LIVE WITH THE COMPUTER

Since each of the parties in an interdependent relationship affects to some degree the other's ability to achieve his goals or satify his needs, major difficulties are likely to arise unless both have positive expectations that the relationship will further these purposes.

— DOUGLAS McGREGOR

The training of employees is probably the most crucial personnel management activity precipitated by computerization. It raises both immediate and long range questions about training policies and procedures. For example, the new emphasis upon systems rather than functional management requires a reevaluation of training objectives, as well as programs to develop technical skills in the short run. The principal sources of training also are subject to change, as exemplified by the growing reliance upon university programs for management personnel. Lines of progression, interfirm mobility patterns, promotion criteria, and performance appraisal procedures are aspects of training also discussed in this chapter.

TRAINING

The need for qualified manpower of all descriptions will increase as more advanced technologies are developed and implemented. Computerization has emphasized this fact by requiring new talents, methods, and skills. The most demanding training needs necessitated by computerization have been for managerial and technical personnel. Hence the following discussion is concerned primarily with management training under computerization.

Objectives

The most significant implication for training precipitated by computerization is that management must think in terms of systems concepts rather than functional areas. Computerization facilitates the re-integration of the managerial process, the focus being on over-all organizational goals rather than on the goals of organizational sub-units or personalities. These trends will have a significant impact upon training programs for managers.[1] Forrester comments on this change in emphasis:

> In the past, with management considered more of an art than a profession, education and practice have been highly fragmentized. Manufacturing, finance, distribution, organization, advertising and research have too often been viewed as separate skills and not as part of a unified system. Too often management education consists of gathering current industrial practice and presenting it to the student as a sequence of unrelated subjects. Similarly in his work in industry the manager specializes within departments where his experience perpetuates the atmosphere of unrelated compartmentalization.
>
> The next big step in management education will be in the development of a basis for fitting together the many management functions into a meaningful whole. Around this central core specialized subjects and experience will take on more significance. Men can be developed more rapidly. They will be able to start from a point now accessible only through long training or fortuitous experience.[2]

In keeping with this concept of future management training, Forrester outlines the major objectives of the Industrial Dynamics program at the Massachusetts Institute of Technology:

---

[1] The current revision of engineering school curricula is a relevant example. Several leading schools are pioneering in an effort to decrease course specialization and to increase the emphasis on broad scientific areas. The pace of technological advance quickly makes obsolescent particular engineering skills. A broad knowledge of the underlying sciences, experience in independent thinking, and problem solving skills are basic. Many business schools, reacting to criticism of the vocational nature of their curricula, are currently revising their programs.

[2] Jay W. Forrester, "Industrial Dynamics," *Harvard Business Review* 36:no. 4, 38 (July-August, 1958).

1) To develop in the manager a better intuitive feel for the time-varying behavior of industrial and economic systems. . . .

2) To provide a background showing how the major aspects of a company are related to one another, so that the developing manager can derive the greatest benefit from his work experience.

3) To help predict the future course of an existing organization.

4) To improve the future prospects of a company.[3]

According to Forrester, managers will have to plan more effectively to effectuate these objectives. This planning must include the personal development of a manager as well as the physical development and adjustment of an organization. To meet the job demands of new computerized corporate systems,

> . . .(T)he arguments are persuasive that some 25 per cent of the total working time of all persons in the corporation should be devoted to preparation for their future roles. This means time devoted to competence some five years in the future and does not include the learning that may be a necessary part of the immediate task. Over a period of years this study would cover a wide range—individual and group psychology, writing, speaking, law, dynamics of industrial behavior, corporate policy design, advances in science and engineering, and historical development of political and corporate organizations—the extent and sequence being tailored to the individual person.[4]

Bize also addresses himself to the training needs of managers in light of present and future technological developments. In Bize's view industrial leaders of tomorrow will have to develop four attributes not currently emphasized. First, managers must increase their knowledge of man for technical and material advance. Second, managers' imagination and innovative abilities must be developed more systematically. Third, managers must understand their culture in order to facilitate adaptations in

---

[3] *Ibid.*, p. 66.

[4] Jay W. Forrester, "A New Corporate Design," *Industrial Management Review,* 7:no. 1, 16 (Fall, 1965).

their organization. And fourth, managers' training must relate more to the formation of character and cultivation of the desire to initiate action.[5]

The objectives for management training outlined above imply a formidable reorientation of its basic purposes. It is noteworthy that as the technical requirements of managerial positions become more complex and demanding, the emphasis should be placed upon the broader aspects of the job.

At a time when increasing demands for technical skills tend to focus attention upon further specialization of functions, there is considerable evidence that the primary problem of managing complex organizational systems will be in developing managers who possess a far broader view of operations.[6] The most difficult training problem is how to develop managers who are proficient in areas other than technology, yet who have a good grasp of the technical features of their jobs.

Current Training Activities

Current training programs reflect short run company needs for technical skills related to computerization rather than the long run objectives cited above. The technical problems of evaluating computers and applying them to a firm's operating procedures have pre-empted training endeavors. Training activities for various employee classifications are discussed below.[7]

Top Management: The training of top executives in the sur-

---

[5] Pierre Bize, "Automation and the Scientific Management of Enterprises," *Views on Automation* (Paris: Organisation for European Economic Cooperation, 1957), 32-33.

[6] Managers are required increasingly to relate internal operations and environmental influences to achieve organizational objectives. See H. Igor Ansoff, "The Firm of the Future," *Harvard Business Review*, 43:no. 5, 176 (September-October, 1965) and "1970 — Ready or Not It's Coming," *Administrative Management*, 27:no. 1, 15 (January, 1966).

[7] For a detailed breakdown of electronic data processing training in twenty firms studied by the Bureau of Labor Statistics, see "Adjustments to the Introduction of Office Automation," *Bureau of Labor Statistics Bulletin Number 1276* (Washington, D.C.: United States Government Printing Office, United States Department of Labor, May, 1960), 48-50. The B. L. S. categorizes the various programs under these headings: Planning and Programming Jobs, Console Operators, and Auxiliary Equipment Operators.

veyed firms and as reported in the literature is best described as an orientation to electronic computers. Indoctrination customarily lasts up to forty hours, with the emphasis placed upon the characteristics of the equipment. This training usually takes place during the feasibility study phase of the computerization process. The purpose is either to study alternative equipment or to become familiar with the computer which the firm soon will purchase or rent. Usually the training is under the direction of the equipment manufacturer.

The majority of the equipment manufacturers offer, in addition to one or more programming courses, a short executive orientation course. A portion of these courses is usually devoted to touring installations, showing the equipment. The balance is spent in describing electronic data processing systems, with special reference to the manufacturer's own product. This instruction will be pertinent and informative as far as it goes.

Ideally, the executive orientation course should consist of about forty hours of classroom instruction in diverse brands and types of data processing equipment.[8]

Is this type of training appropriate or sufficient to meet executives' needs? The consequences of the fact that top management has remained too distant from computerization have been cited numerous times. The failure of top managers to take a more active role in computerization is perpetuated by the absence of effective training for this group. Their technical familiarization training does not, of course, include study of the manpower and organizational implications of computerization for their firm's paperwork procedures.

Middle Management: Middle management training relative to computerization closely parallels that cited above for top managers. The major difference is that training may be longer and more technical, since it is designed for line managers who will be in charge of computerized procedures.

Key middle management training in the use of electronic data processing systems is a relatively new discipline and its content is still not fully standardized.

[8] Roger Nett and Stanley A. Hetzler, *An Introduction to Electronic Data Processing* (Glencoe, Illinois: The Free Press of Glencoe, 1959), 208.

> Generally, it attempts in a three or four week course, to wed computer techniques with the analysis and design of organizational systems.[9]

Typically, the courses encompass developing an appreciation of the principles of computerization, the technical abilities of the computer, and a rudimentary knowledge of systems and programming activities.

Two somewhat novel approaches to middle management training are reported in the literature. Both involve a system of rotation, whereby young managers are familiarized with computer-oriented management problems. Rush reports that his company utilizes a rotation system to train line managers in the technical aspects of computerization.

> In several installations, promising young men are being rotated through data-processing work as part of their development. One of our largest refineries, which has had a long history of success with a rotation system, has extended the program to include a year or more of programming experience for future managers.[10]

In the second example Gustafson reports on "criss-cross management" developed by a firm to promote flexibility in middle management.

> To adapt to the new system, a training program was started five years ago to build versatility into a staff of 125 management people so they would be able to cross departmental lines. Known in the organization as criss-cross management, the system is described by Robert Koch, the manager, as follows:
> "This is the process of using supervisory personnel to solve company-wide problems in policy and procedure so they will accept changes because they are part of the changes and are helping to make them. We have found that there is no better formula for avoiding resistance to change than to have the people make the change themselves."[11]

---

[9] *Ibid.*, p. 206.

[10] Carl H. Rush, "Standard Oil Company (New Jersey): Organizational Development," George P. Schultz and Thomas L. Whisler, eds., *Management Organization and the Computer* (Glencoe, Illinois: The Free Press of Glencoe, 1960), 200.

[11] Philip Gustafson, "What Management Is Learning from Computers," *Nation's Business*, 46:no. 11, 62 (November, 1958).

None of the surveyed firms has attempted to utilize rotation of middle managers as a means to develop in them both a technical knowledge in depth and a greater breadth of view.

Lower Management: Of all members of management in the surveyed firms, the first-line supervisor has been afforded the least formal orientation to computerized operations. Although he has been the most directly affected by computerization, he has been the most neglected by way of training.

In several of the surveyed firms, one- or two-week training programs are being scheduled for supervisors; this is usually done only after top and middle managers have been trained. Although this technical training is beneficial, the changes in the supervisor's job demand additional training in managerial skills as well. It is important for the line supervisor to understand the technical features of computerization, especially if he is to cooperate effectively with staff specialists in developing, implementing, and supervising computerized procedures. To this end, technical training should be augmented. The effort made to train supervisors to handle the non-technical conditions and problems they face on their jobs should be increased as well.

Staff Specialists: Systems analysts and programmers have, of necessity, received a great deal of specialized training in the application of electronic computers to information processing. Staff specialist training was administered for all the surveyed firms but one by the manufacturers of their equipment.

Of all staff specialists, programmers receive the most training. The largest proportion of electronic data processing training "spaces," for example, required in all government agencies are for students in beginning and advanced programming courses.[12] For firms using large scale electronic computers,

> Each manufacturer, before his equipment is released
> for marketing, must have developed what has come to
> be known as a programming course. These courses

---

[12] "Use of Electronic Data-Processing Equipment," *Hearings before the Subcommittee on Census and Government Statistics of the Committee on Post Office and Civil Service, House of Representatives* (Washington, D.C.: United States Government Printing Office, 1959), 121.

usually consist of a brief description of a system's components and their interrelationships and they then move rapidly on to machine language, machine instructions, problem flow charting, and the coding of problems in machine language. The essentials of programming are usually covered in less than a hundred hours and the remainder of the course is given over to practice programming. A "thesis" problem may be assigned to each student, which is of such length that he can reasonably expect to complete and machine-test it during the final days of the course....Programmer courses for large scale systems are generally from 160 to 240 hours duration. Some manufacturers have found that a single programming course suffices, since experience on the job is the main element in the development of skill. Others...have found valuable a second or advanced course. This instruction follows a period of practical experience thus making it possible to resume the study of theory on a more tangible basis.[13]

Training for programming medium and small scale electronic computers is essentially the same. Because these systems are less complex, programmers typically require only forty to eighty hours of instruction.

Maintenance, as pointed out before, presents no great training problem. In the surveyed firms adequately trained technical specialists have been provided by the manufacturer as part of the rental service, or were hired by the firm from the manufacturer when the electronic computer was purchased.

Clerical Employees: Mechanization of paperwork has necessitated the training of large numbers of clerical employees. An International Labour Organisation study aptly details the experience in the United States with regard to training.

The growth of large undertakings gave rise to more systematic methods of job classification based on specific requirements.... These developments, coupled with the expansion of clerical work and shortage of manpower, and the growing use of office machines, resulted in proliferation of commercial schools in industrialized areas

---

[13]Nett and Hetzler, *op. cit.,* pp. 204-206. See also Roger C. Vergin, "Staffing of Computer Departments," *Personnel Administration,* 28:no. 4, 9 (July-August, 1965).

offering courses in machine operation, shorthand, and other business techniques. Manufacturers of office equipment organised training courses for operators, as a source of supply for purchasers or offered to train the latter's own employees. In some countries, courses of training for clerical employment were introduced into the secondary schools.[14]

A Bureau of Labor Statistics study supports the view that little retraining has been necessary for employees transferred to computerized operations. In the twenty firms surveyed by the B. L. S.,

> With one exception, formal programs to retrain employees affected by the electronic computers for other clerical positions were apparently not considered necessary. . . . All companies reported that they tried to transfer such employees to clerical positions comparable in duties and skill to the positions held before the introduction of the computers. Such positions generally required only a relatively short period of on-the-job instruction to familiarize the employee with new forms and procedures.[15]

The B. L. S. findings confirm my observations in the firms I surveyed. Typing, keypunching, and general clerical skills possessed by employees prior to computerization have sufficed on the new jobs. Only for several non-management jobs in the computer center has new, specialized training been required.

Console and auxiliary equipment operators were given special training to meet the technical demands of computerized operations. This was primarily on-the-job training for periods lasting as long as a year. In some of the larger systems, these operators were given training similar to that afforded systems analysts and programmers. The number of operators is small, and no training difficulty was reported.

Training Sources

Four sources are available to a firm to meet training needs

---

[14]"Effects of Mechanisation and Automation in Offices," *Report III* (Geneva: International Labour Office, 1959), 70.

[15]"Adjustments to the Introduction of Office Automation," *op. cit.*, p. 27.

created by computerization: equipment manufacturers, the firm itself, universities, and other miscellaneous organizations.

Equipment Manufacturers: The bulk of training in the computerization art is probably carried out by the electronic computer manufacturers. These manufacturers provide far more than equipment. They also render numerous services. For instance, most large electronic computer manuafacturers provide services for: 1) feasibility studies, 2) selection of proper equipment, 3) systems analysis, 4) maintenance, and 5) training for managerial, operational, and clerical employees.

The International Business Machines Corporation reported that in 1960 it had conducted its two thousandth one-week course on I.B.M. systems for a total of 63,043 executives. In addition, 100,000 customer operating personnel had been trained during 1959.[16]

During 1965 I.B.M. enrolled 154,963 of its customers' employees in training programs, including 10,880 executives. The executive program still is a one-week course, and the other courses run from one day to three weeks for operating, programmer, systems, and middle management personnel. The training programs are held in I.B.M.'s twenty-one education centers and 130 branch offices across the country. For the period 1961 through 1965, approximately 680,000 client employees were trained, about 30,000 of these being top executives.[17]

The surveyed firms have relied almost exclusively upon the equipment manufacturers to orient executives and middle managers and to train systems analysts, programmers, operators, and clerical employees. In addition, each surveyed firm usually has hired at least one former employee of an equipment manufacturer. This practice is not frowned upon; the equipment manufacturers recognize it as a cost of selling and renting their electronic computers.

The consulting firm hired by the Bureau of the Budget

16 "Education for Action," *Harvard Business Review,* 38:no. 2, 40-41 (March-April, 1960).
17 Data were obtained by telephone interview with an I.B.M. executive.

cautions against relying too heavily on the equipment manufacturers to train managerial personnel:

> The role assigned to the manufacturers, namely, giving skill training to programmers and operators, still appears to be a sound one, with certain modifications. ...The real job as far as management personnel is concerned is that of acquainting them with the management significance of A.E.P.S. and of upgrading them in the management skills necessary to make a computer installation effective. On this part of the job the Government should definitely not depend upon the manufacturers. However, when this particular group of trainees is ready to get the story about the performance characteristics of the hardware itself, the existing facilities of the manufacturers for conveying this understanding should be used.[18]

The inadequacy of present management training, previously cited, supports the above statements. Additional sources for training are discussed below.

Intra-firm Training: The major training method within the surveyed firms was on-the-job training. It was utilized, to some degree, for developing systems analysts, programmers, and middle managers. The method was used most in training console and auxiliary equipment operators and clerical employees.

On-the-job training is still practical, but its use in the surveyed firms is restricted somewhat. Most of the employees trained on the job, holding positions cited above, possess skills and experience which make this kind of training feasible.

Intra-firm training programs have some advantages over other training methods when the program can be tailored to meet fairly specific and company-oriented requirements. Training designed to meet broad objectives or to prepare for new technological developments probably can be met more efficiently by other means.

Universities: The surveyed firms utilize university courses to a small extent for training personnel for computerization. In the near future managers and specialists will be trained in larger numbers in the universities.

---

[18] "Use of Electronic Data-Processing Equipment," *op. cit.,* p. 134.

In the long run fuller exploitation of the possibilities of assistance from the universities of the country offers the most important outside resource for meeting the vast training load which is indicated by the returns of this study.[19]

Many universities now provide training opportunities at their computer centers for students, faculty members, and private business employees. A working knowledge of the computer is being required in numerous fields of study including business education. The exposure is one which emphasizes the computer as a high-powered tool to extend the creative capabilities of human beings.

Miscellaneous Sources: The final training category includes various groups which have contributed to computerization training of employees. While the surveyed firms have made use of these additional sources, it is difficult to determine the degree of participation and the impact.

Professional associations such as the American Management Association and the Systems and Procedures Association are included in this category. In addition, the services of numerous consulting firms are available to a firm to help meet its training needs. Some individuals have been enrolled in correspondence courses to aid in training.

PROMOTION AND MOBILITY

Computerization of work routines affects manpower movements within a firm. The utilization of employees and their lines of progression within a firm, the hiring of manpower for various levels of the organization from without a firm, and in general the criteria for advancement have undergone significant change.

Internal Mobility

In the past the movement of employees within a firm tended to be fairly well defined. Job progression in the departmentalized form of organization was generally prescribed by tradition;

---

[19] *Ibid.,* p. 135.

probably little variation occurred except at the upper levels of middle and top management. For instance, in unionized firms, a problem often arose when one of the career ladders or lines for advancement became blocked by senior employees who were not promotable. In many firms these career ladders also provided the route by which the most capable were able to progress to the very top of the organizational pyramid.

These traditional avenues for job progression have changed over time to meet changing organizational manpower needs; one major force for change has been the increasing professionalization and job specialization necessitated by advancing technology. Computerization, therefore, has not brought about a major change in mobility patterns in a firm; but it has reinforced the trend for revision. The exact impact of observed changes in the mobility of employees in computerized offices is not yet fully known; but certain truisms, such as the popular belief than an office boy can some day become president of the company, merit reevaluation.

Clerical Employees: The introduction of the computer into office work has had three major implications for clerical employees. First, the number and variety of jobs open to clerical employees have been altered. Many lower rated jobs are eliminated under E.D.P. Thus, the room for movement and progression, everything being equal, is affected.

Second, the upper limit for clerical positions is relatively higher. Programming positions are considered to be management positions; but even if this were not the case, the great majority of clerical employees do not qualify for these new positions. Experience in coding, keypunching, filing, or checking is not as important in the new programming positions as are certain analytical qualities and educational background. Therefore, for the majority of clerical employees programming jobs are outside the area of reasonable expectations.

In this regard, the same situation exists for console operators in the computer center. The requirements for these positions, and for closely related counterparts, restrict the possible number of clerical employees or lower rated employees in the computer center who can aspire to fill them.[20]

The third and final point is that the new, higher rated clerical and lower management positions, e.g., systems analysts, can be filled only by clerical employees who acquire the special skills and training required by *off the job* preparation. It appears that some supervisory jobs still can be filled from the ranks.

Management Employees: In many respects the impact of computerization on internal mobility and opportunity for promotion for management employees is similar to that for clerical employees. The demand for professional and technical skills by computerized firms is increasing. The requirements for the new and changing management jobs also affect traditional patterns of internal mobility.

In computerized systems design and operations, the line of progression is becoming distinct, and qualified personnel usually come from specific functional areas. For instance:

> The computer team will form the nucleus of computer know-how in the company. If a computer is acquired as a result of this study, the members of the computer team will logically hold the key positions in programming and installing the computer.[21]

Rush points out that in some cases management employees in other areas of a firm are reluctant to take a position closely related to computerization.

> We have not yet established career lines which show where a person goes after a successful period in computer work. As a result, some people, when asked to enter the field, have declined on the grounds that it would remove them from the "main stream" of the

---

[20] Most of the programmers and analysts came from closely related types of jobs. About half of them were formerly in accounting and associated professional work. Only a relatively small proportion had previously been engaged in routine clerical work....

Of the console and auxiliary equipment operators, the largest proportion had been transferred from occupations related to machine tabulation work.

From "Adjustments to the Introduction of Office Automation," *op. cit.,* p. 55.

[21] Frank Wallace, *Appraising the Economics of Electronic Computers* (New York: Controllership Foundation, Incorporated, 1956), 24.

company. Others have said they do not want to be branded as "machine men" when their careers are in economics, accounting, plans administration, technical or scientific fields, etc. Yet these are often the very people we want, because of their subject matter experience and other qualifications.[22]

Thus, computer-oriented management jobs tend to be restricted to applicants with highly specific technical skills and specialized interests. The implications of computerized systems for line department managers are not clear as yet.

According to one view mobility within management ranks will be facilitated by E.D.P.:

> Professionalization of middle management would have repercussions on top management, but perhaps not of great significance. The paths between top management and middle management would change, perhaps in ways which would facilitate up and down mobility. Top management is increasing its use of staff, and the increasingly professionalized middle managers should be able to move more easily than they do now into the top management staff areas as well as into higher line positions.[23]

On the other hand, Leavitt and Whisler suggest that mobility between middle and top management positions will decrease under computerization.

> Thus, in effect, we think that the horizontal slice of the current organization chart we call middle management will break in two, with the larger portion shrinking and sinking into a more highly programmed state and the smaller portion proliferating and rising to a level where more creative thinking is needed.[24]

Obviously, if Leavitt's and Whisler's view prevails, middle managers will find it increasingly difficult to progress from within to the "creative" level of an organization.

---

[22] Carl H. Rush, "Standard Oil Company (New Jersey): Organizational Development," George P. Schultz and Thomas L. Whisler, eds., *Management Organization and the Computer, op. cit.,* p. 204.

[23] Alex Orden, "Man—Machine—Computer Systems," George P. Schultz and Thomas L. Whisler, eds., *Management Organization and the Computer* (Glencoe, Illinois: The Free Press of Glencoe, 1960), 86.

[24] Harold J. Leavitt and Thomas L. Whisler, "Management in the 1980's," *Harvard Business Review,* 36:no. 6, 45 (November-December, 1958).

To date there has not been any radical change in the mobility patterns and opportunities of management employees in
the surveyed firms. Line and staff managers not directly responsible for E.D.P. have been affected to the degree to which
they had to comprehend computers to meet their changing
job requirements. Mobility, in these cases, depends upon
varying degrees of technical competence and understanding of
computerized procedures.

As for the manager who is directly concerned with the
computer or systems, mobility, as in any other specialized area
of company operations, is fairly well defined by job requirements. In this case it is quite natural to expect that training,
experience, and job skills will play an important role in upward
mobility.

The question of whether horizontal movements across
career lines of progression are impeded by increasing levels of
technology in the office is an old one which undoubtedly will
receive more attention as computerization is extended.

Inter-firm Mobility

Lockwood comments on the job skills and mobility of clerks
before the rationalization of office work.

> The highly individual nature of business methods
> introduced him to a routine peculiar to the firm in which
> he started his career. He definitely acquired skills, but
> it was difficult to say exactly what they were, or to
> compare them with those of other clerks. His maturing
> experience would be peculiar to his own firm, often
> highly valuable to his particular employer, but relatively
> worthless outside. Promotion was given and respon-
> sibility added, not by virtue of his progressive certifica-
> tion, but in accordance with his employer's estimation of
> his merit and worth — in other words, by the value of a
> particular clerk to a particular employer in a particular
> business routine.[25]

Lockwood adds that bureaucratization provides an alternative to the labor market in rationalization of office workers.

---

[25] David Lockwood, *The Blackcoated Worker* (London: George Allen and
Unwin, Limited, 1958), 82.

The means to this end are procedures which impersonally establish job description and evaluation, criteria for performance appraisal, and job specifications. The crux of Lockwood's thesis is that rigid and impersonal standards lead to bureaucracy. In this scheme, impersonality of employment arrangements is equated with a labor market situation because impersonality is the major social facet of a labor market.[26]

What Lockwood obscures is the greater perfection of the labor market for office workers, primarily because increasing mechanization has led to less reliance on the personal factor in making manpower decisions within a firm. The uniform standards used by today's offices in utilizing, hiring, paying, and evaluating its personnel are made possible largely by technological changes in information processing. Common technologies among firms enable office workers to take advantage of economic incentives to improve their position by moving from one firm to another with a minimum of inconvenience and risk. The increased mobility of office workers also heightens competition among firms for manpower and leads, therefore, to a more perfect labor market situation.

Increasing professionalization and the establishment of common standards for specialization of management personnel within and among firms correspond to the developments observed above with regard to clerical workers. The transferability of managerial, professional, and technical skills from one firm to another, although greatest at lower levels in the organization, will increase at higher levels also with advancing mechanization.

Leavitt and Whisler point out that with an increasing proportion of higher level positions mobility patterns will change. For instance, they believe that the number of entry points into a computerized firm will increase at higher levels in the organization, that the sources for qualified managers will be greater in number, and that there will be less reliance on company

---

[26] *Ibid.*, p. 85.

training for promotion.[27] Forrester states that organizational developments now taking place will provide an individual with greater opportunity for movement within a firm. There may be less movement between firms because entry will be more difficult.[28] The survey data corroborate the general thesis of greater mobility within a firm, but no evidence of restraint upon entry was noted.

These tendencies toward greater employee mobility among firms under advancing technology undoubtedly will prompt serious questions about personnel policies which attempt to tie the employee to a particular firm. The entire area of fringe benefits may merit scrutiny in firms where turnover rates have increased due to the greater interchangeability of employees among firms.

Promotion Criteria

The criteria for promotion have been affected by computerization in the same way as have selection criteria; the factors have remained essentially the same, but the emphasis among them has varied to meet changed manpower requirements. In fact, the criteria and the relative shifts among them are the same in the internal selection process for higher rated positions as in the selection process for new employees. The discussion which follows deals with three special problems related to applying these criteria within a firm. The three problem areas are: 1) seniority, 2) obsolete skills, and 3) age.

Seniority: The decreasing reliance on previous job experience as a prerequisite for job progression is upsetting to personnel in those organizations where time with the company typically assured promotion. For instance:

---

[27] Leavitt and Whisler, *op. cit.,* p. 47. For example,
   One factor which is assuming increasing importance as automation progresses, and which has an unfortunate effect on the opportunities for advancement from within the undertaking, is the practice of filling posts of higher responsibility, especially at the executive level, by professionally trained people brought in directly from the outside.
From "Effects of Mechanisation and Automation in Offices, II," *International Labour Review*, 81:no. 3, 267 (March, 1960).
[28] Forrester, "A New Corporate Design," *op. cit.,* pp. 12-13.

During the conversion there were occasions where seniority had not outweighed other factors in the selection of people for promotion. Some examples were the selection of the managers of the accounts division and the tabulating (machine accounting) division. The managers of these two divisions each had 17 years of service with the company compared with an average of more than 30 years of service of the managers of the other divisions. These promotions had been exceptions to the traditional code, and had been based on the fact that this was a new area of work where different skills and abilities were required.[29]

Other manifestations of this type have been cited previously: the assistant manager who actually runs the department, the creation of special staff positions, and the line role played by staff specialists in the management of operational, computerized procedures. The increasing functional specialization associated with the management of non-computerized procedures also tends to limit the types of experience which would prepare an employee to assume broader responsibilities.

The downgrading of seniority raises a more difficult problem which, to date, largely has been ignored by management. The shifting of unpromotable manpower or the creation of unproductive jobs does not efficiently or even adequately resolve the dilemma of how to utilize manpower with long company service. One means by which to alleviate this situation is an expanded and well planned retraining program.

Obsolete Skills: Updating manpower skills is a national problem. Individual firms have engaged in retraining programs to the advantage of both the firm and its employees. The increasing rate of technological change will, doubtless, cause attention to be focused more on retraining as a means to insure efficient utilization of the nation's and an individual firm's manpower.

In the surveyed firms there were few problems with the transfer and promotion of clerical workers. The retraining in-

---

29 Harold Harlow Craig, *Administering a Conversion to Electronic Accounting* (Boston: Division of Research, Harvard University Graduate School of Business Administration, 1955), 74.

volved was usually of short duration, and most employees readily accepted promotions requiring the acquisition of new skills. Older clerical employees sometimes were reluctant to be trained for jobs, even with promotion, primarily because they felt either that they could not handle the new responsibilities, or that they preferred a less demanding job which would require little personal adjustment. Since no clerical employees in the surveyed firms feared being laid off, they could afford to refuse retraining.[30]

Management personnel with long service had much the same options as clerical employees. The surveyed firms have carried those who would not acquire new skills or who are not capable of further training to keep up with their responsibilities or to seek promotion. An editorial on this general phenomenon appeared recently:

> It takes enlightened management — with the ability to know obsolescence when it sees it, to understand the causes and do something constructive about it. It takes realistic management, too — with the stamina to tell those of limited potential that the job has grown too big for them; that they must at last vacate it.[31]

Leavitt proposes four methods for attacking managerial obsolescence. First, attempt to retrain displaced managers. Second, support executives in power with young assistants and shorten the working years of executives. Third, automate management. And fourth, differentiate management into classes and assign tasks and educate them accordingly.[32]

Under advancing technologies younger managers will face harsher pressures to prepare themselves for changing job responsibilities. Professional and technical men in all fields undergoing rapid technological change are learning that train-

---

[30] For a discussion of alternative organizational policies dealing with employees affected by computerization, see Russell J. Cooney, "Manpower Planning for Automation," *Public Personnel Review*, 26:no. 3, 154 (July, 1965).

[31] "Management Obsolescence," *Administrative Management*, 27:no. 3, 17 (March, 1966).

[32] Harold J. Leavitt, "Dealing with Management Obsolescence," in "Computer-Based Management for Information and Control," *American Management Association Bulletin 30* (New York: American Management Association, 1963), 51-52.

ing as a continuous process is fast becoming a requisite of advancement.

Progress with automation will tend to call for educational qualifications in a greater proportion of jobs, and so will tend to make it more difficult to advance through experience gained on the job. In some industries even supervisors may require qualifications that can be acquired only at educational institutes. It seems, therefore, to be increasingly important for industrial firms to find potential managers and technicians in their ranks and give them the necessary training for promotion, either within or outside the firm, so keeping the line of advance open.[33]

All employees are not equally equipped to accept or to participate to the same degree in programs to update skills enabling them to accept new positions. The older employee presents a special problem in this regard.

Age: The utilization of older employees under conditions of rapid change presents difficulties which often receive tardy attention.[34] Older employees, with few notable exceptions, find adaptation very difficult.

In a few exceptional instances older employees who had been stymied in one job for a long period of time found salvation in computerization. These employees were offered and accepted job opportunities for a new career with different and challenging responsibilities. Individuals, thought by management to have reached their peak, suddenly blossomed into employees whose contribution to the firm increased considerably. While these employees are in the minority, a firm errs when it fails to make a sincere effort to provide job opportunities for older workers displaced by computerization.

The tendency to discount the maturity, past experience, and other assets of older employees, as new technological developments are introduced, implies that new barriers may be raised to their promotion and em-

---

[33] *Automation* (London: Department of Scientific and Industrial Research, 1956), 79.

[34] For an excellent over-all treatment of the characteristics of E.D.P. employees and the implications of E.D.P. for older employees, see Chapters X and IV in "Adjustments to the Introduction of Office Automation," *op. cit.*

ployment. From the evidence presented, however, it is clear that a fixed age limit would exclude some qualified older individuals who could be successfully retrained for the new positions.[35]

All these comments notwithstanding, computerization favors the younger employee. The B.L.S. has found that:

> Relatively few persons 45 and over were employed in electronic data processing. The median age of both groups was about 32 years, but only 10 per cent of the employees in electronic data processing were age 45 and over, compared with 23 per cent of those in the affected unit. Newly hired persons for electronic data processing were younger, with a median age of 26, and no persons age 45 or over were hired for these new positions.[36]

Mann and Williams report that physical disabilities as well as age hinder internal mobility:

> As the reassignment program gained momentum, a review of factors — such as age and physical disability — were the principal deterrents to a candidate's placement. It became apparent that some of the old white-collar desk jobs had attracted many individuals with physical disabilities such as speech or hearing difficulties, arthritis, or heart conditions. Some employees had entered the company with such difficulties; others had developed them during their tenure. Many of the new jobs required communication with others including the use of telephones, standing at machines, and a considerable degree of training.[37]

Physical disability was not mentioned in the surveyed firms as being a problem of particular magnitude. In many instances, however, management representatives noted that many of the new jobs entail new physical demands, such as increased bending, walking, and lifting.

---

[35] *Ibid.*, p. 64.

[36] *Ibid.*, p. 52.

[37] Floyd C. Mann and Lawrence K. Williams, "Observations of the Dynamics of a Change to Electronic Data-Processing Equipment," *Administrative Science Quarterly,* 5:no. 2, 244 (September, 1960).

PERFORMANCE APPRAISAL

Performance appraisal procedures in the surveyed firms have been relatively unaffected by computerization. Most firms utilize fairly standard forms in evaluating employee performance. The process typically consists of rating, reviewing, and discussing an employee's work record. The factors considered are related to the job and the conduct, personality, and potential of the employee. The rater checks off the appropriate point on a scale indicating the relative standing on each factor, and an over-all rating is then assigned.

There has been much speculation in the literature as to the impact of computerization upon the evaluation of performance. For instance:

> At the same time, the whole top management effort is likely to be a more explicit one, with decisions more readily exposed to examination. As noted earlier, this development puts those with authority very much on the spot and may lead to more discerning judgements about the quality of the job being done at the top of the organization.[38]

The idea that evaluation criteria and data will make judgment more exact is applicable to all levels of the organization, even where job responsibilities tend to be intangible.

The difficulties of evaluating programmers have caused attention to be focused on the need for improved appraisal procedures. Several approaches to this problem are suggested by Conway, Gibbons, and Watts: 1) traditional subjective evaluation by superiors, mentioned above, 2) determination of proficiency as indicated by solving test problems, 3) rigid adherence to project completion dates, and 4) a detailed record of the time required to de-bug programs.[39]

Evaluation procedures for clerical employees have remained

[38] Thomas L. Whisler and George P. Shultz, "Information Technology and Management Organization," George P. Shultz and Thomas L. Whisler, eds., *Management Organization and the Computer* (Glencoe, Illinois: The Free Press of Glencoe, 1960), 18.

[39] B. Conway, J. Gibbons, and D. E. Watts, *Business Experience with Electronic Computers* (New York: Controllers Institute Research Foundation, Incorporated, 1959), 91-93.

relatively unchanged. The increasing capability to define and to measure individual output has been noted previously, as has the kind of employee desired; and the factors considered in selecting him can be prescribed more specifically. These trends indicate that personal attributes should receive less attention in the appraisal process.

In one of the surveyed firms a novel approach was developed by a systems group to define job responsibilities and to measure work performance.

An Experimental Approach to Job Description and Evaluation

An "integrated position guide" was designed for managerial personnel. While the guide was developed by a technical staff department rather than by the personnel department, the approach can be used by the entire organization.

The Concept: A matrix is used to plot the positions and levels against the tasks to be performed within the organizational unit. Thus, the left, vertical column contains position titles in order of salary levels. The horizontal, top box contains the major work tasks of the department. The degree to which any single job involves one of the job tasks is indicated by the percentage of time on the job the incumbent is expected to devote to the particular task. For example, a computer coder, grade 5, is expected to spend a minimal amount of time on corporate citizenship, managing, and supervising; most of his time on computer coding and programming; and a minimal effort on computer systems and organizational analysis.

The Factors: The noteworthy factors considered when measuring job performance are these: 1) the clarity with which the employee interprets organizational objectives with regard to himself and his subordinates; 2) management confidence as exemplified, e.g., by the time lapse between critical reviews by superiors; 3) flexibility, or the ability to change activities to suit organization needs; 4) careful consideration of systems concepts, e.g., understanding of business systems (technical aspects), computer systems, and organization of men in making decisions; 5) the extent to which "visual imagination" is used;

6) effectiveness in communicating ideas; and 7) the extent to which policies and procedures are adhered to *or* initiative is assumed to change them.

The Tasks: Individual tasks are listed on separate sheets of paper. The most interesting task recognizes the importance of planning and integrating the man-business-computer systems complex. After the task objectives are stated, the factors to be considered are listed.

Advantages: The systems group feels that its concept offers several important advantages. It is simple, speedy, uniform, flexible, and eliminates repetition. In regard to its flexibility, it is believed that individual ability and organizational needs may be coordinated more easily through frequent revision of the position guides. Evaluation based on the explicit factors cited above will be improved appreciably thereby.

This concept, although no panacea for the evaluation process, makes several valuable contributions. First, the fact that the need for a new process to define and to evaluate job duties was recognized by a technical staff department is encouraging. As in other instances the personnel department was not conversant with these needs and was not consulted for help. Second, the factors selected comprise a sound basis for evaluation. These factors are less personal in nature and reflect the changing dimensions of managerial responsibilities. And third, this new approach is simple and can be revised easily. A changed job description would entail merely issuing new task sheets. Presumably, duties can be revised by joint consultation of superior and subordinate; but questions of salary would require satisfying the less flexible salary procedure requirements of the personnel department. The discussion of this plan is necessarily cursory. Nevertheless, it is obvious such new approaches to personnel procedures can be developed by imaginative managers.

PART IV
ONWARD, ALWAYS ONWARD

Chapter XIII

COMPUTERIZATION: PRESENT AND FUTURE

As the computer becomes more imbedded in the fabric of business, as management molds these general-purpose machines to the configuration of individual corporate goals and objectives, it becomes increasingly dangerous to look to industry averages for guidance in proportioning computer effort. The alert management group will find useful guidelines in the experience of other organizations. But it will be the company that shapes the computer to its own destinies — influenced perhaps but not awed by the practices of others — that will find itself most competitive and best prepared to meet the challenges of the future.

— JAMES W. TAYLOR
NEAL J. DEAN

Computerized information processing is a relatively new technological development. It is only within the past fifteen years that computers have been used in the processing of large quantities of information. Only within the last few years have computerized information systems become fairly common. Integrating electronic data processing into their operations efficiently has presented managements with serious problems and vast opportunities. The present impact and the future implications of computerization now can be chronicled on the basis of more experience with the new technology.

The purpose here has been to summarize the impact of computerization on the firm and to discuss the resultant implications for management. With this goal in mind, the specific objectives were to evaluate the impact of computer technology on information processing, management, and personnel policies and practices. The objective was to formulate some general conclusions by contrasting and integrating data from the literature with data collected from firms where computers have been introduced.

The conclusions are discussed below within the following three major categories: 1) information processing, 2) management and the work process, and 3) manpower management. The final section of this chapter contains comments upon some future developments connected with computerization.

INFORMATION PROCESSING

The major aspects of computer technology and its applications to information processing are summarized below.

Information Technology

Computers have been applied most widely to processing information. Since its introduction in 1950 E.D.P. has rapidly grown in use; in the years ahead its use will expand even more. The entrance of new firms into the industry and sales forecasts both indicate a sharp rise in the manufacture of computers. In addition, computer technology is increasingly available to small firms.

Computerization is the most recent major technological development in information processing. Mechanization of information handling has been undertaken seriously by firms for over half a century. The evolution of mechanization during these years has encompassed three distinct phases: 1) machines which performed a single operation or function, 2) multi-purpose or multi-function machines, and 3) common language machines. Computerization is a refinement of the third phase of mechanization. Computers improved upon prior machines by being faster and more accurate, and by the ability to store information.

The advancing level of office technology has serious manpower implications for the firm. Manpower problems created by technological change are of particular importance because of projected changes in the economy, the population, and the labor force. These predictions are being confirmed by the changing composition of the firm's work force. For instance, technological change promotes a relative increase in executive, managerial, professional, and technical manpower as compared to unskilled and semi-skilled manpower. The survey data support this view that the firm's total manpower skill needs are upgraded with advancing technology.

Management of Systems and Procedures

Systems and procedures as a recognized function, especially as applied to paperwork, is relatively new in most firms. The growth of systems activities closely parallels the application of computers to information processing.

Computerization is a long, complicated, and difficult process. Systems analysts are involved throughout the major phases of conversion to E.D.P., that is: 1) planning, 2) feasibility study, 3) program preparation, and 4) operation.

The technical aspects of conversion accentuate the need for manpower and organizational planning, which has been almost totally neglected by the firm. Top management has failed to develop policies to guide systems activities or to become actively involved with them. Middle managers trained in systems, initially permitted to implement computer technology pretty much as they wished, are coming under closer line management control. Organizational barriers to innovation are often handled on a personal basis, rather than in a planned and well-thought-through manner. Top management has been forced to recognize the non-technical aspects of computerization because some of the anticipated savings failed to materialize. Top management has resorted to off-the-cuff guidance, a paternalistic philosophy, and the protection of obstructionists, all of which impede computerization and create difficult problems for systems analysts.

Moreover, in the organization and control of systems activities, there has been little adherence to the principles of organizational theory. Lack of systems planning and ill-defined systems analyst responsibilities lead to jockeying for advantageous position by managers affected by E.D.P. Such a fluid situation encourages politically oriented maneuvering. Computer blackmail, the E.D.P. committee as a manipulative device, rival systems, and control of vital information are all manifestations of the strategies and weapons of conflict in such political warfare.

Systems approaches vary, but transcription of the old procedure plus some innovation was the characteristic approach adopted. The reasons for this conservative approach to E.D.P. were the need for the firm to learn while implementing the new technology, and the desire to obtain production as soon as possible. The lack of trained personnel, the need for accuracy, and technical difficulties associated with integrating the computer into operations were also important determinants of the systems approach adopted.

The initial programs placed on the computer were the most routine, the simplest, and in many cases, those which had been the most highly mechanized before computerization. Payroll, accounts receivable and billing, and accounts payable were computerized most frequently. Organizational and human factors, rather than machine limitations, were the most important restraints on the systems approaches taken and the programs converted.

Management of Computer Operations

Computers have not yet been fully integrated into the firm's organizational structure. In most instances management of computer operation is under the control of the financial chief. However, if the responsibility for E.D.P. is *not* under the control of a single functional area, the higher the organizational position and status of the computer center, the more innovative the systems group's approach, the broader the applications, and the more advanced the equipment. There are signs that E.D.P. will not remain under functional control, but, rather, will be placed under the administrative division, or will become a separate service department altogether.

Computerization has encouraged the trend toward centralized information processing. This trend has been reflected in the surveyed firms by the creation of new, enlarged, information processing centers, the expansion of old centers, and the consolidation of others. The degree of centralization appears to be dependent upon 1) the degree of prior mechanization and centralization of machine operations, 2) a firm's industrial organization, 3) production inputs and outputs, and 4) the existence of company-wide policies, procedures, and forms.

Centralized information processing implies centralized decision-making, but this need not be the case. Evidence was presented which suggests that decentralized decision-making may be enhanced under computerization. In any case, the computer can be used to help implement either centralization or decentralization decision strategies.

Management of Change

The management of rapid and significant change, that results for example from office innovations after computerization, has been handled badly in the surveyed firms. Manpower and organizational planning do not offer a panacea for the problems of organizational change, but they can provide a framework with which to predict problems and to plan for their amelioration. Planning activities, carried on as a continuing process, can also disclose new or emerging factors to be taken into consideration, permitting quicker accommodation to them.

These planning responsibilities are not recognized as an important top management responsibility in the surveyed firms. Therefore, the development of appropriate organizational structures, proper delegation of responsibility and authority, and the establishment of relevant policies and procedures are neglected. Even the formal trappings of planning activities, such as policy and procedure manuals, training programs, and job descriptions are absent in some of the surveyed firms. The direct results of the failure to plan are delayed efficiencies from E.D.P. and duplication and waste of a firm's resources.

Inadequate planning for computerization is reflected also in the lack of enlightened consideration of the human factor in the management of change. In most of the surveyed firms, employees have been given fairly extensive general information about computerization. There is, however, very little communication in regard to changes in organization and responsibilities. The participation of interested and affected personnel at all levels of the organization is minimal and badly organized. The positive aspects of the change to computerization were not stressed; hence, the favorable attitudes most employees possess toward improvement was not capitalized on.

In organized firms the unions generally were not hostile toward computerization. Existing contract provisions have sufficed to protect union members in most cases. Labor market conditions and clerical employee characteristics are such that the unions have not been placed in political difficulty by taking a progressive approach to the problems created by E.D.P. The fact that no employee in the surveyed firms was laid off because of E.D.P. contributed to good union-management relations both during and after the conversion process.

The personnel department plays a sterile and inconsequential role in the management of change in most firms. The personnel department was not consulted, and generally had little or no idea of the organizational and manpower problems associated with computerization. Several factors which contributed to the impotence of the personnel function are: 1) the unsatisfactory organization of the function, 2) the predominance of unrelated administrative responsibilities, and 3) the low status of the personnel representative relative to other managers.

MANAGEMENT AND THE WORK PROCESS

The impact and the implications of computerization for line and staff management and the work process are summarized below.

Line Management and Computerization

Two alternative ways of managing, policy management and

management by rule and regulation, were compared. Analysis indicates that policy management is not inconsistent with computerization, and that it may even make policy management more feasible. The impact of E.D.P. on line management, to date at least, does not preclude or devaluate decentralized decision-making, participative management, communication and consultation, and a non-paternalistic view of lower management and rank and file employees.

Top management has been affected only incidentally, to date, by computerization. The data from the surveyed firms and the literature are consistent, predictions excluded. There is agreement that there is more time available for planning, policy formulation, and innovation by top management. There are differences, however, on the appropriate over-all managerial philosophy and approach to organizational problems raised by E.D.P.

Top management in the surveyed firms maintains that there is more time for planning, since less time is required to oversee E.D.P. operations. Computerization has increased the accuracy and speed and improved the quality of information processing. Nevertheless the over-all impact of E.D.P. on top management has been slight because of 1) the relatively early state of E.D.P., 2) the fact that integrated data processing is only now being implemented, and 3) the general lack of participation through policy planning.

Middle management has been affected to a greater degree than top management. Middle management structure has remained essentially the same, but the centralization of machine operations and the computerization of procedures have resulted in numerous reassignments and transfers. There has not been, however, any general movement of *classes* of middle management jobs, either upward or downward.

As a result of computerization, middle management job responsibilities involve more planning, coordination, and personnel administration. The middle manager's evaluation of these changes is that personal judgment is more important, while day-to-day supervision of operations is less important;

scheduling to meet computer operations is of paramount importance in managing a computerized department; and, the job of a middle manager is more interesting, demanding, and rewarding, while the level of performance can be determined more easily.

Lower management has been affected most by E.D.P. Some supervisory skills have become obsolete; less time is spent on direct supervision of employees; and more time is spent on personnel administration matters. The job itself is more technical and complicated; and the supervisor must be more adaptable to change.

Not many older supervisors have been displaced by computerization. Yet higher managers have not planned for the reassignment of these supervisors. Therefore the severity of their dislocation has been disproportionate.

Staff Management

Computerization induces and supports the trend toward the development and management of a systems rather than a functional approach to organization. This trend emphasizes the need to reevaluate the usefulness of the line-staff principle of organization.

Two views were discussed as possible alternatives. The first predicted the separation of the staff, professional, and creative functions from the line and personnel adminstration functions. The second view predicted a blurring of line-staff distinctions, and foresaw the increasing use of a team approach to systems development and management.

The systems specialist is the staff manager most involved in computerization activities. Good relationships with line management are essential for efficient implementation of E.D.P. Yet, the role and duties of systems specialists in the surveyed firms are ill-defined; and there are no policies to facilitate cooperation. The assignment of responsibility typically is nebulous and results in conflict and confusion between systems analysts and line managers.

No dominant pattern for working relationships between systems specialists and line managers has been established in the surveyed firms. The particular working relationships appeared to depend upon the extent of the procedural change, the traditional method of implementing changes, and the presence or absence of functional groups to deal with the systems problems raised by E.D.P. The project or team approach, after evaluation, appears to offer the most promise in meeting the systems development and management requirements of computerization.

Some evidence from the literature and the surveyed firms suggests that final responsibility for systems leadership should rest with the line organization. All phases of systems activities, however, require the contribution and cooperation of both line and staff managers.

Changing Features of the Work Process

The nature and form of office rationalization precipitated by computerization were analyzed by establishing a framework within which to examine work process changes. The framework consisted of four factors: 1) integration, 2) formalization, 3) standardization, and 4) social context.

The degree of integration in the work processes of the surveyed firms has been only slightly altered by computerization. The flow of work is slightly more continuous. The work load over the cycle has tended to be more even, and the time lapse between work elements has been decreased by E.D.P. Formalization has increased, with closer scheduling of work activities, further routinization of work tasks, greater reliance upon procedures, rules, and regulations. Standardization, too, has increased under computerization. Further subdivision of work tasks has been made possible by computerization, which allows more precise measurement of performance, and quicker and more accurate error detection, also. Job enlargement consistent with efficiency was instituted by several surveyed firms.

Finally, the social aspects of work also have been changed by computerization. The computer determines the work pace for some jobs. Supervision has been depersonalized through the increased use of operations manuals, procedures, and rules. Many low paying and low status jobs have been eliminated by computerization, while higher rated clerical jobs have increased in number. Some of the higher paid and higher status clerical jobs have been eliminated by E.D.P. Professional and technical jobs have increased in number as a result of the introduction of computers into clerical operations.

Traditional social and economic distinctions between plant and office work have been narrowed by computerization. Computerized information systems have linked blue collar and white collar work more closely.

MANPOWER MANAGEMENT

The efficient provision of goods and services requires competent utilization of human resources within a firm. Three major manpower considerations in a computerized firm are: 1) recruitment, selection, and mobility, 2) conditions of employment, and 3) training and development of manpower.

Manpower Requirements

The modification of some traditional staffing policies and procedures has been required in computerized firms. The recruitment of clerical and machine operator employees has not been difficult, but the recruitment of managerial and technical employees often has been troublesome. These positions entail new skills for the development and management of computerized procedures. So far these positions represent a small percentage of the entire employee population, yet the recruitment of qualified applicants for positions such as programmer has been probably the major manpower problem faced by computerized firms.

Initially most of the surveyed firms recruited from within to fill the new E.D.P. positions. However, the failure of this policy forced the firms to seek applicants from outside. The effort to recruit outside applicants for E.D.P. positions has been probably the biggest contribution of the various personnel departments to facilitating computerization.

The traditional selection process and criteria were modified to meet the new requirements of E.D.P. positions. The customary selection procedure had included a promotion from within policy, and weighted company experience heavily as a factor to be considered. The shortcomings of this approach under computerization forced the surveyed firms to establish better criteria. Social and personal criteria were downgraded, while greater emphasis was placed upon educational qualifications, test results, and ability. Union contract provisions in the surveyed firms stressed both ability and seniority in selection procedures, and therefore did not hamper management in implementing its revised approach to selection.

Placement procedures were altered little by computerization. Where the work team approach was utilized by a firm, orientation of new employees was made easier. Positions which required greater technical skills or proficiency necessitated less accommodation by the employee to company ways of doing business. In such cases the new employee has received some or all of his training before being hired. Temporary placement is more important, since, under computerization, bad performance by a permanent employee creates a more difficult and expensive problem.

Replacement transfers represent one of the most sensitive areas that are aggravated by a technological change. These transfers have not been adequately planned for in the surveyed firms. First-line supervisors and highly paid clerical employees are affected most by the dislocations that result from computerization. Involuntary separations are rare, but disguised separations due to E.D.P. may be more common than supposed.

Conditions of Employment

On the whole, salaries, hours, and conditions of work have not been affected greatly by computerization. Nevertheless, pressures generated by E.D.P. have resulted in some changes. Job analysis and evaluation procedures are unchanged, by and large. Past experience and skill are less important than before, while more emphasis is placed upon accountability, mental capacity, and potential. Actually, job description and evaluation have proceeded very slowly for all jobs affected by computerization. The one exception is programming which has been treated by the surveyed firms as a special case because of strong labor market forces.

It is difficult to generalize about job skill levels and upgrading. However, structural changes have occurred in the surveyed firms. The average for all graded positions appears to be higher, and there are fewer lower rated clerical positions. The method of payment in the computerized offices has not been changed.

Computerization has had little or no effect on the hours worked, except for specific groups of employees. Management and general clerical employees have experienced no change in hours, and no pressures for change were observed. Machine room employees have experienced some changes in hours. Generally where shiftwork existed before, it was continued but not expanded. Where shiftwork did not exist previously, it was not introduced after computerization.

Nevertheless, the possibility exists that more office employees will work on multiple shifts in the future. As additional procedures are computerized, relatively fewer employees are required; and as information technology advances, the use of multiple shifts may be expanded.

The increasing mechanization of operations in the office has brought working conditions closer to those that exist in the plant. While office working conditions, even in those areas most affected by E.D.P., still are generally good, several work-oriented conditions such as fatigue, the pace and rhythm of the new work discipline, noise, and nervous strain are increasing under E.D.P.

Manpower Development

The most crucial training needs created by computerization are for managerial and technical personnel. Clerical training has been affected only slightly by E.D.P. A major shift in training objectives was noted also. The trend toward reintegration of the management process in computerized firms has highlighted the need to think in terms of systems instead of functional management. The new training goals stress the desirabilty of developing creative, imaginative, and innovative employees. The major training problem is the development of managers capable of supervising both the personnel and technical aspects of the job.

Current training activities in the surveyed firms stress short run technical skills rather than the long range needs of systems management referred to above. Therefore, top management training in E.D.P. has consisted largely of orientation and familiarization with the technical systems. Training on the broader organizational aspects of E.D.P. has been notably lacking.

Middle manager training has been similar to but longer and more technical than that provided top managers. It is essentially the same in all the surveyed firms. Lower management has received the least formal orientation and training for E.D.P. Supervisory job changes have mostly been related to personnel administration. Even when technical training had been given, it was not sufficient or appropriate. Staff specialists require and receive much technical training in E.D.P. Clerical employees, except for a small group of machine operators, require no special training.

Four major training sources are utilized by the surveyed firms. Equipment manufacturers provided the bulk of E.D.P. training. Intra-firm training is mostly on-the-job training for machine operators and clerical employees. In most instances these employees' prior skills and experience have fitted them for their new E.D.P. positions. University training courses are utilized to a small degree by the surveyed firms, and the trend is toward greater use of this training source in the future. Finally, various miscellaneous sources, such as professional associations and consulting firms, are used to assist in training personnel.

Mobility within a firm has been affected by computerization. The number and variety of clerical jobs have been reduced, and off-the-job training has become more essential for progression into management. For managerial employees, the new technical lines of progression are fairly specific. The full impact of E.D.P. on line manager progression is not as yet clear, but no radical changes in mobility patterns were observed in the surveyed firms.

Inter-firm mobility has been increased by E.D.P. Technological advance typically increases the transferability of skills and experience between firms. Higher levels of management undoubtedly will become more mobile as computerization deepens within firms and is incorporated by additional firms.

The changed criteria for promotion under E.D.P. — a greater emphasis on flexibility, less reliance on company experience — create problems for the older worker whose skills have become obsolete. Performance appraisal is focused less on individual personalities and traits, and more upon ability and productivity.

LOOKING AHEAD

The organizational developments chronicled above outline the impressive changes precipitated by computerization. At the same time it is important to note that organizations do not alter their human systems quickly or painlessly. Even radical innovations in a firm's technology often may be compromised by the restraints generated by human abilities and needs. The absorption of computer technology into a firm's operations has been gradual; and therefore, the impact has been modulated.

The meaning of computerization for a firm will continue to be significant but not radical over given short time spans. Particular organizational innovations undoubtedly will have tremendous impact upon a particular work group or procedure, but this has always been the case. The pressure to provide better information at a lower cost surely will increase. Greater efficiency will be facilitated by improvements in both computer software and hardware, as well as increased managerial innovative competence.

The technological threshold is impressive. It portends corporate communications networks — in real time and on line — with direct communication between man and machine. These technical changes will be absorbed by firms, as will other changes that follow, in ways that will alter the familiar patterns of organizational life. In all likelihood, however, the rate of organizational change will continue to permit an orderly adjustment without exorbitant social costs.

BIBLIOGRAPHY

BOOKS

Argyris, Chris. *Organization and Innovation*. Homewood, Illinois: Richard D. Irwin, Incorporated, 1965.

Automation. London: Department of Scientific and Industrial Research, 1956.

Bennis, Warren G. *Changing Organizations*. New York: McGraw-Hill Book Company, Incorporated, 1966.

Bennis, Warren G., Benne, Kenneth D., and Chin, Robert, eds. *The Planning of Change*. New York: Holt, Rinehart and Winston, 1961.

Bize, Pierre. "Automation and the Scientific Management of Enterprises." *Views on Automation*. Paris: Organisation for European Economic Co-operation, 1957.

Blau, Peter M. *The Dynamics of Bureaucracy*. Chicago: University of Chicago Press, 1955.

Brech, E. F. L. *Management*. London: Sir Isaac Pitman and Sons, 1956.

Bright, James R. *Automation and Management*. Boston: Division of Research, Harvard University Graduate School of Business Administration, 1958.

Burck, Gilbert, *et. al.*, eds. *The Computer Age and Its Potential for Management*. New York: Harper and Row, 1965.

Canning, Richard G. *Installing Electronic Data Processing Systems*. New York: John Wiley and Sons, Incorporated, 1957.

Conway, B., Gibbons, J., and Watts, D. E. *Business Experience with Electronic Computers*. New York: Controllers Institute Research Foundation, Incorporated, 1959.

Craig, Harold Harlow. *Administering a Conversion to Electronic Accounting*. Boston: Division of Research, Harvard University Graduate School of Business Administration, 1955.

Croome, Honor. *Human Problems of Innovation*. London: Department of Scientific and Industrial Research, 1960.

Diebold, John. "Automation as a Management Problem." *Automation and Society*. Jacobson, Boone, and Roucels, eds. New York: Philosophical Library, 1959.

Drucker, Peter F. *The Practice of Management*. New York: Harper and Brothers, 1954.

Feigenbaum, A. V. "The Approach, Analysis and Design of a System." *Ideas for Management*. C. Gordon, ed., for the Systems and Procedures Association. Forge Valley, Massachusetts: The Murray Printing Company, 1959.

Goodman, L. Landon. *Man and Automation*. Baltimore: Penguin Books, 1957.

Hattery, Lowell G. *Executive Control and Data Processing*. Washington, D.C.: Anderson Kramer Associates, 1959.

Hattery, Lowell G. and Bush, George. *Electronics in Management*. Seattle: University of Washington Press, 1956.

Hill, Samuel E. and Harbison, Frederick. *Manpower and Innovation in American Industry*. Princeton: Princeton University, Industrial Relations Section, 1959.

Kennedy, Thomas. *Automation Funds and Displaced Workers*. Boston: Harvard University Press, 1962.

Killingsworth, Charles C. "Cooperative Approaches to Problems of Technological Change." *Adjusting to Technological Change*. Somers, *et. al.*, eds. New York: Harper and Row, 1963.

Laubach, Peter B. *Company Investigations of Automatic Data Processing*. Boston: Division of Research, Harvard University Graduate School of Business Administration, 1957.

Lockwood, David. *The Blackcoated Worker*. London: George Allen and Unwin,

Limited, 1958.

McDonough, Adrian M. and Garrett, Leonard J. *Management Systems*. Homewood, Illinois: Richard D. Irwin, Incorporated, 1965.

McGregor, Douglas. *The Human Side of Enterprise*. New York: McGraw-Hill Book Company, Incorporated, 1960.

Mecham, Alan D. and Thompson, Van B., eds. *Total Systems*. Detroit: American Data Processing, Incorporated, 1962.

Mehl, Lucien. "Automation in Public Administration." *Views on Automation*. Paris: Organisation for European Economic Cooperation, 1956.

Men, Steel and Technical Change. London: Department of Scientific and Industrial Research, 1956.

Michael, Donald N. *Cybernation: The Silent Conquest*. Santa Barbara: Center for the Study of Democratic Institutions, The Fund for the Republic, Incorporated, 1962.

Mills, C. Wright. *White Collar*. New York: Oxford University Press, 1951.

Moore, Wilbert E. *Industrial Relations and the Social Order*. Revised ed. New York: Macmillan Company, 1951.

Nett, Roger and Hetzler, Stanley A. *An Introduction to Electronic Data Processing*. Glencoe, Illinois: The Free Press of Glencoe, 1959.

Neuschel, Richard F. *Management by System*. New York: McGraw-Hill Book Company, Incorporated, 1960.

Newcomb, Dorothy Perkins. *The Team Plan*. New York: G. P. Putnam's Sons, 1953.

Optner, Stanford L. *Systems Analysis for Business and Industrial Problem Solving*. Englewood Cliffs, New Jersey: Prentice-Hall, Incorporated, 1965.

Pigors, Paul and Myers, Charles A. *Personnel Administration*. 5th ed. New York: McGraw-Hill Book Company, Incorporated, 1965.

Redfield, Charles E. *Communication in Management*. Chicago: University of Chicago Press, 1958.

Rice, A. K. *Productivity and Social Organisation*. London: Tavistock Publications, Limited, 1958.

Shallenberger, Frank K. "Economics of Plant Automation," *Automation in Business and Industry*. Grabbe, Eugene M., ed. New York: John Wiley and Sons, Incorporated, 1957.

Shultz, George P. and Whisler, Thomas L., eds. *Management Organization and the Computer*. Glencoe, Illinois: The Free Press of Glencoe, 1960.

Simon, Herbert A. *The Shape of Automation*. New York: Harper and Row, 1965.

Smith, J. Sanford. *The Management Approach to Electronic Digital Computers*. London: McDonald and Evans, Limited, 1957.

Steel Workers and Technical Progress. Paris: European Productivity Agency of the Organisation for European Economic Cooperation, June, 1959.

Taylor, George W. "Collective Bargaining." *Automation and Technological Change*. John T. Dunlop, ed. Englewood Cliffs, New Jersey: Prentice-Hall, Incorporated, for the American Assembly, 1962.

Tead, Ordway. *Administration: Its Purpose and Performance*. New York: Harper and Brothers, 1959.

Thurston, Philip H. *Systems and Procedures Responsibility*. Boston: Division of Research, Harvard University Graduate School of Business Administration, 1959.

Urwick, L. F. *Leadership in the Twentieth Century*. London: Sir Isaac Pitman and Sons, Limited, 1957.

Wallace, Frank. *Appraising the Economics of Electronic Computers*. New York: Controllership Foundation, Incorporated, 1956.

Woodward, Joan. *Management and Technology*. London: Department of Scientific and Industrial Research, 1958.

PERIODICALS

"A Boost for the Man in the Middle." *Business Week*. 1899:85-89. January 22, 1966.

Abruzzi, Adam. "The Power of Automation." *Automation*. 3:no. 12, 38-42. December, 1956.

Ansoff, H. Igor. "The Firm of the Future." *Harvard Business Review*. 43:no. 5, 176. September-October, 1965.

"An Updated Look at Optical Scanning and Its Uses." *Administrative Management*. 27:no. 2, 26-27. February, 1966.

"A Steel Company's Date with a Data Machine." *Business Week*. 1757:142-146. May 4, 1963.

Brabb, George J. and Hutchins, Earl B. "Electronic Computers and Management Organization." *California Management Review*. 6:no. 1, 33-42. Fall, 1963.

Bright, James R. "Are We Falling Behind in Mechanization?" *Harvard Business Review*. 38:no. 6, 93-106. November-December, 1960.

————. "Does Automation Raise Skill Requirements?" *Harvard Business Review*. 36:no. 4, 85-98. July-August, 1958.

Brooker, W. M. A. "The Total Systems Myth." *Systems and Procedures Journal*. 16:no. 4, 28-32. July-August, 1965.

Buckingham, Walter. "The Human Side of Automation." *Business Horizons*. 3:no. 1, 19-28. Spring, 1960.

Burack, Elmer H. "The Impact of the Computer on Business Management." *The Business Quarterly*. 31:no. 1, 35-45. Spring, 1966.

Burck, Gilbert. "The 'Assault' on Fortress I.B.M." *Fortune*. LXIX:no. 6, 115, 198ff. June, 1964.

Burlingame, John F. "Information Technology and Decentralization." *Harvard Business Review*. 39:no. 6, 121-126. November-December, 1961.

"Computers Move Up in Personnel Ranks." *Business Week*. 1886:118. October 23, 1965.

"Computer Time-Sharing Goes on the Market." *Business Week*. 1892:116. December 4, 1965.

Conant, Eaton H. and Kilbridge, Maurice D. "An Interdisciplinary Analysis of Job Enlargement: Technology, Costs, and Behavioral Implications." *Industrial and Labor Relations Review*. 18:no. 3, 377-397. April, 1955.

Cooney, Russell J. "Manpower Planning for Automation." *Public Personnel Review*. 26:no. 3, 151-155. July. 1965.

Dearden, John. "Can Management Information Be Automated." *Harvard Business Review*. 42:no. 2, 128-135. March-April, 1964.

————. "How to Organize Information Systems." *Harvard Business Review*. 43:no. 2, 65-73. March-April, 1965.

————. "Myth of Real-Time Management Information." *Harvard Business Review*. 4:no. 3, 123-132. May-June, 1966.

Delehanty, George E. "Office Automation and the Occupation Structure." *Industrial Management Review*. 7:no. 2, 99-109. Spring, 1966.

"Desk Work Gets Faster Countdown." *Business Week*. 1887:91-93. October 30, 1965.

Diebold, John. "ADP — The Still-Sleeping Giant." *Harvard Business Review*. 42:no. 5, 60-65. September-October, 1964.

――――. "The Boss Will Always Be Human." *Business Week*. 1875:100-102. August 7, 1965.

――――. "The New World Coming." *Saturday Review*. XLIX:no. 30, 17-18. July 23, 1966.

――――. "What's Ahead in Information Technology." *Harvard Business Review*. 43:no. 5, 76-82. September-October, 1965.

"Doubling the Freight Car's Workday." *Business Week*. 1894:122-126. December 18, 1965.

"Education for Action." IBM advertisement in *Harvard Business Review*. 38:no. 2, 40-41. March-April, 1960.

"Effects of Mechanisation and Automation in Offices: I." *International Labour Review*. 81: no. 2, 154-173. February, 1960.

"Effects of Mechanisation and Automation in Offices: II." *International Labour Review*. 81:no. 3, 255-273. March, 1960.

"Effects of Mechanisation and Automation in Offices: III." *International Labour Review*. 81:no. 4, 350-369. April, 1960.

"Eighth Annual Report on E.D.P. Salaries." *Business Automation*. 13:no. 6, 36-47f. June, 1966.

Evans, Marshall K. and Hague, Lou R. "Master Plan for Information Systems." *Harvard Business Review*. 40:no. 1, 92-103. January-February, 1962.

Ever, Jacob. "A Corporate Time-Shared Computing System." *Industrial Management Review*. 6:no. 2, 71-79. Spring, 1965.

Faunce, William A. "Automation in the Automobile Industry: Some Consequences for In-Plant Social Structure." *American Sociological Review*. 23:no. 4, 401-407. August, 1958.

"Finding New Ways to Make Autos." *Business Week*. 1880:190-198. September 11, 1965.

Fiock, L. R., Jr. "Seven Deadly Dangers in E.D.P." *Harvard Business Review*. 40:no. 3, 88-96. May-June, 1962.

Fish, Lounsbury S. "Decentralization Reappraised." From a forum, "Organization Planning — Decentralization Reconsidered." *Management Record*. 22:no. 4, 14-17. April, 1960.

Forrester, Jay W. "A New Corporate Design." *Industrial Management Review*. 7:no. 5, 5-17. Fall, 1965.

――――. "Industrial Dynamics." *Harvard Business Review*. 36:no. 4, 37-66. July-August, 1958.

"From One Machine: 100 Days' Work in 8 Hours." *U.S. News and World Report*. LXI:no. 8, 11. August 22, 1966.

Garrity, John T. "Top Management and Computer Profits." *Harvard Business Review*. 4:no. 4, 6-8ff. July-August, 1963.

Ginder, Charles E. "Why Automation?" *Office Executive*. 34:no. 10, 9-15. October, 1959.

Gray, Arlen. "Problems of Adjustment in the Automated Office." *Personnel*. 41:no. 4, 43-48. July-August, 1965.

Griffin, W. H. "Staffing an E.D.P. Installation." *Personnel*. 42:no. 3, 60-66. May-June, 1965.

Gustafson, Philip. "What Management Is Learning from Computers." *Nation's Business*. 46:no. 11, 38-39f. November, 1958.

Helfgott, Roy B. "E.D.P. and the Office Work Force." *Industrial and Labor Relations Review*. 19:no. 4, 503-516. July, 1966.

Hill, Walter A. "The Impact of E.D.P. Systems on Office Employees: Some Empirical Conclusions." *Academy of Management Journal*. 9:no. 1, 9-19. March, 1966.

Hoos, Ida Russakoff. "When the Computer Takes Over the Office." *Harvard Business Review.* 38:no. 4, 102-112. July-August, 1960.

"How Computers Liven a Management's Ways." *Business Week.* 1926: 112-116f. June 25, 1966.

Irwin, Patrick H. and Langham, Frank W., Jr. "The Change Seekers." *Harvard Business Review.* 44:no. 1, 81-91. January-February, 1966.

Jones, Gardner M. "Organizational Consequences of E.D.P." *Business Topics.* 7:no. 4, 23-27. Autumn, 1959.

Jones, Gilbert E. "From the Thoughtful Businessman." *Harvard Business Review.* 38:no. 6, 16f. November-December, 1960.

Karsh, Bernard and Siegman, Jack. "Functions of Ignorance in Introducing Automation." *Social Problems.* 12:no. 2, 141-150. Fall, 1964.

Kaufman, Felix. "Data Systems That Cross Company Boundries." *Harvard Business Review.* 44:no. 1, 141-145f. January-February, 1966.

————. "E.D.P. and the Disenchanted." *California Management Review.* 1:no. 4, 67-73. Summer, 1959.

Kilbridge, M. D. "Do Workers Prefer Larger Jobs?" *Personnel.* 37:no. 5, 45-48. September-October, 1960.

Kurshan, Daniel L. "Central Staff as a Control Agency." From a forum, "Organizational Planning — Decentralization Reconsidered." *Management Record.* 22:no. 4, 9-14. April, 1960.

Lawrence, Paul R. "How to Deal with Resistance to Change." *Harvard Business Review.* 32:no. 3, 46-57. May-June, 1954.

Leavitt, Harold J. and Whisler, Thomas L. "Management in the 1980's." *Harvard Business Review.* 36:no. 6, 41-48. November-December, 1958.

Lee, H. C. "Do Workers Really Want Flexibility on the Job?" *Personnel.* 42:no. 2, 74-80. March-April, 1965.

————. "Electronic Data Processing and Skill Requirements." *Personnel Administration.* 29:no. 3, 49-53. May-June, 1966.

Lee, Hak Chong. "On Information Technology and Organization Structure." *Academy of Management Journal.* 7:no. 1, 204-210. September, 1964.

"Little Big Honeywell." *Forbes.* 94:no. 10, 25. November 15, 1964.

"Looking Ahead: Managing in 1980." *Iron Age.* 193:no. 13, 83. March 26, 1964.

Lucking, Walter T. "The Function of Executive Management." From a forum, "Organization Planning — Decentralization Reconsidered." *Management Record.* 22:no. 4, 7-9. April, 1960.

MacDonnell, J. J. "The Administration Executive." *Office Executive.* 34:no. 8, 79-82. August, 1959.

Machaver, William. "Introduction." From a forum, "Organization Planning — Decentralization Reconsidered." *Management Record.* 22:no. 4, 6. April, 1960.

"Management Obsolescence." *Administrative Management.* 27:no. 3, 17. March, 1966.

Mann, Floyd C. and Williams, Lawrence K. "Observations of the Dynamics of a Change to Electronic Data-Processing Equipment." *Administrative Science Quarterly.* 5:no. 2, 217-256. September, 1960.

Martin, Norman H. and Sims, John Howard. "Thinking Ahead: Power Tactics." *Harvard Business Review.* 34:no. 6, 25f. November-December, 1956.

McCreary, Edward. "Countertrend to Decentralization: Top Management Tightens Controls." *Dun's Review and Modern Industry.* 74:no. 1, 32-34. July, 1959.

Megginson, Leon C. "The Human Consequences of Office Automation." *Personnel.* 37:no. 5, 18-26. September-October, 1960.

Miles, Stephen B., Jr. and Vail, Thomas E. "Thinking Ahead: Dual Management." *Harvard Business Review.* 38:no. 1, 27f. January-February, 1960.

Moore, Leo B. "How to Manage Improvement." *Harvard Business Review.* 36:no. 4, 75-84. July-August, 1958.

Morse, Gerry E. "Pendulum of Management Control." *Harvard Business Review.* 43:no. 3, 158-160ff. May-June, 1965.

Mumford, Enid. "Clerks and Computers; A Study of the Introduction of Technical Change." *Journal of Management Studies.* 2:no. 2, 138-152. May, 1965.

Neuloh, Cetto. "Paving the Way for Technological Change." *Personnel.* 34:no. 5, 21-26. March-April, 1958.

"Next in Banking: Pay Bills by Phone." *Business Week.* 1889:82-86. November 13, 1965.

"1970 — Ready or Not It's Coming." *Administrative Management.* 27:no. 1, 15. January, 1966.

Odiorne, George S. "Company Growth and Personnel Administration." *Personnel.* 37:no. 1, 32-41. January-February, 1960.

"On-Site Systems Top 30,000 Mark." *Business Automation.* 13:no. 2, 54-56. February, 1966.

Protzel, Harvey W. "Personnel Problems in Data Processing Systems: The Approach of Top Management." *Computers and Automation.* 14:no. 8, 16-17. August, 1965.

"Real-Time, On-Time and Realism." *Administrative Management.* 27:no. 1, 15. January, 1966.

Rico, Leonard. "Automation and Manufacturing Employment: A Reappraisal." *Management of Personnel Quarterly.* 5:no. 1, 5-9. Spring, 1966.

————. "The Dynamics of Organizational Innovation." *Industrial Management Review.* 5:no. 1, 3-16. Fall, 1963.

————. "The Staffing Process and the Computer." *Management of Personnel Quarterly.* 1:no. 5, 32-36. Autumn-Winter, 1962.

"Rx for Hospitals — Computers." *Business Week.* 1863:142-144. May 15, 1965.

Schlesinger, Lawrence E. "Personnel Specialists and Change, Monks or Missionaries?" *Personnel Administration.* 28:no. 4, 3-5f. July-August, 1965.

Selwyn, Lee L. "The Information Utility." *Industrial Management Review.* 7:no. 2, 17-26. Spring, 1966.

Shaul, Donald A. "What's Really Ahead for Middle Management?" *Personnel.* 41:no. 6, 10-12. November-December, 1964.

Slater, Lloyd E. "Instrumentation." *Office Executive.* 34:no. 10, 44-46. October, 1959.

Slater, Robert F. "Thinking Ahead: How Near Is the Automatic Office?" *Harvard Business Review.* 36:no. 2, 27f. March-April, 1958.

Stahl, O. Glenn. "The Network of Authority." *Public Administration Review.* 18:no. 1, 2-4. Winter, 1958.

Stieber, Jack. "Automation and the White-Collar Worker." *Personnel.* 34:no. 3, 8-17. November-December, 1957.

Swanson, Chester A. "Functional Approach to Mechanized Data Processing." *Office Executive.* 34:no. 10, 40-43. October, 1959.

Thayer, Clarence H. "Applying an Automation Philosophy." *Automation.* 6:no. 1, 44-49. January, 1959.

Thurston, Philip H. "Who Should Control Information Systems?" *Harvard Business Review.* 40:no. 6, 135-140. November-December, 1962.

"Uncommon Denominator." *Systems and Procedures Journal.* 17:no. 3, 5. May-June. 1966.

"Univac Thinks Small — But Fast." *Business Week*. 1921:173-174. June 25, 1966.

Uris, Auren. "Fitting Today's New Specialist into Your Plant Organization." *Factory*. 117:no. 9, 224-226f. September, 1959.

Vergin, Roger C. "Staffing of Computer Departments." *Personnel Administration*. 28:no. 4, 6-12. July-August, 1965.

Watson, Arthur K. "The Administrative Revolution and Creative Management." *Office Executive*. 34:no. 8, 11-13. August, 1959.

Weber, C. Edward. "Change in Managerial Manpower with Mechanization of Data-Processing." *The Journal of Business*. 32:no. 2, 151-163. April, 1959.

"Where the Computers Care, Too." *Business Week*. 1906:140-146. March 12, 1966.

Whisler, Thomas L. "The 'Assistant-to' in 4 Administrative Settings." *Administrative Science Quarterly*. 5:no. 2, 181-216. September, 1960.

_____."The Manager and the Computer." *The Journal of Accountancy*. 119:no. 1, 27-32. January, 1965.

UNITED STATES GOVERNMENT PUBLICATIONS

"A Case Study of a Modernized Petroleum Refinery." *Bureau of Labor Statistics Report Number 120, Studies of Automatic Technology*. Washington, D.C.: United States Government Printing Office, United States Department of Labor, 1957.

"Adjustments to the Introduction of Office Automation." *Bureau of Labor Statistics Bulletin Number 1276*. Washington, D.C.: United States Government Printing Office, United States Department of Labor, May, 1960.

A Study of the Impact of Automation on Federal Employees. Prepared by the United States Civil Service Commission and Referred to the Subcommittee on Census and Government Statistics of the Committee on Post Office and Civil Service, House of Representatives, Eighty-Eighth Congress, Second Session. Washington, D.C.: United States Government Printing Office, August. 1964.

Canning, R. G. *Production Control through Electronic Data Processing: A Case Study*. Washington, D.C.: United States Government Printing Office, United States Department of Commerce, Office of Technical Services, May 1, 1954.

Hardin, Einar. "The Reactions of Employees to Office Automation." *Monthly Labor Review*. 83:no. 9, 925-932. September, 1960. Washington, D.C.: United States Government Printing Office.

Inventory and Cost Data Concerning the Utilization of Automatic Data Processing (ADP) Equipment in the Federal Government for Fiscal Years 1959, 1960, and 1961. Washington, D.C.: United States Government Printing Office, The Executive Office of the President, United States Bureau of the Budget, May, 1960.

Inventory of Automatic Data Processing (ADP) Equipment in the Federal Government. Washington, D.C.: United States Government Printing Office, Subcommittee on Census and Government Statistics of the Committee on Post Office and Civil Service, House of Representatives, 88th Congress, October 25, 1963.

"Management Decisions to Automate." *Manpower/Automation Research Monograph Number 3*. Washington, D.C.: United States Government Printing Office, United States Department of Labor, Office of Manpower, Automation, and Training, 1965.

Manpower Challenge of the 1960s. Washington, D.C.: United States Government Printing Office, 1960.

New Views on Automation. Washington, D.C.: United States Government Printing Office, 1960.

Riche, Richard W. and Alli, William E. "Office Automation in the Federal Government." *Monthly Labor Review*. 83:no. 9, 933-938. September, 1960. Washington, D.C.: United States Government Printing Office.

"The Impact of Office Automation in the Insurance Industry." *Bureau of Labor Statistics Bulletin Number 1468*. Washington, D.C.: United States Government Printing Office, United States Department of Labor, 1966.

"The Rising Levels of Education Among Young Workers." *Monthly Labor Review*. 88:no. 6 ,625-628. June, 1965. Washington, D.C.: United States Government Printing Office.

"The Social Impact of Computers." *Congressional Record*. 10:no. 149, H4051-A4053. August 3, 1964. Washington, D.C.: United States Government Printing Office.

"The Introduction of an Electronic Computer in a Large Insurance Company." *Bureau of Labor Statistics Report Number 2, Studies of Automatic Technology*. Washington, D.C.: United States Government Printing Office, United States Department of Labor, 1955.

"Use of Electronic Data-Processing Equipment." *Hearings before the Subcommittee on Census and Government Statistics of the Committee on Post Office and Civil Service, House of Representatives*. Washington, D.C.: United States Government Printing Office, 1959.

NEWSPAPERS

Acheson, Dean. "Thoughts about Thought in High Places." *New York Times*. Sec. 6, pp. 20f. October 11, 1959.

"Automation Seen Affecting Bosses." *New York Times*. p. 29. April 4, 1966.

Freeman, William M. "High Executives Grow in Number." *New York Times*. Sec. 3, p. 5. October 9, 1960.

Janson, Donald. "Automation Stirs Machinists' Union." *New York Times*. Sec. 3, p. 125. October 9, 1960.

Zipser, Alfred R. "R.C.A. Sales of Data Systems Running 200% above '59 Level." *New York Times*. Sec 3, p. 1. September 25, 1960.

Zipser, Alfred R. "Young Blood and Office Machines." *New York Times*. Sec. 3, pp. 1 and 12. November 20, 1960.

MISCELLANEOUS

"Automation in the Metal Trades." *Report II*. Geneva: International Labour Office, 1956.

Baldwin, George B. and Shultz, George P. "Automation: A New Dimension to Old Problems." *Proceedings of Seventh Annual Meeting of Industrial Relations Research Association*. Madison: Industrial Relations Research Association, December, 1954.

Barkin, Solomon. "Discussion of Part V, Automation, Productivity, and Industrial Relations." *Proceedings of Seventh Annual Meeting of Industrial Relations Research Association*. Madison: Industrial Relations Research Association, December, 1954.

Beaumont, Richard A. and Helfgott, Roy B. "Management, Automation, and People." *Industrial Relations Monograph Number 24*. New York: Industrial Relations Counselors, 1964.

Canter, Ralph R. "Automation's Impact on Future Personnel Policies." *Proceedings of First Conference, Research Developments in Personnel Manage-*

ment. Los Angeles: University of California, 1957.

"Collective Bargaining Problems." *Automation and Major Technological Change, Publication Number 18.* Washington, D.C.: The Industrial Union Department, AFL-CIO, April 22, 1958.

"Computer-Based Management for Information and Control." *American Management Associatin Bulletin 30.* 1963.

Coughlin, Howard. *Testimony on Automation by Howard Coughlin, President, Office Employees International Union, AFL-CIO, before the Subcommittee on Automation and Energy Resources of the Joint Economic Committee.* July 1, 1960. (Mimeographed.)

Dale, Ernest. "The Decision-Making Process in the Commercial Use of High-Speed Computers." *Cornell Studies in Policy and Administration.* Ithaca: Cornell University, Graduate School of Business and Public Administration, 1964.

Diebold, John. "The Basic Economic Consequences of Automation for the State of New York." *Governor's Conference on Automation, June 1-3, 1960.* New York: The State of New York, 1960.

Drucker, Peter F. *Managing the Educated.* Paper presented to the alumni of the Washington University Graduate School of Business Administration Management Development Conference. January 14, 1959.

"Effects of Mechanisation and Automation in Offices." *Report III.* Geneva: International Labour Office, 1959.

"Establishing an Integrated Data-Processing System." *Special Report Number 11.* New York: American Management Association, 1956.

Gallagher, James D. "Improving the Organization and Management of the Data-Processing Function." *The Changing Dimensions of Office Management, Report Number 41.* New York: American Management Association, 1960.

"General Electric Company Contract Proposals to International Union of Electrical Workers." *Daily Labor Report.* 170:F-1-5. August 31, 1960.

Higginson, M. Valliant. "Managing with E.D.P.: A Look at the State of the Art." *American Management Association Research Study 71.* New York: American Management Association, 1965.

"Impact on Union Size, Structure and Function." *Automation and Major Technological Change, Publication Number 19.* Washington, D.C.: The Industrial Union Department, AFL-CIO, April 22, 1958.

"Increasing Automation Usually Cuts Needs for Skilled Men, Bright Says." *Daily Labor Report.* 169:A-7-8. August 30, 1960.

"Information Processing." *Proceedings of the International Conference on Information Processing, Paris, June 15-20, 1959.* Munich: United Nations Educational, Scientific, and Cultural Organization, 1960.

Kreithen, Alexander. "Total Information Systems." *Data Processing Yearbook, 1965.* Detroit: American Data Processing, Incorporated, 1964.

Leavitt, Harold J. "Dealing with Management Obsolescence," in "Computer-Based Management for Information and Control." *American Management Association Bulletin 30.* New York: American Management Association, 1963.

Memorandum Number 18-11. Lawrence, Massachusetts: United States Treasury Department, Internal Revenue Service, Northeast Service Center, March 27, 1958. (Mimeographed.)

Myers, Charles A. "The Impact of EDP on Management Organization and Managerial Work." Working paper, Alfred P. Sloan School of Industrial

Management, Massachusetts Instiute of Technology, September, 1965.

"Office Equipment." *Standard and Poor's Industry Surveys.* Sec. 2, PO10. May 12, 1966.

Place, Irene. "Administrative Systems Analysis." *Michigan Business Report Number 28.* Ann Arbor: Bureau of Business Research, University of Michigan School of Business Administration, 1957.

Reintjes, J. T. "Automation — Its Forms and Future." *Third Annual Week-End Conference, District Number 1 — United Steel Workers of America, Congress of Industrial Organizations.* Paper presented at Industrial Relations Section, Massachusetts Institute of Technology, Cambridge, May 22, 1955. (Mimeographed.)

Report of the Committee on New Recording Means and Computing Devices. Chicago: Society of Actuaries, September, 1952.

Stein, Charles, Jr. "Some Organizational Effects of Integrated Management Information Systems." *The Changing Dimensions of Office Management, Report Number 41.* New York: American Management Association, 1960.

Taussig, J. N. "EDP Applications for the Manufacturing Function." *American Management Association Research Study 77.* New York: American Management Association, 1966.

"The Third Generation Computer." *American Management Association Bulletin 79.* New York: American Management Association, 1966.

Touraine, Alain, *et. al.* "Workers' Attitudes to Technical Change; An Integrated Survey of Research." *Industrial Relations Aspects of Manpower Policy.* Paris: Organisation for Economic Cooperation and Development, 1965.

Tower, James W. "Incentive Patterns of Executive Compensation." *Notes and Quotes.* Hartford: Connecticut General Life Insurance Company, 1960. (From *Bulletin Number 28, Addresses on Industrial Relations.* Ann Arbor: The University of Michigan, 1960.)

Weinberg, Nat. "Practical Approaches to the Problems Raised by Automation." *Trade Union Seminar on Automation.* Paris: Organisation for European Economic Cooperation, 1957.